MOTIVE FOR A MISSION

MOTIVE FOR A MISSION

The Story Behind Hess's Flight to Britain

JAMES DOUGLAS-HAMILTON

With a Foreword by
ALAN BULLOCK

Macmillan
St Martin's Press

SBN boards: 333 12260 7
Library of Congress Catalogue Card No.: 75-145429

First published 1971 by
MACMILLAN AND CO LTD
London and Basingstoke
Associated companies in New York Toronto
Dublin Melbourne Johannesburg and Madras

Printed in Great Britain by
ROBERT MACLEHOSE AND CO. LTD
The University Press, Glasgow

To
Squadron Leader Lord David Douglas-Hamilton
killed on operations 2 August 1944

CONTENTS

PART III: THE FATE OF ALBRECHT HAUSHOFER

LIST OF ILLUSTRATIONS

Between pages 96 and 97

ACKNOWLEDGEMENTS

THE author and publishers wish to thank the following who have kindly given permission for the use of copyright material:

George Allen and Unwin Limited and Houghton Mifflin Company, Boston, for extract from *The Memoirs of Dr Eduard Beneš (1954)* by Eduard Beneš; The Revd Dr Eberhard Bethge for permission to quote from a personal letter and from *Dietrich Bonhoeffer, A Biography* (Collins 1970); The British Broadcasting Corporation and Mrs Temple for extract from *The Broadcast by the Revd Dr William Temple, Archbishop of York, 2nd October 1939*; Cassell and Company Limited and McClelland and Stewart Limited, Canada for extract from *The War Speeches* Vol II of Sir Winston S. Churchill; Cassell and Company Limited and Houghton Mifflin, Boston for extracts from *The Reckoning: The Eden Memoirs* by the Earl of Avon, and extracts from *Their Finest Hour* and *The Gathering Storm* from the Second World War Vols II and III by Sir Winston S. Churchill; Chicago Daily News for extracts from *The Ciano Diaries (1947)*; Collins Publishers and Curtis Brown Limited for extract from *Ambassador on a Special Mission* by Viscount Templewood; Sefton Delmer for extracts from *Black Boomerang*; Doubleday and Co. Inc., for extracts from *Total Power* by Edmund Walsh; Hamish Hamilton for extracts from *Black Record – Germans Past and Present* by Sir Robert Vansittart; Dr Karl-Heinz Harbeck for permission to quote from his unpublished thesis: *Die Zeitschrift für Geopolitik, (Kiel 1963)*; Professor Dr Heinz Haushofer for permission to quote from *The Hartschimmelhof Papers*, and to reproduce *Albrecht Haushofer's Peace Plan (1941)* and *The Sonnets of Moabit*; Sir Alan Herbert C.H. for poem 'Hess' from *Let Us Be Glum* by A. P. Herbert (Methuen 1941); Dr Rainer Hildebrandt for extracts from *Wir Sind Die Letzten (1950)*; H.M.S.O. for extracts from *Hansard, Documents on German Foreign Policy 1918–45* Series D. Vols XI and XII, and also from *Trials of German Major War Criminals at Nuremberg*; Professor Rolf Italiaander for extracts from *Besiegeltes Leben* (*1949*), and from *Akzente eines Lebens* (Carl Schunemann Buchverlag Bremen); Dr Ursula Laack (nee Michel) for permission to quote from her unpublished thesis: *Albrecht Haushofer und Nationalsozialismus*, (*Kiel 1964*); E. P. S. Lewin for extracts from *Hitler – The Missing Years* (*1957*) by Ernst Hanfstaengl; Paul List Verlag, Munich for extracts from *Das Spiel Um Deutschland* (*1953*) by Fritz Hesse; The National Archives of U.S.A., Washington for extracts from *Speeches and Discussions in 1941*; Gerald Reitlinger and The Viking Press, Inc., for extracts from *The S.S. Alibi of a Nation* by Gerald Reitlinger; The Royal Institute of International Affairs, Chatham House for permission to quote from *Albrecht Haushofer's lecture 29th April 1937*, which was given to a private off the record meeting; Martin Secker and Warburg Limited and Simon Schuster for extracts from *The Rise and Fall of the Third Reich* (*1960*) by William Shirer. David Higham Associates and Butterworth for, *The Case of Rudolph Hess* by J. R. Rees; Deutsche Verlags Anstalt, Stuttgart for, '*In Memoriam—Albrecht Haushofer*' by Walter Stubbe, in an article from The Quarterly Bulletin for Contemporary History, (Munich, July 1960); Atlantis Verlag for '*Memoirs*' by Ulrich Von Hassell (1948); Professor von Weizsaecker for *In Memoriam Albrecht Haushofer* by Carl F. von Weizsaecker. The publishers have been unable to trace the copyright holders of some extracts but will be pleased to make the necessary arrangement at the first opportunity.

The author also wishes to thank the Wiener Library and everyone who has given him information; in particular he wishes to thank Mr Theodore Kay for his kind and invaluable help in translating and checking the authenticity of the original German documents, including *The Sonnets of Moabit*.

Foreword by Alan Bullock

FOREWORD
by
Alan Bullock

THE flight of Rudolf Hess to Britain in May 1941 remains one of the most bizarre episodes in the history of the two Great Wars. It is clear that Hess acted out of loyalty to Hitler rather than from treachery and that he hoped, by securing British agreement to a peace settlement, to restore the standing with his master which he had lost to other, more forceful rivals. There are still plenty of puzzling questions left, however. Where did Hess get hold of such an idea in the first place? How could a man who still ranked as Hitler's Deputy and was one of his oldest and closest associates so misjudge Hitler's reaction to an independent initiative of this kind? Did he act alone or were there others who knew what he was planning? Was he genuinely deranged, as he later tried to make his captors believe, or only shamming? Why did he pick on the Duke of Hamilton to approach? Had there been earlier contacts between them? And why was Churchill – as well as Hitler – apparently embarrassed by the whole affair?

The author of the present book starts with an unusual advantage. The second son of the Duke of Hamilton, he was brought up, so to speak, on the inside of the British half of the story and was so fascinated by it that after graduating from Oxford he determined to make as thorough an investigation as he could of the German side and then put the two together. This is how I come to be writing the preface to his book, for, along with Sir John Wheeler Bennett and other historians, I was consulted by James Douglas-Hamilton on possible lines of research to follow and have been able to watch his study develop and assume its final shape.

In fact, if the book contained no more than the documents made available by the Duke of Hamilton and the account of the British side of the affair which his son has reconstructed, it would still make highly interesting reading. How Churchill received the news is worth publication by itself alone. But the research which James

Douglas-Hamilton has carried out into the German background
has opened up an equally interesting side of the story.

The problem was to know where to begin. There was a well-
known connection between Hess and Professor Karl Haushofer,
the founder of geopolitics, and the Haushofer papers seemed to
provide an obvious way into the German material. This proved to
be a lucky strike. In the letters preserved by Heinz Haushofer at
Hartschimmelhof, and in the Haushofer papers found in the
Federal Archives at Koblenz and the Manuscript Division of the
Library of Congress, the author has found new evidence, not
before published in English and only partially explored in German,
which fits together with the Hamilton material to throw light on
much that was hitherto obscure in the Hess affair.

The interest of James Douglas-Hamilton's book, however, does
not end there. The link between Hitler's Deputy and the Duke of
Hamilton was Albrecht Haushofer, the son of the Professor and a
man who played in his own right a certain part – although of an
equivocal nature – in the German Resistance. Albrecht Haushofer,
unlike his father, had no illusions about the character of the Third
Reich and its leaders, but he was tempted by the belief that he
could do more good by remaining in office and trying to work
against it from within than by going into exile – a dilemma faced
by many other Germans. No one was more scathing about the
mixture of motives in his decision than Albrecht Haushofer
himself. The result was disastrous. He was distrusted by the
Nazis, distrusted by the Resistance, and worst of all came profoundly to distrust himself and to hate, without being able to back
out of, the role he had adopted.

After Hess's flight, Albrecht Haushofer had little doubt that it
was only a matter of time before he would be put to death. His
ability to survive even for a limited period depended solely on his
usefulness to Himmler in the plans the SS leader kept in mind for
a possible compromise peace with Britain. All he could do was to
set down in his letters to his mother and later in the poems he
wrote in prison (the Sonnets of Moabit) a record of his thoughts
and self-analysis without illusion and without concealment. None
of this, so far as I know, has been translated into English and James
Douglas-Hamilton has wisely decided to include the most striking
passages in full. Haushofer's fate was a direct result of his involvement in the Hess affair and is as much a part of its history as the

subsequent trial and imprisonment of Rudolf Hess in Spandau. Unlike Hess, however, Albrecht Haushofer has left behind one of the most illuminating human documents to survive from a period of history which in its conflict of loyalties searched men to their roots.

So a book which had its origin in a young man's personal interest in a curious and sensational episode ends by working out the contrast between the fate of these very different men, Rudolf Hess and Albrecht Haushofer, both caught up in events too big for them, both seeking unsuccessfully a way out which led in Hess's case to his trial by the Allied Court at Nuremberg and subsequent imprisonment for life in Spandau, in Haushofer's to summary execution by the SS in the very last days of the war. In the course of his account, the author provides the fullest and most convincing explanation I have seen of why Hess came to make his flight to Britain, the circumstances in which the plan was conceived and why Hess picked on the Duke of Hamilton as his contact in Britain.

For a young man publishing his first book this is a considerable achievement. James Douglas-Hamilton has carried out his researches and written his account in the intervals of starting a career as an advocate. I admire the pertinacity with which he has carried out his undertaking and the judgement with which he has overcome problems of arrangement which would have taxed any author, however experienced. I hope his book will have the success it deserves and that he will use his gift for historical inquiry to go on and write more.

ALAN BULLOCK

St Catherine's College,
Oxford.

Prologue

PROLOGUE

T H E news that Germany had lost the World War came as a terrible shock to virtually all Germans. It meant the end of the monarchy and led to the establishment of a Republican regime which had to bear the immense unpopularity of men surrendering to enemy demands, first through the Armistice, and later through the Treaty of Versailles. Attacks against the Republican Government came from extremists of the left who wished to institute a Communist way of life, and, more important, from a fanatical right. It was openly hinted that it would be a patriotic duty to destroy a regime which had accepted unpalatable peace terms. This mood was widespread, especially amongst those who had fought at the Front. One such man was Major-General Karl Haushofer, who resolved to play his part in the destruction of the Treaty of Versailles, through his teachings in German universities.

Karl Haushofer was a patriotic German General, brought up in the traditions of the Imperial German Army. While in Tokyo as a military attaché from 1908 to 1911 he had learnt Japanese, made himself an expert on South and East Asia, and came to believe that the struggle for a nation's life was little more than a contest for space on the world's surface, and that the British and Japanese had appreciated this fact better than the Germans. It struck him that his countrymen had never known where their frontiers should lie, and had never had a boundary sense driven into them. When the war came he served on both Eastern and Western Fronts, rose to the rank of Major-General, and in 1918 supervised the return of the Thirtieth Bavarian Reserve Division from Alsace to Bavaria. It seemed to him that Germany was like a powerful man whose limbs had been amputated by her enemies, that the nation had been left prostrate, encircled and suffocating, and that more Lebensraum, or living space, would be the panacea for all her troubles.

Karl Haushofer acquired his degree of Doctor of Philosophy in 1913 at the University of Munich, graduating *summa cum laude* in Geography, Geology and History. In 1919 he decided that he would institute the new Science of Geopolitics, in fact the study of Political Geography seen from the point of view of the German State. It was a form of geographical Imperialism, and sought to bring about what German Nationalists thought of as a more logical arrangement of political boundaries. In his own words, 'Geopolitics wants to and must become the Geographical conscience of the State'.[1]

Many of Haushofer's ideas came from Ratzel, Kjellen, Mahan and Mackinder, the basic ones being that the state is a biological organism which grows or contracts, and that in the struggle for space the dynamic countries swallow up the weak. In order to be self-supporting Germany must have autarchy and Lebensraum, and hence Geopolitics must become the doctrine of National Self-Sufficiency. Haushofer was a product of Bismarck's nationalist, reunified, resurgent Germany, but unlike Bismarck he had no strictly limited and precise aims as to the furthest practicable extent of German expansion. Hence German Geopolitics, if only on account of its vagueness, was never and could never be more than a pseudo-science. It was merely an attempt to set an academic stamp on claims that land in which Germans had settled was German, and that regions in which German was spoken ought to be German, or, at least for cultural purposes, a German sphere of influence.[2]

It was to the frustrated nationalism of a defeated country that Professor General Karl Haushofer was appealing in learned academic language, and in 1921 he became Professor of Geopolitics. Many of his students had come to hear him after the war, embittered that all the fighting had been in vain. Many believed the myth that the troops at the Front had been stabbed in the back by a cowardly Government. Many of them looked upon the workings of German democracy as a bottomless swamp. It was no wonder that Karl Haushofer was hailed by his disillusioned, angry and alienated students, who believed that he was giving them a sense of vision. One of these students was Rudolf Hess.

Hess, the son of a wealthy German merchant was born on 26 April 1894 in Alexandria where he stayed for the first dozen years of his life, before being sent to school at Godesberg on the Rhine.

He later served a business apprenticeship in Hamburg and went to Switzerland to study French. He reacted strongly against his father's wish that he should become a merchant, and in 1914 at the outbreak of war escaped to join the German Army as an eager volunteer. He served in the Sixteenth Bavarian Reserve Infantry Regiment, which consisted mostly of students. Under poor leadership it suffered terrible losses, but Hess and Hitler, who were still unknown to each other, came through alive. While the latter remained a Corporal, Hess rose to the rank of a Lieutenant and, after being wounded twice, became a pilot in the German Air Force in 1918.

Rudolf Hess was a fanatical young man in search of a father-substitute and a cause. He found in the course of the next few years two such substitutes, Haushofer and Hitler. The former gave him an educational training, the latter a cause. After the war Hess enrolled as a student of economics at the University of Munich, attended the lectures of Karl Haushofer, and brooded over the downfall of his country with a burning intensity. He devoted much of his energy to the distribution of anti-semitic pamphlets, and to other political activities, which led to the overthrow of the Soviet regime in Munich in 1919. He expressed his aggressive mode of thought in a prize-winning essay on the theme 'How Must the Man be Constructed who will lead Germany back to her Old Heights?'

He wrote: 'When all authority has vanished, only a man of the people can establish authority. . . . When necessity commands, he does not shrink from bloodshed. . . . In order to reach his goal, he is prepared to trample on his closest friends. . . .'[3] In 1920 Hess heard Hitler speak: he heard the voice thundering forth, and found himself wondering: 'Was this man a fool or was he the man who would save all Germany?'[4] He decided to join the Nazi Party, and became an intimate friend of Hitler.

In 1923 he was involved in the planning of the unsuccessful Beerhall Putsch on 8 November, when he tried to protect Hitler from armed reprisal by detaining prominent members of the Bavarian Cabinet as hostages. On the next day, while Hitler was preparing to march into Munich, Hess was sent into the foothills of Southern Bavaria with his hostages, who were at one point threatened with death. When the news of the failure of the Putsch reached them Hess and his guards melted away.[5] He made his

way to Karl Haushofer's home, Hartschimmelhof, in the Bavarian
Alps, where he was given refuge, and it was with Karl Haushofer's
help that Hess escaped to Austria – favours which Hess would
never forget.

In due course Hitler was sentenced to five years' imprisonment in
Landsberg Prison, which lasted in practice less than nine months.
Hess returned, was given a very lenient sentence, and he too
arrived in Landsberg, where Hitler had already started to dictate to
Emil Maurice *Mein Kampf*. Hess soon supplanted Maurice as
Hitler's principal secretary and typist. At this time Karl Haushofer
paid a few visits to his former pupil Hess, bringing him reading
material. Hess had been the Professor's personal assistant at the
Institute of Geopolitics, and while Karl Haushofer thought that
Hess's 'heart and idealism were greater than his intellect', he also
regarded him as 'my favourite pupil'.[6] During his visits to Hess in
Landsberg, Karl Haushofer had occasional conversations with
Hitler, and as a result certain geopolitical ideas were transmitted to
Hitler either directly or indirectly through Hess.[7] Even so Hau-
shofer and Hitler differed in temperament, character and con-
viction, being from completely different worlds.

Karl Haushofer belonged to the military aristocracy and
believed in government by an old-fashioned paternalistic imperial
elite, and therefore he looked upon Hitler as a vulgar if resourceful
upstart. Unlike Hitler, Haushofer was certainly not an extreme
racialist; he had married Martha Mayer-Doss who was half-
Jewish. Martha came from the family of George Mayer, a Jewish
merchant of Mannheim, and she bore Haushofer two sons, Albrecht
and Heinz. Moreover in foreign policy Haushofer wanted an
Overseas Empire with a strong Germany in Middle, South and
South-East Europe. Like many German Generals he desired
co-operation with Russia and competition against the British
Empire for Lebensraum. Hitler on the other hand believed that
Germany must either ally with Russia against Britain or with
Britain against Russia. In his own mind he was quite certain that it
would have to be the latter. Whatever happened Germany must not
dissipate her energies by expanding South or Overseas. The Third
Reich would have to gain territory in the East, and would stretch
across the Russian steppes and plains. Hitler wrote in *Mein
Kampf*:

If European soil was wanted by and large it could be had only at the expense of Russia. . . . For such a policy as this there was but one ally in Europe – England. Only with England covering our rear could we have begun a new Germanic migration.

No sacrifice should have been too great in winning England's friendship. We should have given up all thought of colonies and seapower and avoided competition with British industry. . . .[8]

Although Karl Haushofer did not write, revise or review *Mein Kampf*, he did provide Hitler with a formula and certain well-turned phrases which could be adapted, and which at a later stage suited the Nazis perfectly. Even the vagueness of Karl Haushofer's Geopolitics would be advantageous to Hitler. In German University circles it served as a ponderous intellectual smokescreen, obscuring the aims of Nazi Foreign Policy. Meanwhile Hess's total allegiance was transferred from Karl Haushofer to Hitler. When Hitler was released from Landsberg Hess remained with him as his Secretary, and his influence was great, for he had become the initiator of the Fuehrer cult. He started calling Hitler 'Der Chef', then 'Fuehrer', and soon the greeting 'Heil Hitler' became commonplace.[9]

Most Nazis saw Hess as a coming man, as he was with Hitler almost every day, taking care of Hitler's personal affairs. Goebbels recorded in his Diary on 13 April 1926 '. . . Hess: the most decent, quiet, friendly, clever reserved: Alone with Hess. Talk, He is a kind fellow'.[10] Goering on the other hand loathed Hess as a rival and the dislike was mutual. Both Hess and Goering had been pilots, and Hess was jealous of Goering, who in the First World War had commanded the famous Richthofen Squadron. Goering pictured himself as a man of action who despised intellectuals, and in a muddled way Hess fancied himself as an intellectual expert on Geopolitics.[11]

In the late 1920's and early 1930's Hess fulfilled two important tasks. He was good at collecting funds for the Nazi Party, and at spying on Hitler's behalf. Hess also managed the Adolf Hitler Industrial Fund, into which certain business interests paid large sums. On 15 December 1932 Hess was put in charge of a Central Party Commission, and four months later in April 1933 Hitler appointed Hess 'my deputy with the power to take decisions in my name in all questions relating to the conduct of the party'.[12] As such Hess was able to help his old friend Karl Haushofer with the Ausland Organisations which were set up, within Germany and elsewhere, to foster contracts and comradeship between Germans in the Reich and German minorities outside.

In a sense Karl Haushofer's work with these organisations such as the V.D.A., namely the Verein für das Deutschtum im Ausland (the League for German Nationals Abroad) was merely the practical application of his geopolitical teachings in the service of Pan-German Imperialism. The activities of the V.D.A. were not lost on Hitler who knew only too well that the twenty million Germans outside the Reich could be used in schemes of territorial aggrandisement for the Third Reich. On 12 February 1934 Hess established the Volksdeutsche Rat (the Volksdeutsch Council) with Karl Haushofer as its President. Under Hess's authority the Foreign Organisation of the National Socialist Party, the Foreign Institute and the V.D.A. began to organise Germans outside Germany.[13]

While Hess collaborated with Karl Haushofer in guiding the work of the Ausland Organisations, he devoted all his energies to the service of Hitler. At no time was this more clear than during the Night of the Long Knives, on 30 June 1934. Between 1933 and 1934 Hitler was faced with the problems of resolving the bitterness between S.A. and Army and of determining the succession to President Hindenburg. Roehm, Chief of Staff of the S.A., and some of the other S.A. leaders represented those disillusioned Nazis who wanted to enrich themselves at the expense of capitalists, landlords and Civil Service bureaucrats, and Roehm wanted to reconstitute the Army under his own authority. However, Hitler had to succeed Hindenburg in order to obtain absolute power, and to do that he had to keep on good terms with the Army; this meant that the ambitions of Roehm and certain S.A. leaders would have to be curbed.

The attempts of Hitler and Hess to conciliate did not produce the intended results,[14] and in Munich on the morning of 30 June 1934 the local leaders of the S.A. were collected, under the direction of Hess and Bormann. On the evening of the same day Sepp Dietrich, the Head of the S.S. Leibstandarte Adolf Hitler arrived at the Stadelheim Prison with a shooting squad. He showed Frank, the Bavarian Minister of Justice, a list of the names of 110 persons which were believed to be underlined with Hitler's pencil. Frank telephoned to Hess at the Brown House protesting, and Hess said he would approach Hitler. Hess telephoned back to say that Hindenburg had given Hitler emergency powers, and he read over the phone the names of nineteen persons who would have to be destroyed. These nineteen were summarily murdered and Roehm was dealt with later.[15]

Of all the Nazi leaders Hess was the most retiring, and therefore his public image was less bloodthirsty than that of Himmler or Goering. There were many Germans who thought that he was an 'intellectual', an 'honest man' and 'the conscience of the Party'.[16] It was no doubt for this reason that Hess was chosen to give a public justification for the Night of the Long Knives. The speech which he delivered at Koenigsberg on 8 July was broadcast by all German broadcasting stations:

> 'Special thanks of the movement are due to the S.S. who in these days honouring their slogan "Our Honour is our Loyalty" carried out their duties in an exemplary manner. . . .
>
> Who can now doubt that every youngster in the Hitler Jugend looks upon the Fuehrer as his ideal who particularly in those days acted like a heroic ideal figure of youth. . . .

Hess then touched upon the delicate subject of the guilty men:

> In an hour when the German people's being or not being was at stake, the extent of individual guilt could not be measured. Despite its harshness, it has a deep sense if mutinies in the Army are punished by decimation, that is the execution of every tenth man, irrespective of whether he was guilty or innocent.[17]

He may have had in mind one incident in which he was involved. In Munich on the evening of 30 June, Dr Willi Schmid, who was a music critic for the newspaper the *Muenchener Neueste Nachrichten*, was taken away from his flat by four S.S. men. A few days later a coffin was returned with his body inside, accompanied by orders from the Gestapo to keep it closed. Dr Schmid's misfortune had been to possess the same name as Willi Schmidt, a leader of the local S.A., who was shot by another group of S.S. men. When the S.S. sent the widow some money she refused to accept, and eventually Hess went to see her. He said that he was sorry about the mistake, and asked her to think of the death of her husband as 'the

death of a martyr for a great cause'.[18] He was obviously anxious
that such incidents should be hushed up.

In the early 1920's two men had exercised great influence over
Rudolf Hess, Karl Haushofer and Hitler. After 1923 the Professor
General receded into the background and remained the paternal
friend, while Hess had become one of Hitler's most fanatical
supporters. By the late 1920's Karl Haushofer was no longer the
major influence in Hess's life, but the two men remained close, and
Hess came to know Karl's son Albrecht, a brilliant student of
Foreign Affairs. In years to come this acquaintance between
Rudolf Hess and Albrecht Haushofer was to result in unexpected
consequences.

The Work of
Albrecht Haushofer

'*Rudi Hess and his equals are beyond help.*'
Albrecht Haushofer's letter to his father 8 June 1932.

'*I sometimes ask myself how long we shall be able to carry the responsibility, which we bear and which gradually begins to turn into historical guilt or, at least, into complicity. . . .*
'*There will be much violent dying and nobody knows when lightning will strike one's own house.*'
Albrecht Haushofer's letter to his parents 27 July 1934.

'*Perhaps we shall manage to chain the fuming titan to the rock.*'
Albrecht Haushofer to Fritz Hesse after the Remilitarisation of the Rhineland 1936.

'*The disappointed fury over the missed war is now raging internally. Today it is the Jews. Tomorrow it will be other groups and classes.*'
Albrecht Haushofer's letter to his mother 16 November 1938.

'*I am very much convinced that Germany cannot win a short war and that she cannot stand a long one.*'
Albrecht Haushofer's letter to the Duke of Hamilton 16 July 1939.

'*I can only live in two different forms: as a mind in the service of lying or as a body in the service of murder.*'
Albrecht Haushofer's letter to his mother 23 December 1939.

Early Days

IN 1933 Hess began to be influenced by Albrecht, Karl Haus-hofer's eldest son. Although he could not know it then, Albrecht would decisively affect the course of his life a few years later.

Because of the unwitting role he was to play, Albrecht is a character worthy of close examination; he was certainly one of the most fascinating and mysterious of all characters lurking behind the scenes of the Third Reich. It was hard for his acquaintances to judge whether he was a scholar, geographer, poet, musician, playwright, resister of Nazism or staid official in the German Foreign Office, but all who knew him agreed that he was a man of huge ability. Allen Dulles wrote that Albrecht Haushofer 'was fat, whimsical, sentimental, romantic and unquestionably brilliant'.[1] It was said of him that his friendships were of an uncertain kind and that he would often put an end to them in a mood of angry despair.[2] His friend Dr Carl von Weizsaecker wrote 'He could be compared to an elephant: weighty, clever, very clever and if necessary cunning.'[3]

Albrecht Haushofer was much closer to his half-Jewish mother than to his father the Professor General, with whom he did not always get on well. His father at times complained that his son would never make a German soldier, and the mother often had to smooth over relations between them. His letters to his parents tell a great deal, but it is his personal letters to his mother which are the most revealing, as he confided in her in a way which he did not with anyone else.

In 1917, at the age of 14, he attended the Theresien Gymnasium in Munich, where he was a solitary who did not integrate with his schoolfellows, mainly because they could not keep pace with him intellectually. One of his contemporaries asked him what he wished to become and without a moment's hesitation he replied 'German Foreign Minister'.[4] Such confidence caused irritation amongst

those around him, but they recognised that he had exceptional
qualities. In 1920 several of his age-group were celebrating the end
of the school term and Hermann Heimpel, a friend, leaves us a
glimpse of this strange man:

> Later Albrecht Haushofer made a great speech. He spoke of
> Germany, so full of love that it was unexpected, of the rest of the
> world, of stones and stars, of history and the future, with a dark
> seriousness as if he were carrying the wisdom of millenia and
> entering it in the book of the future: he spoke as if something
> was to happen. He appeared to be without hope, sombre and
> sweet. Since the others could not completely understand the
> speech but fully agreed with it they kept silent.[5]

At the age of nineteen at Munich University Albrecht Haushofer
passed his Doctor's degree *summa cum laude*. In 1924 he finished
his studies in History and Geography at Munich and submitted
his dissertation *Alpine Pass States*, which was not published until
1928. Many of his father's ideas appear in it, but the word 'geopolitics' does not. Unlike his father he wished geopolitics to have
the character of an exact science; it should not simply be a crude
tool for political propaganda. Consequently, in most of his future
writings he treated geopolitics and political geography as being
on the same level.

Like many Germans he felt rootless and insecure in spite of his
academic successes. He wrote to his mother on 25 May 1923
'. . . But I am sometimes troubled, young as I am, by the thought
whether I shall ever find a refuge, a home, or whether I shall
always be and remain a rootless person, a bird of passage. . . .'[6] In
the summer of 1924 he went to Berlin and became assistant to the
well-known geographer, Albrecht Penck. There, many doors were
opened to him on account of his father's reputation, and he grew
into his father's circle of contacts. In 1925 he became the Secretary
General of the Berlin 'Society for Geography', a post which he
held for the rest of his life, and in 1926 he became Editor of the
Periodical of the Society for Geography in Berlin. He lived at 23
Wilhelmstrasse, the premises of the Society for Geography, in
an official flat on the top floor. During these years he travelled
widely, visiting all the European countries, North and South
America, the Near, Middle and Far East and the Soviet Union,
but it was his trips to Britain that he enjoyed most.

Politically Albrecht Haushofer was a Bismarckian patriot, with a hankering for a Constitutional Monarchy in the sense of an idealised Bismarckian State. He intensely disliked revolutionary movements, an attitude which had its roots in his memories of Munich in November 1918. At that time an attempt had been made by a group of leftist intellectuals, led by Kurt Eisner, to seize power in Bavaria by setting up a Soviet Republic. The Reichswehr had intervened and General Ritter von Epp, a friend of Karl Haushofer, put down the revolt, but not before many hostages had been shot by the revolutionaries at the Luitpold Gymnasium. On 7 November 1928 Albrecht Haushofer wrote to his parents from Berlin: 'That winter ten years ago means something to me which I shall never get rid of while I live — an inexhaustible source of hatred, distrust, anger and scorn.'[7]

He also resented the Versailles Treaty and regarded the policy of fulfilment of the provisions of this Treaty as being too high a price for Germany to pay. As for the Treaty of Locarno of 1925, guaranteeing the frontiers of France and Belgium, he dismissed it sceptically as being 'the seal affixed to an existing situation'[8] which would happily be broken by either side at the first opportune moment. He wanted a revision of frontiers and wrote in 1926 that a 'lively participation of the German people, constructive and formulative, was not possible if present day frontiers are to be maintained'.[9] The Polish Corridor driving a wedge through Germany was a particularly bitter grievance to him. 'The present day solution of the Vistula problems', he wrote, 'is unpleasant for Danzig, damaging for Germany and far from satisfying for Poland.'[10]

Haushofer saw a future Germany as a co-ordinating power in middle, east and south-east Europe, the area between the Baltic and the Adriatic, including the Baltic States, Poland, Czechoslovakia, Hungary and the Balkan States. Situated between two powerful neighbours, Germany and Russia, these East European countries had traditionally fallen within the sphere of influence of either Germany or Russia. As German enclaves still formed an important part of the population in each of these states, Albrecht Haushofer saw them as potential clients of Germany in the economic field.

As a southern German who had a deep attachment for the Alps, he hoped that Austria and Germany would come closer together

B

through a process of gradual evolution, until eventually an
Anschluss would take place. In 1931 an attempt was made at the
height of the Depression to form a German–Austrian Customs
Union. The plan was thwarted through the opposition of France,
supported by the countries of the Little Entente, and the International Court of Justice at the Hague rejected it.

This made Albrecht Haushofer regard France as the dedicated
enemy of Germany. Had not France guaranteed the frontiers of
Belgium, Poland and those of the Little Entente States, and was not
France preventing Germany from collaborating with Austria and
from exercising a decisive economic influence in south-east
Europe? Was it not symptomatic of the desire of the French
Government to want to prevent Germany from ever becoming a
strong European Power and to keep her isolated?

He did not consider Russia as a possible target for armed
aggression, or as a potential ally. The only country with which he
wished close co-operation was Britain. In a letter to his parents
dated 30 July 1930, he expressed his views on both Russia and
Britain in a language which few Russians would have liked:

> So my first impression of Russia is one of terrible poverty and
> oppression, a partly purposeless, partly systematic cultural de-
> cline of enormous proportions. On the other side the accumula-
> tion of sinister power and growing economic strength (partly
> through ruthless exploitation of large natural resources, partly
> however, through an undeniably systematic large scale recon-
> struction) in a few entirely or nearly barbaric hands.
>
> The national character however has not changed. The Russian
> is still indolent, lazy, dull, unclean and unpunctual. Many
> things may be recognised in many fields; and the danger must
> not be underestimated.
>
> To make common cause with Moscow is according to my
> impressions completely out of the question as long as the entire
> structure of our political mentality remains unchanged.[11]

Britain fared much better in a letter dated 9 November 1930
written to his parents from London. From the way in which he
expressed himself he was obviously enjoying himself, as though the
seemingly self-confident British way of life was one to which he
would have liked to belong, even if he did not wholly understand it.

And now London. General impression: envy for the country
which still has so many men to steer her history. I have at last
seen almost all important leaders, to many of them I have
spoken personally: e.g., Lord Allenby with whom I had a
brilliant conversation for an hour without knowing who he was....

Splendid the old Earl of Crawford and Balcarres, a Scot of
ancient descent – one of the wisest men I ever met ... Chamberlain who actually makes a less distinguished impression:
Churchill, who has become fat and who looks more like a clever
clown than a Statesman. . . . The German Embassy with the
young Count Bernstorff and the young Prince Bismarck makes
in comparison a rather paltry impression – the welcome was
exceedingly cordial.[12]

He idealised the British two-party system of Government and
saw in it a complete contrast to the Weimar Republic, which had
been weakened through the frequent occurrence of party political
splintering (he referred to President Hindenburg as the 'sentry in
front of the bankruptcy trustee's office'[13]). He especially liked
what he understood to be British flexibility and pragmatism. He
believed that 'for every political aim there are hundreds of forms;
but he who insists on sticking to one will be stunted'.[14] He thought
that an appreciation of this outlook had been the key to the successes
of Bismarck and the British.

To Haushofer's way of thinking co-operation with Britain was
essential and any war in Europe unthinkable. In any large-scale
war there could not in his view be any victors – only death and
destruction. In her own interests and in the interests of European
civilisation Germany must achieve her aims through peaceful
means.

The peoples of Europe are in a position in which they have
to get on together lest they all perish; and although one realises
that it is not commonsense but emotional urges which govern
the world, one must still try to control such urges. If one is
forced to get on with others in a certain space, one does not have
to love them. But it will be well not to exasperate one another.
The risk would be too great. [15]

In Germany he saw the weaknesses of the Weimar Regime;
his play *And thus Pandurion Is Governed*, written between 1930 and

1932, deals with the unhappiness of coalition crises, and is set against the background of the French invasion of the Ruhr. He had already tried to influence diplomats and members of the Weimar Cabinets by means other than the stage. On 26 October 1929 he proudly wrote to his mother: '. . . The "People and Reich" essay has indeed attracted some attention . . . all really political people have at last recognised me as a personality in my own right, and no longer a son of my father. . . .' [16]

On the same day he wrote a long letter to his father stating his respect and even admiration for Stresemann, the foreign minister. Albrecht had corresponded with him and regarded him as a leader of moderate nationalism.

> . . . For years now Western [German] policy was made with sacrifice after sacrifice in order to get a free hand in the East one day – now, in the few weeks since Stresemann's death, our last means of pressure in the Poland negotiations has been thrown overboard. . . .
>
> Everybody who sails under the direct flag of the Right is not even listened to owing to the anxiety psychosis into which Hugenberg and Hitler have plunged the people. . . . I must confess that four weeks ago I could not have considered how deep the desire for Stresemann's return must be. He was certainly not a great man, but among the blind he was certainly one-eyed. . . .

He mentioned his desire to intrigue behind the scenes and to keep on speaking terms with Hess and the Nazis, in case any information could be gleaned from them.

> I intend to have a determining voice, but not in the foreground of the platform. I am still too young for that and the general situation is not *yet* tense enough. . . .
>
> Do you know by any chance things about Hess, which are not confidential but none the less interesting and which may be passed on? Please do not mention that I have asked. [17]

It was significant that Albrecht Haushofer wrote to his father on 4 November 1929 'What you write about the extreme right coincides with my own impressions. It may become necessary to exert influence there one day.' [18] On 25 February 1930 he wrote to his mother, with a certain faith in his own ability, and with a few reservations about his father:

> I wish you had borne me a little more stupid. . . . A little more convinced of the 'correctness' of what I say – perhaps like my father who is certainly not vain, much less vain than I am myself – who delivers his teachings only with the downright provoking conceit of conviction.[19]

Albrecht Haushofer was doing all that he could to keep every option open, although he had little in common with the Nazis. He did not mind mixing and collaborating with extreme Nationalists, such as his father's friends. In November 1931 he started to work for the *Zeitschrift für Geopolitik*, the journal which his father edited. While his father wrote the 'Reports from the Pacific World', Albrecht wrote the 'Reports from the Atlantic World'.

On 30 May 1932 Bruening's government resigned, producing in Albrecht Haushofer a deep pessimism about Anglo–German relations and the future of Germany. He wrote to his mother on 3 June 1932: 'It is not my fault nor that of others that today the entire German position in the Anglo–Saxon countries is a heap of debris. . . . Let us see how we can get through mill torrent 2, the beginning of which we now experience. I do not think that in the end there will still exist a German Reich.'[20]

Unlike many Germans he had no faith in or liking for Nazi ideas and ideology. On 8 June he wrote to his father that 'Rudi Hess and his equals are beyond help'.[21] He had no time for the Government of Papen, and wrote on 25 July 'Mr. Von P. is a nonentity . . . whose description of "untested efficiency" one can unhesitatingly change into "tested inefficiency"'.[22]

Even at this time Haushofer completely underestimated Hitler and Nazism. 'Now we just have to await what the elections will bring. I do not believe in a swastika majority and I have the curious idea that this possibility would be the only one of which Adolf the Great is afraid, like a small child.'[23] The strength of popular support for Nazism puzzled him, and on 16 February 1932 he wrote to his parents: 'Today the Right is demagogised to such an extent that nothing can be expected from it and experience and responsibility lie in the middle. It is a strange situation.'[24] He had reached the view that support for Nazism was only a phase. He was soon to be disillusioned.

2 Protection from Hess: 1933

ALBRECHT Haushofer was confronted with a serious dilemma when the Nazis came to power. There were three possibilities open to him. He could oppose Nazism openly, and run the risk of being killed and of causing persecution to his family. He could flee the country and express himself without let or hindrance from abroad, or he could work for the regime in one capacity or another, in the hope of influencing the course of events in a peaceful direction.

He never seriously thought of open opposition to the Nazi regime, since any hostility might have produced a violent reaction, and have landed him in a concentration camp. Albrecht knew how ruthless the Nazis could be, and he had no reason to believe that the matter would be left there. At the very least his internment and fate would have caused great embarrassment to his family, especially to his half-Jewish mother, of whom he was very fond. He did not wish to take risks which might involve harm to her, physical or otherwise. This left him with the choice of either leaving Germany or of working for the Third Reich. The possibility of emigration was carefully considered, but it did not appeal to him, as he felt that he would be running away, and that outside Germany he would not be in a position to alter the actions of the German leaders.

The third course, that of working for the regime in the hope that he might tone it down, was an option more in accordance with his temperament and outlook. His intellectual vanity was such that he imagined he might be able to manipulate those with authority in the Reich. Yet however confident he was in his own ability, he was apprehensive. During the first months after the Nazi accession to power he adopted a waiting attitude, tinged with pessimism. In spring 1933 he wrote 'the only consolation is very negative, that is the conviction that we are approaching such a great general catastrophe that personal catastrophes will no longer count'.[1]

There is no doubt that he had no enthusiasm for his leaders. On 22 February 1933 he wrote to his mother complaining of Goering's threatening demands and offers to François-Poncet, the French Ambassador in Berlin, and the frustration which it caused Von Neurath, the German Foreign Minister.

> Politics for the amusement of father: Latest performance of Mr G[oerin]g: He goes to François-Poncet off his own bat, demands the return of the Corridor; if Poland responded favourably, one would assist her in conquering the Ukraine. F.-P. smiles and asks that the matter be given to him in writing. And he gets it! Two hours later a smiling Russian Ambassador shows it to the desperate Mr Von N[eura]th. These are the saviours of the nation.[2]

Yet he was prepared to co-operate with the Nazis as he felt that there was no turning back for Germany. On 17 March he wrote to his parents from Berlin:

> As matters stand today, one has to wish them full success; because the boats are burned – a state which in itself is extremely uncomfortable – and one has to become familiar with the coast-line, even if it appears to be very adventurous at first. Reasonable persons are always out of place in revolutionary periods. And that will not change so soon. . . . [3]

He was rudely brought to his senses on 7 April 1933 when the Nazi regime passed the Civil Service Laws which excluded those of non-Aryan origin from public office within the Reich. As a person in part Jewish this news hit Albrecht Haushofer like a blow from a hammer. By German law he was at most only a second-class citizen. He may well have felt that if he chose to stay in Germany his chances of becoming German Foreign Minister were negligible, and that in the long run his career was already finished. The whole Haushofer family was affected, but Albrecht and his mother felt it most bitterly, and on 12 April Albrecht wrote to his mother:

> When I examine the human side – honestly! there is not much left at all. . . . The special faith in humanity has become thin, terribly thin.[4]

On 19 April he wrote again to his mother, expressing a sense of resignation, indifference and dread.

. . . and yet I cannot write otherwise than in a mood of
a completely resigning philosophy of life, to which the individual life, especially one's own, has become indifferent and
alien. . . .

Desires? Hopes? You yourself see clearly enough what will
yet come to pass. In small circles as well as in the large one. Why
should one throw dust into one's eyes? Afterwards it will be a
poor consolation that one has foreseen and known everything
with clear and alert common sense. For father and for Heinz –
who both have deeper roots in the soil – it will be more difficult. . . .[5]

On 7 May his resentment at his father's passive acceptance of a
racist policy bubbled over in a letter to his mother, and his intentions were almost suicidal:

I am glad about the optimism of father and of Heinz, although
I do not understand it. . . . The way our German world develops
I see no possibilities of activity for myself. . . .

But these are only the external things. Internally it looks like
this: I now stand on a narrow strip of land which remains when
one becomes indifferent to one's own existence, and when on
the other hand there is no compelling reason for taking an active
step towards non-existence.

I cannot really say very much regarding father's political
letter. I am glad that he sees possibilities of activity for himself
to a certain extent – in the same state which disqualifies his
sons from the Civil Service (I have very carefully read the new
Ordinance to the Civil Servants' Act, I do not notice much
relaxation in them). But we judge matters too differently for me
to be able to say anything in respect of this attitude, in respect
of his standing up or not standing up for people.

You cannot plane wood without producing shavings is a very
fine proverb; but when some of the shavings are personally
known to you, things look very different. I only do not know
whether I should envy or admire the blindness which does not
see how near to us already is the blade of the plane.[6]

On 26 May he wrote to his mother saying that he saw no future
for himself, and that his position as editor of the periodical of the
Society for Geography in Berlin was threatened:

And here we are back at the topic, which is unavoidable today and which I have avoided in my last letters solely for the reason that you have written to me that I should not undermine father's passably positive frame of mind. If it has to be mentioned at all, I cannot deny that now as before I take a very gloomy view of the future in general as well as of my own in particular. In this state which makes second-class human beings out of us, who in the interest of expediency should not exist, there is no activity for us. Because our position is based on the fact that our descent is either not known or ignored. That is no basis for any life-work of quality. Any position grudger – and how many of them do exist today – can have us thrown out. . . . If, for instance, the Emergency Aid Association is forced to make the granting of subsidies to journals dependent on the pure Aryan descent of the editor – a procedure which is entirely conceivable – then my position here will come to an end.

Then I shall be faced with the problem of whether to crawl away in the quiet with the remainder of my fortune and to live just as long as this remainder lasts or whether to make the attempt to find shelter somewhere abroad, which would neither be easy in practice, nor easy for me personally.[7]

This was the first time that the thought of emigration seriously occupied him, but as a patriotic German it was unattractive, and he rejected the idea. He was in despair until June 1933, when Hitler's Deputy Rudolf Hess intervened personally. Hess issued protective letters to the two sons of the Professor General, so that the Nazis would refrain from attacking them. Hess was glad to help his old tutor and friend, who had sheltered him after the Beerhall Putsch, and he took it for granted that his sons would be patriotic Germans.

Following Hess's action, Albrecht wrote to his parents on 22 June, a long and important letter which showed that while he was prepared to work for the regime he remained basically hostile to Nazism in all its forms.

R. H. [Rudolf Hess] has not yet phoned. . . . I find it touching that he engages himself so strongly in the whole matter, while on the other hand I cannot quite understand it either (seen from his angle). Because either one enacts such a Law (and in doing so, considers which class of human beings is thereby affected)

B2

or one does not enact it: if one enacts it at all, one also has to implement it.

This is, however, just a psychology, which is no longer valid today. That it is no longer valid in this case is, of course, fortunate for our family circle, especially for those members of it who are fortunate enough to have a bad memory. Unfortunately, I have a good one and I shall not forget the experience of being turned out, even though it was only a spiritual and not an actual dismissal, and even though I am now smuggled back again in the wake of H's [Hess's] peasant cunning and of father's personal authority. Because it is nothing else after all.

I am now completely clear on the point that I am fundamentally not suited for this new German world. . . . I am opposed in all essential aspects to the human type which, above all, is represented as valid in the younger generation. You know that I am not completely without passion, but it is a different passion of coldness, of stillness, of abstraction – i.e. the exact opposite of that which the emotional type ruling today can understand and need. He, whose faith in human society approximately agrees with Schopenhauer's fine parable of the porcupines – is unusable for the rulers of today.

There is no personal future for me in the new Germany, because humanly I can agree as little with the new people as perhaps Erasmus of Rotterdam could with the Anabaptists or even with the Lutheran Protestants.

Since the new state now renews the totality demand of absolutism, probably no cultural sphere free of government intervention will be left at all . . . nothing else will remain for me but a retreat into a potentially dead corner, from which in the best case a secret invisible background operation may be thought of.

In the case of geopolitics I have the strong fear that it is too near the motive of power to be acceptable to me in the long run. For the last half-year every report is an agony for me, over which I ponder for days in order to distil the necessary compromise between truth, inner conviction and the permissible.

Nothing very positive will therefore result from the friendship of R. H. [Rudolf Hess]. . . .

In the best case, I foresee for myself a state of quietness and resignation, which will undoubtedly last for years. A position publicly visible would only be a danger today, but I do not believe that it would occur to anybody to call me there. Because most of the persons in authority today do not know me and the few who know me can understandably do without me as easily as I can do without them. The best possible relationship is a friendly emphasised distance.

I write all this for once quite openly noting father's disappointment. . . . You, Mother, will undoubtedly understand this in every detail.[8]

Contrary to what he wrote, something more did result from Karl Haushofer's friendship with Hess. Albrecht Haushofer received the offer of an official post in Germany as a lecturer in Political Geography at the Berlin High School for Politics through the help of Hess. He was also asked by Hess to attend talks at Danzig as the latter's representative in June 1933, and at the end of that month Albrecht wrote to his parents giving the reasons for his decision to work for the regime:

Inhibitions:

Lack in me of National Socialist philosophy of life. Lacking faith in the ability to teach and to find contact with the young generation. Compulsion to make a whole series of compromises in questions of opinion; loss of a good deal of both inner and external freedom.

Incentives:

Increased possibility of practical activity: improvement of my position in the sense of external prestige and of middle class significance of titles.

Compulsion to be active:

In a certain sense increase and safety of external freedom of movement, both financially as well as in respect of freedom to travel, which one must grant to the holder of this position.

You see, it is all rather muddled up, but it is, after all, a fact that the incentives are all on the side of my worldly *vita activa* – while the inhibitions are just inhibitions of my character. That I could accomplish many things better than others, that in this position a tolerably reasonable person is better than an unreasonable one, that I probably possess the necessary skill to create for myself further influence from this activity, that (and this is said really more for you than for myself, because your external need for my prestige is greater than my own) the then existing combination of external position would for quite a number of years serve as an absolutely satisfactory basis – all that I know of course. The question is whether I could manage to jump over the internal shadow, and if I do, how it will end.[9]

He had accepted the post and would have to pay a high price for his action. He knew he would have to compromise his principles on a vast variety of issues, and that knowledge humiliated him and made him lacking in self-respect. Having accepted the post at the Berlin High School his doubts were increased rather than diminished. It appears that Goebbels, Reich Minister of Propaganda, regarded him as a Jew and referred to him as such. Albrecht at any rate wrote to Goebbels saying that his father was 'personally well-known to the Reich Chancellor and the Deputy of the Fuehrer'.[10] Hess's 'protective' letters, to the effect that the Haushofer sons were honorary Aryans, were sent to the Ministry of Propaganda. On 22 July, Albrecht wrote to his mother about the precariousness of his own existence:

> I only see very clearly, and much clearer than Father and my brother, the shakiness and insecurity of such a basis for all practical activity. What will happen if Father's friend should lose his influence one day?
>
> When I enter the new activity, I shall have to face such a measure of sacrifice of inner conviction, of silence and of swallowing that I am unwilling further to increase this measure with open eyes by acquiring the truly false odour of a Party Member.
>
> You, Mother, will understand that the whole matter presents for me a great inner predicament. I do not ask of Father to understand it. If the matter materialises, to which I have said 'Yes' now – then I shall pay for the external activity (and for the satisfaction of your ambition for me) a price, which is so high, that during the night it sometimes causes me long hours of wakefulness. . . .[11]

On 5 August he wrote to his mother as a man who was trying to rationalise his position:

I have never deceived myself on the point that political life in all conceivable forms exacts compromises and sacrifices of attitude. . . .

You are quite right: we have only a choice between evils, and everything I do is, after all, but an attempt to come to terms with the present evil as best I can. . . .[12]

Albrecht could only exist in the Third Reich provided that he concealed his real views from the Nazi High Command, and thus his relationships with senior Nazis were necessarily hypocritical. On 7 September 1933 he wrote a significant letter to Rudolf Hess, which represented a turning point in his life:

. . . A messenger of the Ministry for Propaganda called to bring me a letter . . . in which is contained the final permission for my appointment to the High School for Politics. Now I may add a short personal word to you.

I know what I have to thank you for. It is not so much the position as such – much as it is appropriate to the possibilities of what I can accomplish – it is the deliverance from an inner plight, of the seriousness of which I cannot speak. We – my brother and I – are indebted for your intercession, to which it is solely attributable that we have not been swept onto the dump as Germans of inferior value. You will understand when I say that it is very difficult for an internally proud and sincere person to be indebted to such a degree, that he examines himself carefully before he begs or lets somebody else beg for him. I could not have accepted this extraordinary favour – not even for my father's sake – if I did not feel certain that in case of need I would be capable of full personal effort for you as a person. On the face of it perhaps all this may be very remote. It is an inner necessity for me to affirm this to myself and for once also to be allowed to express it to you.[13]

These were words which would have their importance for both Albrecht Haushofer and Hess, and in spite of Hess's protection the subject of anti-semitism was a particularly awkward topic for Albrecht. In this connection he was in an unusual position. On the one hand it was advantageous to him that his father had a standing in Germany as an impeccably patriotic general and founder of German geopolitics: on the other hand it was a great disadvantage to him that his mother was half-Jewish, because his part-Jewish origin excluded him from all meaningful public activity – prior to Hess's intervention. Even after Hess had made him an honorary Aryan he was treated by the other Nazi leaders with reserve.

There were two strains of thought running through his mind. The strain of patriotism came from his father, who would support his country whatever it might do. The other and more sympathetic strain of hatred of all forms of violence came from his half-Jewish mother, who feared Nazism on account of its fanatical racism and vicious excesses. Although Albrecht was much closer to his mother and respected her outlook much more than that of his father, he had submitted to his father's influence, contrary to his mother's advice. He became Hess's personal adviser and by mid-1934 was installed by Hess in the Dienststelle Ribbentrop, a Nazi Foreign Affairs Bureau, under the control of Hess as the head of the Nazi Party.

As a part-Jewish person in a country which discriminated against all Jews, Albrecht Haushofer was not prepared to fight against Nazi discrimination, and run the risk of being dropped by Hess and whisked into a concentration camp. Instead he was bending over backwards to make himself acceptable as a loyal German subject, in the hope that he might mitigate the effect of Nazi racial policy.

In the spring of 1934 he wrote a laboured and cautiously worded memorandum for Hess: 'Ideas for a differentiating Solution of the Non-Aryan Problem',[14] in which he wished to prevent discrimination against all Jews in Germany, by suggesting an annexe to the Civil Service Law of April 1933. He argued that there were Jews who should be regarded as Germans, and exceptions made in their case. Broadly speaking his suggestions would have given to established German Jewry the rights of citizenship, but not to those Jews who had immigrated into Germany within the last few decades. It may well be that he thought that this was as far as he dare go in suggesting an easing of the 'anti-Semitic' legislation.

In 1933 there were about half a million Jews living within the Reich, and about one-fifth of them did not possess German citizenship. All of them were subject to discrimination after April 1933. Albrecht Haushofer in his proposals suggested that approximately two-fifths of the Jewish population in Germany, which incidentally included his mother's family, should be exempted from the Civil Service Laws and should be accepted as Germans, while the other three-fifths of German Jewry, that is more than 300,000 persons, would be excluded from the rights of citizenship. Haushofer was engaged in special pleading on behalf of those in a similar predicament to himself, and he gave a brief summary of the document which he wrote for Hess a year later in a letter to his father, dated 14 January 1935:

> I have the impression that in the near future a decision in principle on the State Citizenship Act will be forthcoming in the Reich Ministry of the Interior. (Remarks of Frick, confidential information from the Ministry.) What matters . . . is the ultimate finding of a form for the exceptions deemed necessary.

Enclosure:

Should in the near future an ultimate form of non-Aryan Law in the scope of a state citizenship legislation of the Reich Ministry of the Interior ensue, it has to be examined whether the existing rules of the Civil Servants Act could not be made more flexible by a permissive provision. Such provision could look as follows. . . .

In special cases persons, who according to the Act . . . are non-Aryans and in respect of whom none of the existing saving clauses are applicable can also be recognised as Germans. Such a recognition can be granted:

(a) in the case of children of war participants (perhaps in the case of children of holders of high war decoration);

(b) in the case of persons who can prove that all their non-Aryan ancestors were domiciled in the present Reich territory since 1815;

(c) in the case of persons who are of non-Aryan descent only in respect of one parent or grandparent, if it can be proved that among their non-Aryan ancestors of the first to the third generation there are personalities who have deserved well of the German people.

Such recognition should be granted:

(1) in cases of persons, where instances (a) (b) and (c) apply simultaneously;

(2) in cases of persons, whose recognition as Germans is proposed by one of the highest Reich authorities or by the

leadership of the National Socialist German Workers
Party. . . .[15]

It is not known whether Hess reviewed with any seriousness the
document which Albrecht Haushofer had previously written for
him. Certainly it had no effect. Hess had no hesitation in signing
the Nuremberg Race Laws and the Reich Citizenship Law. These
laws dismissed all persons of Jewish origin from public office, the
only exceptions being those very few like Albrecht Haushofer who
were directly protected by the Nazi leadership and who were considered to be temporarily indispensable.

Albrecht Haushofer was not technically a member of the Nazi
Party, but he was compromising with Nazism. He might have
argued and probably did argue that it was better to save some
people from discrimination, and he may have intervened personally on behalf of Jews whom he knew. Even so, these attempts
were hardly more than specks of dust in a flood. In any case he
was working for Hess, who was helping to direct the flow of the
Nazi tide.

3 Personal Adviser: 1934

ALBRECHT Haushofer appeared to be only a lecturer in Political Geography in Berlin, but in fact behind the scenes he saw a lot of Hess, and acted as the latter's personal adviser, his policy being 'Let us educate our masters.'[1] He gave advice to Hess on a large range of topics, three of the most important being the position of unpopular persons in the Reich, matters relating to Volksdeutsch activity with Germans outside the Reich, and Germany's relations with foreign countries, especially with Britain and the U.S.A.

On 24 August 1933 Albrecht wrote to Hess asking that Nazi threats to the life of former Chancellor Bruening should cease:

> ... A very delicate matter ... I now learn that a personality, who lives completely withdrawn in the inland, but has still got a very great name abroad, H[einric]h B[ruenin]g, has to fear for his personal safety. ... I need not say what reactions a personal accident to B[ruening] would have abroad – Could you take care of internal restraint?[2]

This letter may well have saved Bruening's life; and on 7 September 1933 Albrecht Haushofer wrote to Hess: 'For your intervention *in re* B. sincere thanks!'[3]

Albrecht also tried to exert influence in Volksdeutsch affairs, in which his father and Hess were deeply involved. On 8 October 1933 he wrote to his father: 'The form of the supreme control for German nationality questions established by you in co-operation with Rudolf Hess appears to me decidedly hopeful.'[4] On 14 October the Volksdeutsch Council appointed by Hess had its first meeting under the chairmanship of Karl Haushofer, and Albrecht became his father's representative in Berlin.

Albrecht also acted as Hess's representative on a number of occasions. Between 18 and 19 June 1934 he went as the representative of the Volksdeutsch Council to Danzig in order to

induce German groups in Poland to accept a joint programme – the
Zopot Agreement – and then reported back to Hess.[5] On 19
September 1934 he arranged the first meeting between Hess and
Henlein, the leader of the Sudeten German Party.[6] It is even
thought that from 1935 onwards Hitler based some of his formu-
lations in Volksdeutsch politics on statements submitted to him
by Hess and prepared by Albrecht Haushofer.[7]

Through Hess, Albrecht attempted to settle disputes between
the Volksdeutsch Council and other aggressively Nazi organisations
such as the Hitler Jugend, the Ausland Organisation of the
N.S.D.A.P. under Gauleiter Bohle and the S.S. under Himmler.
Albrecht was opposed to Gleichschaltung or co-ordination under
the Third Reich's regime, as he did not want Volksdeutsch work
in countries outside Germany to be converted into Nazi Fifth
Columnist activity. For this reason he attempted to resist the
pressures on the V.D.A. from Nazi sources, and on 3 November
1933 he wrote to his father: 'There is no harm in your energetically
intervening once again to prevent hotheads and intriguers in the
Hitler Jugend from smashing up the Overseas German Youth
Movement. . . .'[8]

On 20 November 1933 Albrecht again wrote to his father,
mentioning that it was difficult in a totalitarian regime for the
leaders to discriminate between accurate information and false
propaganda.

> I again have an appointment in the next few days with our
> friend Rudolf Hess. . . . Generally the problem of how to learn
> the truth is very much more burning for the leadership of an
> absolutist state than for that of a liberal one. . . .[9]

Haushofer feared that even if Hess did learn the truth his power
to act independently of Hitler was negligible, and that Hess did
not have as much influence with Hitler as he had had before the
Nazis had come to power. After a meeting with Hess, he wrote
'Hess gives the impression of being full of goodwill, but I do not
have the impression that this will suffice.'[10] Yet Albrecht remained
willing to collaborate with him, and in the spring of 1934 he wrote,
to his father: 'Our great friend Hess is really a blessing. I recently
saw him for a short while and had a pleasant discussion with him
on all kinds of topics.'[11] In contrast he wrote to his mother on the
same day as though he were apologising for himself:

The political volcano, yes I understand how you see it. But against this, without the worth of our friend, who is a constant source of solace amidst all the unpleasantness, we would have been entirely excluded, and neither insectology nor Etruscology would have saved us from being evicted. [12]

He allowed himself to be caught up in abstractions, which blanketed his mind against the inhumanities inherent in Nazism. He wrote of Hess: 'There is a strange charm in his personality; whenever he is there, a friendly veil falls over all the grey and black of the present.' [13]

Still Albrecht could see that the V.D.A. was gradually being Nazified, and that the Volksdeutsch Council, under his father, as the only relatively moderating influence, was losing its grip. In June 1934 Karl Haushofer, acting with Albrecht's approval, warned Hess that if the Volksdeutsch Council no longer had jurisdiction over the Volksdeutsch outside Europe, there would be severe repercussions in the U.S.A. and the British Dominions. [14] On 15 August 1934 Albrecht Haushofer wrote to his father that Bohle's activities at the head of the Nazi Ausland Organisation would stir up hatred for the Germans in foreign countries:

You can tell our friend Hess without hesitation that I too would have told him that we shall get a nasty foreign political swarm of wasps about our ears, if we give the all-clear to Bohle....[15]

The dispute with Bohle arose over his refusal to acknowledge the difference between Volksdeutschen (persons of German ethnic origin, but citizens of other countries) and Reichsdeutschen (German citizens living abroad). The Volksdeutschen came under the jurisdiction of Karl Haushofer and the Reichsdeutschen under that of Bohle, and Bohle was attempting to extend his own power, much to the irritation of both Haushofers. On 18 January 1935 Albrecht wrote to his father, referring to the latter's impending discussion with Hess on the possibilities of limiting the ambitious movements of Bohle:

. . . Our superior will not get peace either, unless he puts Bohle in his place. . . .

P.S. The fact that our relationship to Ribbentrop . . . is

excellent, is yet another indication as to where the source of the discord lies.[16]

Soon after Hess told Bohle to restrict his attentions to Reichsdeutschen. Even so the Volksdeutsch Council did not succeed in co-ordinating Volksdeutsch organisations and Hess decided to reactivate it. During 1935 the Volksdeutsch Council disappeared, and soon after, in 1936, the Volksdeutsch Centre, with which the Haushofers were also connected took over the functions of the Volksdeutsch Council. This centre was a Party office established by Hess with the intention that it should co-ordinate all Volksdeutsch agencies. From the outset Bohle and the Nazi Ausland Organisation were hostile; Himmler and the S.S. were more so.

In December 1936 Karl Haushofer wrote to Hess pointing out that the substitution of S.S. and Gestapo officers for other men in the V.D.A. would have an effect of far-reaching proportions, and he suggested that Hess should obtain a personal decision from the Fuehrer.[17] But unknown to the Professor General, Hitler had already decided to centralise control over subsidies for Volksdeutsch organisations[18] and it is likely that Hess had received instructions which directly contradicted Haushofer's warnings. At any rate in early 1937 the Volksdeutsch Centre was superseded by a new and sinister organisation which had erupted on to the scene.

This was the Volksdeutche Mittelstelle, V.O.M.I. (the Centre for Racial Germans), and it was controlled by one of Himmler's minions, S.S. Obergruppenführer Lorenz. In 1936 Hitler had decided that the alleged grievances of the Volksdeutschen in Austria, the Czech Sudetenland and Poland should be exploited. To do this it was necessary to have effective control over the various Ausland Organisations, and Himmler was the right man for the job as far as Hitler was concerned. 1937 was an important year for Hess and the Haushofers, for after the creation of V.O.M.I. effective control over the Volksdeutsch passed from Hess to Himmler. The overall charge in Volksdeutsch affairs still remained with Hess for a few more years, but from 1937 on the real power lay with the Reichsführer S.S. It soon became apparent that Himmler was not slow to organise the German minorities outside the Reich through V.O.M.I., so that these minorities might serve as useful pawns in any Nazi military action for extra Lebensraum.

Albrecht Haushofer was not unaware of what was happening

around him, and he felt that his only security lay in serving as a useful adviser to Hess, in return for which Hess continued to protect him. On 27 March 1935 Hess sent Albrecht a copy of a letter from a Frau Schultz who was complaining about the praise given to Albrecht Haushofer's scientific work. She objected in particular to a statement Albrecht had made about Hitler's role in the Beerhall Putsch:

> On the occasion of the fiftieth anniversary of the Geographical Society in 1932 he [Albrecht Haushofer] was a guest in our house. On that occasion he declared that the Fuehrer had cowardly forsaken his comrades in front of the Feldhernhalle in 1923 and had thought only of his own personal safety....
>
> I am at any time prepared to be personally answerable for the above.
>
> Heil Hitler!
Yours faithfully,
H. Schultz.[19]

Hess wrote to Albrecht: 'I should be grateful to you for information as to what I can reply to this. With German salutation!' No doubt Hess was given a 'suitable' answer.

One of the main fields in which Albrecht Haushofer gave advice to Hess was on the subject of Germany's foreign relations with the Anglo-Saxon countries. On 23 August 1933 he wrote a report for Hess on an interview which he had had with Ambassador Dodd of the U.S.A. to Germany. Evidently Albrecht Haushofer foresaw the possible murder of Dolfuss, Chancellor of Austria, which he hoped to prevent:

> I have just returned from a lengthy talk with Ambassador Dodd. He tells me that he will personally do everything to effect an appeasing influence on his Government as well as on London....
>
> One sentence of the talk I must quote to you literally. After having given an assurance that he would do everything to prevent or to suppress incidents, he said: 'Of course the Austrian thing can flare up any moment, and then no help that I can give will be of avail.'[21]

Dodd was referring to the possibility of an attempt by the Nazis to annex Austria by military action, and it was an incident on

25 July 1934 which brought home to Albrecht Haushofer the hypocrisy of his position.

Both Hitler and Hess had wanted to annex Austria at the first available opportunity and plans were made either with the direct approval of Hess as Hitler's deputy or with his connivance. In view of Hess's proximity to Hitler and Himmler, and to the Ausland Organisations which had extensive contacts in Austria, and in view of the mass of information which was accumulated in the Nazi Party's headquarters at the Brown House in Munich, it is inconceivable that Hess was unaware of what was going to happen. Eva Braun wrote in her diary that Hess had given instructions that, in the event of a rising, Chancellor Dolfuss was not in any circumstances to be allowed to survive.[22]

At noon on 25 July 1934 about 150 men of the S.S. Standarte 89, wearing Austrian uniforms, burst into the Chancellery in Vienna and broke into Chancellor Dolfuss's study. Dolfuss knew what they were about and dashed towards a door from his study to a secret passage which had just been blocked up. As he scrabbled desperately with his fingers at the door he was shot down, and as he lay in agony the S.S. refused to allow him either a doctor or a priest: they stood over him watching him choke to death in his own blood. At about 6.00 p.m. Dolfuss died and Austrian forces under Dr Kurt von Schuschnigg recovered control. Some thirteen of the S.S. who had murdered Dolfuss, including Planetta (one of their leaders, who claimed to have fired the fatal shot), were arrested and later executed.

Two days later, on 27 July, Albrecht Haushofer wrote to his parents from Berlin:

> I sometimes ask myself how long we shall be able to carry the responsibility, which we bear and which gradually begins to turn into historical guilt or, at least, into complicity. . . . But all of us are, after all, in a situation of conflicting obligations, from which at best fate can find a way out, and we have to carry on working, even when the task has become completely hopeless.
>
> And now I must try to finish my geopolitics report. How, I do not know. In the evening of the day before yesterday I heard father's radio talk; I must admit it was very sinister to me to hear his sarcastic remark on Dolfuss's accumulation of offices while on the adjoining wave-length it was announced that he was

dead. . . . There will be much violent dying and nobody knows when lightning will strike one's own house.'[23]

In normal circumstances Albrecht would have had no reservations about working for his country as an official. Like most Germans he wanted to see a strong German leadership achieve a modification of the frontiers imposed on Germany by the Treaty of Versailles. In his outlook he has been accurately described as a 'national-liberal-conservative' and at first his attitude towards National Socialism remained ambiguous.[24] He hesitated between acknowledgement of Hitler's effectiveness in restoring German prosperity and self-respect, and a reserve which was developing into a deep-rooted dislike of the methods of the regime. His reservations were on the grounds that its policy was racist and that its leaders were prepared to kill anyone whom they regarded as standing in their way.

He knew that, but for his father's great friendship with Hess, he would have been discriminated against along with others who were of partly Jewish origin. As a person existing under the protecting hand of Hess he was in far too vulnerable a position to protest openly against anti-Semitism and other forms of racism. He thought that any open opposition would be trampled underfoot by the brutality of the Third Reich, and therefore he was compromising. But Albrecht had no love for his leaders, and shortly before the Night of the Long Knives he had a conversation with Rudolf Pechel and Edgar Jung. Pechel, a well-known journalist, reported that Albrecht 'condemned National Socialism and its leaders in such violent terms that Jung remarked that his own and my hatred were puerile in comparison'.[25] In reality Albrecht was doing everything he could to camouflage himself in a world which he viewed with many misgivings. Jung was less skilful in concealing his real views and as a result was murdered by the S.S. on 30 June 1934.

Some time later Albrecht told Steinacher of the V.D.A. that Germany was nearing the abyss with ever-increasing speed, that Hess was a weakling, that Bormann held all threads in his hand and that 'he personally felt like a swindler in the Reich of the S.S.'[26] And still he was allowing himself to be drawn more and more into political activity by Hess.

In spite of his hostility to Nazism, Albrecht thought that with his intellect and ability there was just a remote chance that he

could influence and possibly 'manage' Hess and Ribbentrop, and
through them Hitler, in the interests of peaceful German development.[27] He often used to say that 'Germany could well do with a
Talleyrand', and he may well have fancied himself in such a role.[28]
He probably imagined that he might be able to outwit Hitler and
the Nazi leadership in much the same way that Talleyrand had
doublecrossed Napoleon. Albrecht, however, had a disability in
Hitler's eyes which Talleyrand did not have for Napoleon.
Albrecht was of partly Jewish origin in a country whose leadership
was determined to treat Jews as deadly enemies, and he could not
avoid being regarded as an object of suspicion in official circles.

He saw the clouds of war gathering on the horizon and wrote
to his mother on 8 August 1934 saying he believed he might have
to face a choice of emigration, suicide, death, or staying behind
and compromising himself to such an extent that life would become unbearable.

> There are historical necessities and I do not believe enough
> in miracles to expect that just in our lifetime that which has
> again and again been proved through millenia of human history
> should become invalid. Actually, nobody has ever reproached
> me for lacking the courage to foresee developments.
>   I also see in this the possibilities of my own fate very clearly:
> there are many possibilities, but among them only few that are
> 'positive'. Here is a small selection of what is possible:
>   A violent end from outside by chance or by intention;
>   Economic decline to a point where life stops;
>   Internal destruction through permanent time-serving;
>   A voluntary exit.
>   All that is within. . . .[29]

He also feared that geopolitics would be used as the intellectual
excuse for German expansion, not just in areas where Germans
were in the preponderance, but in Europe as a whole, and he
dreaded the prospect of another war:

> When I then look into our geopolitics, I sometimes shudder
> at the way we take 'We' in the greater sense and 'We' in the
> smaller sense. You will, no doubt, understand what I mean.[30]

He had hopes that the regime might eventually slow down and

even abandon ideas of war, but these were very distant hopes. Besides, he was a man in continual conflict with himself, and for as long as he worked for the Nazi regime his inner conflicts were insoluble.

4 Missions for Hitler and Ribbentrop: 1936-7

HANS Jacobsen wrote of Albrecht Haushofer that he 'accepted secret diplomatic missions, so that many called him *"eminence grise"* and many admired his sharp intellect while missing the human warmth, although the latter certainly was not entirely absent in him'.[1]

During 1933 or at the latest 1934 Hess had put Albrecht Haushofer in touch with the former champagne salesman, Joachim von Ribbentrop, who was rapidly rising in the Nazi hierarchy. Hess had Albrecht appointed as an unofficial adviser to the Dienststelle Ribbentrop, a bureau under the immediate control of Ribbentrop and subject to the supervision of Hess. Albrecht was willing to work as an agent for Hess and as adviser to Ribbentrop, as he expected that in this way his chances of influencing foreign policy would be greater than in the German Foreign Office. In early 1935 he wrote a memorandum for Hess, praising the Nazi authorities whose power was used to offset the scarcity of ideas and lack of activity in the Foreign Ministry.[2]

At the time at which Albrecht wrote this document Hitler wanted to short-circuit the German Foreign Ministry in vital negotiations with other countries, because he did not sufficiently trust its diplomats. He thus encouraged Hess and Ribbentrop to recruit a few specialists who could and would operate as the agents of a bureau which would soon become the incubator of Nazi foreign policy.

In April 1936, just after the remilitarisation of the Rhineland, Albrecht submitted a memorandum entitled 'Political Possibilities in the South East' in which he had a number of suggestions to make in relation to Czechoslovakia. He suggested that the Czechs looked upon the Germans as their principal enemy, and because the Czech nation felt itself to be endangered in the event of war the issue whether they could come to an agreement with Germany was occupying their minds as a matter of urgency. He put forward five proposals as a basis for negotiations:

1. The conclusion of a ten-year non-aggression pact.
2. A German–Czechoslovak settlement under which Germany would not raise the question of frontier revision in return for which total cultural autonomy for the Sudeten Germans would be granted.
3. Expansion of German–Czech trade.
4. The conclusion of a 'newspaper peace'.
5. Attempt to put forward joint proposals on the Hapsburg question.[3]

Albrecht Haushofer hoped that negotiations would lead to the granting of concessions for Germans living in the Czech Sudetenland, would reduce the influence of France and Russia in Czechoslovakia, and would pave the way for German development along peaceful lines.

The proposals in this memorandum interested Ribbentrop and Hitler, and in the autumn of 1936 Albrecht and the aristocrat Graf zu Trauttmannsdorff were chosen as possible envoys should secret negotiations with President Beneš of Czechoslovakia materialise. Trauttmannsdorff, acting on Ribbentrop's instructions, asked Dr Mastný, the Czech Minister in Berlin, whether talks under the name of 'cultural agreement' would be acceptable to President Beneš.[4] The reply came back that under certain circumstances direct talks with Hitler's envoys could proceed. Trauttmannsdorff and Albrecht Haushofer were ordered to conduct the talks in secrecy, and they were strictly forbidden to have any contact with the German diplomatic mission in Czechoslovakia and with the German Foreign Minister, von Neurath.

On 18 October 1936 a meeting took place between Albrecht Haushofer and Mastný. Albrecht advanced the first four of the five proposals set out in his memorandum for Ribbentrop. Mastný went a long way to meet these demands. He admitted that the remilitarisation of the Rhineland had altered the basic tenets of Czech policy, and that while treaty obligations to Russia and France could not be disowned, they should not be interpreted with too much exactitude. Dr Mastný went so far as to accept that Czechoslovakia's borders would only be secure if steps were taken in Czechoslovakia to recognise the German nationality border, and both Mastný and Haushofer spoke about Henlein, the leader of the Sudeten German Party, in an approving manner.

Finally Mastný requested that the strictest secrecy be maintained on the German side, and asked whether Haushofer might be willing to travel to Prague to have a private and informal discussion with President Beneš.[5] Perhaps the Czech Government felt that their Russian friends were not wholly reliable allies and that in the event of a Nazi onslaught on Czechoslovakia, the Russians might fail to come to their aid. On 13 and 14 November talks took place in great secrecy at the Hradschin Castle between President Beneš and his Foreign Minister, Krofta, on the Czech side and Albrecht Haushofer and Trauttmannsdorff on the German. Like Mastný, Beneš and Krofta were prepared to go a long way to placate the Germans, and Albrecht Haushofer's five proposals were answered as follows:

1. President Beneš stated that he was prepared to negotiate a treaty of non-aggression with the Reich. He had been friendly with Germany in the past, and wished to stress in the strongest terms that the Soviet Union could not prevent Czechoslovakia from having an accommodation with Germany.

2. On the subject of cultural autonomy for the Sudeten Germans, President Beneš, while having no admiration for Henlein, wished to satisfy the Sudeten Germans, and asked Haushofer to talk to Krofta. Beneš said that he could take up this question again when Haushofer next visited Czechoslovakia, and it emerged that the Czech Government was in favour of cultural autonomy but hostile to regional autonomy.

3. President Beneš wished to increase trade between Germany and Czechoslovakia.

4. As for a 'Newspaper Peace', such an agreement was desired. An undertaking was given that in the case of a German–Czech understanding, activity by German emigrés in Prague against the Third Reich would not be tolerated.

5. President Beneš repeated his opposition to the restoration of the Hapsburg dynasty in Austria.[6]

Albrecht Haushofer returned to Germany, kept Himmler informed through S.S. General Karl Wolff and prepared his report for Hitler, listing German aims under two columns 'the Attainable and the Unattainable'. The 'Attainable' objectives were numbered:

1. A non-aggression pact between Germany and Czechoslovakia.

2. A neutral Czechoslovakia in the event of a Russian attack on the Reich, possibly arising out of the involvement of Germany and Russia in the Spanish Civil War.
3. A joint policy on the Hapsburg issue.
4. A Press peace and a reduction of the hostile activities of German emigrés in Czechoslovakia.
5. An agreement to increase trade between the two countries bestowing better treatment upon areas in the Sudetenland which had been adversely affected by the Depression.
6. An agreement to give cultural autonomy to the Sudeten Germans and to improve their status.

In general an agreement between the two countries would consolidate German influence in the Danube valley at the expense of French influence, would render a Russian attack on Germany more unlikely and would make a favourable impression in Britain. It might even be possible to make similar agreements with other countries in south-eastern Europe, such as Yugoslavia and Romania.

Albrecht Haushofer argued, however, that if an agreement with President Beneš was not concluded, the Czech Government might believe that the Third Reich's intentions towards Czechoslovakia were sinister. This would lead to the opposite of what was intended, and would strengthen Czechoslovakia's alliances with Russia and France. Therefore, if for some reason the Fuehrer did not wish to conclude an agreement, the talks should be continued and then be abruptly ended by raising the demands of Henlein's Sudeten German Party in the Czech Sudetenland.[7]

From the way in which Hitler renumbered Haushofer's proposals, there is reason to believe that a neutralised Czechoslovakia, a Press peace, a reduction in the unfriendly activities of German emigrés and an agreement to double German–Czech trade appealed to him. For the time being economic advantages might be utilised. But Hitler's most important reaction – indeed his only action of vital importance here – revealed his true intentions. He put a red line through Haushofer's first suggestion for a non-aggression pact; the obvious reason being that Hitler had already decided to smash Czechoslovakia.

Furthermore, Hitler put no number opposite Haushofer's sixth aim. The Fuehrer did not wish to improve the position of the Sudeten Germans. Rather he wished to exploit their grievances and use them against the Czechs.[8]

Hitler wanted to neutralise Czechoslovakia in order to make her an easier prey, and so, as one would expect, Albrecht Haushofer was ordered to make another journey to Prague. On 18 December 1936 he and Trauttmannsdorff again met Beneš, and the conversations centred around the Czech treatment of Germans in the Sudetenland. In a handwritten note, 'Outcome of Prague', Albrecht wrote that President Beneš understood that unless the Sudeten Germans received more favourable treatment, there could be no improvement in German–Czech relations.[9]

On 3 to 4 January 1937, Trauttmannsdorff went to Prague by himself, and after making enquiries drew up a list of the 'minimum demands' of the Sudeten Germans, which ought as he saw it to be acceptable to the Czech Government. On 11 January 1937 he sent the draft of a possible treaty to Albrecht and this was taken to Hitler. The principal piece of new information was that President Beneš did not want a non-aggression pact, but rather an agreement based on the German–Czech Treaty of Arbitration signed on 16 October 1925 at Locarno. President Beneš was in essence offering:

1. That each country should respect the other's Government.
2. That both nations would collaborate in opposing the Communist bloc.
3. That attacks in the Press by one country against the other should cease.
4. That the activities of German emigrés in Czechoslovakia would be suppressed when hostile to Germany.
5. That there should be trade negotiations.
6. That there should be mutual assistance in border relations.[10]

These points were put before Hitler, and on 19 January 1937 Albrecht wrote to his father giving an account of his interview. His words depicted the arrogance of an intellectual who thought that he could manipulate a dictator. He was flattered that Hitler chose to receive him well. In his correspondence with his parents he used Japanese code-names for certain persons, of which 'Tomodachi', meaning friend, was used for Hess, 'Fukon', meaning I will not deviate, for Ribbentrop, and 'O'Daijin', meaning Master Great Spirit, for Hitler.

My own lecture at O'Daijin was this time really a lecture. He listened and asked intelligent questions. The final result was pleasing. Personally he was charming, in his factual attitude more peaceful, more superior than before Christmas. What I notice again and again with him – at least at those times when he adapts himself to the individual and not to mass meetings – is the powerful application of 'commonsense' in the English sense, which occasionally finds excellent formulation.

The dangerous mood of war of December is at least for the moment banished. . . . O'Daijin is now in the mountains, will consider everything once again and will send for me when he is back again. I am naturally anxious to know the result. . . .[11]

However Hitler never followed up the negotiations as Albrecht Haushofer would have liked, and the latter was instructed to let the negotiations drag on monotonously, which meant that Hitler wanted the talks to be terminated. President Beneš understood the position and wrote in his *Memoirs*:

> In the spring of 1937 Goebbels began a systematic and continuous campaign of hatred and revenge against Czechoslovakia, thus showing that Berlin, having failed to persuade us to accept its proposed agreement, had embarked on different tactics: agitation, terror and deliberately planned violence. No definitive reply ever came from Berlin, either then or later.[12]

Haushofer had attempted to divert Hitler's policy into peaceful channels, and yet in spite of all his hopes he had merely served as a willing tool. On 20 April 1937 he wrote to his mother: 'Desires for the future? We shall be lucky if nothing happens. I do not want the next European disaster to find you still alive; nor do I wish it for father.'[13]

In November 1936 the Anti-Comintern Pact between the Third Reich, Italy and Japan was consummated, and not long afterwards Albrecht Haushofer was sent by Ribbentrop on another mission, this time to Japan. His reports had impressed Hess, Ribbentrop and Hitler, and they wanted to be kept well informed, as well as to strengthen the German–Japanese alliance.

In any case Albrecht was suitable for another reason. His father was well known in Japan, his geopolitical writings being very popular. Many of the Japanese were fascinated by geopolitics and thought of themselves as a dynamic space-conquering people at the heart of an expanding empire. Besides, Karl Haushofer, in his writings and personal intervention had played a part in the formation of the alliance between Germany and Japan.[14]

At the end of July 1937 Albrecht's journey to Japan and China took him via North America, and while he was in the Far East he developed a great sympathy for China and her culture. At the end of August 1937 a report was sent by him to Ribbentrop on the war between China and Japan, and he ended by saying: 'In the event of a long confrontation and of a sharp over-straining of Japanese forces together with chaos in China a situation might arise in East Asia which in every respect must be unwelcome to German policies.'[15] He did not want Germany to be too closely involved with Japan's plans for military aggression. In September 1937 he sent another report to Ribbentrop after a short stay in the war zone surrounding Tientsin in China. In his accompanying letter he expressed sympathy for China, as though China were a possible German partner in the Far East. His actual report does not survive, but it would appear likely that he did all he could to diminish the value of a German–Japanese alliance, and advised Ribbentrop to preach moderation to the Japanese.[16]

Haushofer left Japan, and passed his reports in December 1937 to S.S. General Karl Wolff for Himmler, addressed to the Army's General Staff, to the Navy and to the Air Ministry. On his return to Germany he had an interview with Hitler and Hess. They travelled from Munich to Freilassing in Hitler's special train, and discussed points of political interest arising out of his journey. Hitler again received him well, and listened with interest, asking a lot of perceptive questions. However, Hitler was not to be dissuaded from a pro-Japanese policy, hostile to China, and told Albrecht Haushofer that he had decided to place his 'bet on the victors'.[17]

He must have regarded Haushofer as a useful agent and a well-informed expert supported by Hess, but it is unlikely that he trusted him to any significant extent. Conversely, while Hitler may have trusted Hess and Ribbentrop implicitly, it is most unlikely that he regarded them as experts in the same category as Albrecht Haushofer.

Hitler had good reason for not trusting Albrecht. At no time in his life did Albrecht become a member of the Nazi Party, and in order to avoid arousing the suspicion of the Nazi leadership he had to tread warily in trying to achieve German aims through peaceful evolution. A typical example of the veiled way in which he expressed himself was given late in 1937 when he gave a lecture in the House of Airmen in Berlin about his Far Eastern travels. At the end of his talk a young S.S. man demanded an explanation as to why it was that the German Foreign Office of which Albrecht Haushofer was the representative had been unable to prevent the outbreak of the Sino-Japanese War. Professor Rolf Italiaander described the reply:

> Tired, heavy and resigned Haushofer got up. Had this stupid youth not understood what the gist and essence of his lecture had been? Had he not been sufficiently explicit? . . . He said in a quiet, slow and ironical voice: 'Japan and China have, as is known, thousand-year-old cultures. These are best shown in an incomparably distinguished porcelain. I would like to see the European who would be willing to play the bull in a china shop here. I, for one, would certainly refuse.'[18]

Yet in spite of his finer feelings Albrecht knew that the negotiations for a non-aggression pact with Czechoslovakia had petered out, and that his reports from Japan, far from moderating the Japanese, had merely served as useful information for cementing the German-Japanese Axis. When all was said and done he knew that his efforts had not met with success.

5 The Olympic Games and the British: 1936-8

IT was in relation to Britain and the British that Albrecht Haushofer's most important work lay. He frequently visited London, which he undoubtedly enjoyed, and as early as 1932 he had been writing reports on Britain for the German Foreign Ministry. In November 1934 he wrote home: 'The impression of London remains the same; this tradition and all this life. What a pity that in the Bulow era we missed a partnership. This is now gone and past.'[1]

From 1934 onwards he forwarded information on Britain to Hess and he was at hand in the background when British politicians visited Germany. He was present on 30 January 1935 when Hess, Ribbentrop and Field Marshal von Blomberg had a discussion with Lord Lothian on armaments control and also on 26 March when Hitler gave a dinner in Berlin for Anthony Eden and Lord Simon, which was attended by Hess, Ribbentrop, Goering, Goebbels, Von Neurath, the foreign minister, and Schacht, the finance minister.

In April 1935 Haushofer wrote for the *Zeitschrift für Geopolitik* a 'Report from the Atlantic World' showing that he believed it was absolutely essential for Germany to live in a state of peaceful coexistence with Britain:

The final decision on the fate of Europe – as was the case at the turn of the century – is in the hands of Britain. It must be remembered that the decision about the outbreak of war was not made in 1914 but a decade earlier when the British Empire and the German Empire, after vain attempts to establish a common course, began to drift apart. If one asks for the final reasons, one arrives at the mutual distrust for which the language of neither party found a suitable expression . . .

One thing has indeed changed within a generation; while

during the last years of Queen Victoria's reign, public opinion in Britain believed – and perhaps rightly so at that time – that Britain could afford to stay in isolation and not to engage in Europe's political games if these displeased her, this attitude is now of the past. Britain now knows that she cannot dodge European conflicts once these break out.[2]

He was very anxious to avoid another German confrontation with Britain and on occasions his German friends would reproach him for compromising himself by working for Ribbentrop in Britain. Rolf Italiaander criticised him to his face, saying that it was embarrassing to see a man of his calibre collaborating with a vain charlatan like Ribbentrop. Albrecht was silent and then reached for the thesis which he had written: 'Necessities and Aims – Bases of a German Policy in Europe', and read aloud one page:

> In all matters politic there are minima and maxima of the attainable. To know these limits is the iron duty of the political man. . . . Whatever lies outside the attainable – in a wishful dreamland – is reserved for children and prophets. . . . We believe that any explosion in Europe's present situation would be very dangerous for its originator or instigator. . . . Thus there is nothing else left but an attempt to reach an understanding even in questions with regard to which a revenge would seem to be much nearer human nature.
>
> There is nothing more stupid than untimely heroism. But, equally, there is nothing more stupid than an unpremeditated understanding; perhaps the granting of an advantage without any return service. One has to know what one can demand and what one can offer.
>
> It is mortifying when talking with British politicians to hear much clearer opinions about the Danzig Corridor and the chances of its removal, in comparison with those expressed by German circles who feel the fire burning their finger nails.[3]

In 1936 Albrecht Haushofer's views on Britain assumed a greater importance when Ribbentrop was appointed German ambassador in London. This made it necessary for Albrecht to make trips to London as the agent of Hess and assistant of Ribbentrop. A few weeks after the death of the previous German ambassador in London, von Hoesch, Albrecht saw the German Embassy's public relations officer, Fritz Hesse, in London. Hesse was of the impression that Albrecht had gone to England in order to prepare the ground for inviting Lloyd George to visit Hitler in Germany, and also to judge how the British had accepted the remilitarisation of the Rhineland. Both Hesse and Haushofer had written reports warning Hitler of the great dangers involved in expanding the Reich through the use of armed force. Albrecht told Hesse that their reports had had a marked effect on Hitler, which was evident to anyone around Hitler when German armed forces marched into the Rhineland.

Albrecht said that at that time Hitler behaved as though he was experiencing the most anxious hours of his life: 'I would have never thought such hysterical fear and such scenes possible had I not seen them myself. If Neurath had not kept on calming him, Hitler would have quit the Rhineland. . . .' Hesse's reaction was: 'Well, that is not too bad; perhaps he will in future abstain from such unilateral actions through which he could provoke a war.' Albrecht agreed that this was also his hope, however great his fears, and he replied,

> It was well that you also induced Ribbentrop to warn Hitler against a continuation of his *coups*. Hitler will keep peace for some time. But, don't forget his mentality. In a year he will only see his success and will declare all warnings stupid, cowardly and pitiful and all warners crooks. He cannot endure having shown himself weak before others. I think that the days of the Foreign Ministry are . . . numbered . . . I believe that peace is secured for the next two years . . . perhaps we shall manage to chain the fuming titan to the rock.[4]

It was not long after this conversation that Albrecht Haushofer came into contact with a group of British M.P.s who were present at the Olympic Games in Berlin in August 1936. In view of what occurred five years later it is necessary to examine subsequent events.

The British M.P.s included Harold Balfour, Jim Wedderburn, Kenneth Lindsay, and the Marquis of Clydesdale, who became the Duke of Hamilton in 1940. Clydesdale, at one time Scottish amateur middleweight boxing champion, became in December 1929 the second youngest M.P. in the House of Commons. He was a flying instructor in the Auxiliary Air Force, and in 1933 was chief pilot of the expedition flying over Mount Everest, as well as being Commanding Officer of 602 City of Glasgow (Bomber) Squadron. He went to Berlin in August, partly to acquire a picture of the direction in which Germany was moving, but mainly to see something of the Luftwaffe.

It has been incorrectly assumed, even by eminent historians, that Clydesdale met Hess at the Olympic Games in Berlin. Hess did interview one English M.P., Kenneth Lindsay, who wished to know what Hess had meant when he said that King Edward VIII was the only person who could maintain peace in Europe. Hess also gave lunch in his house to the International Olympic Committee, but the only three British officials of the Olympic Games present were Lord Aberdare, Sir Noel Curtis-Bennett and Lord Burleigh.

Hess may have seen Clydesdale across the room when Hitler gave a special dinner in honour of Sir Robert Vansittart. It was well known that Vansittart, as head of the British Foreign Office, had the deepest reservations about Hitler, the Third Reich and the Germans, whom he believed to be preparing for war. Hitler apparently was not only impressed by Vansittart's forceful personality, but also intuitively sensed his enmity and went out of his way to be accommodating for the duration of the Olympic Games. Clydesdale was present at this dinner; and the journalist Ward Price, who was also there, wrote that he remembered seeing Hess talk to Vansittart.[5] It is quite possible that Clydesdale may have been pointed out to Hess as the British aviator who had been the first pilot to fly over Mount Everest.

Yet in spite of the fact that Hess did not meet Clydesdale there was a tenuous and indirect connection between them. Shortly after Clydesdale arrived in Berlin, his youngest brother, David Douglas-Hamilton, who spoke German fluently, appeared, saying that he had met an interesting German, who knew a good deal and might divulge a certain amount – one Albrecht Haushofer.

Later on Clydesdale with some of the other M.P.s met him over dinner and tried to pick his brains. There was no doubt that Albrecht Haushofer was clever, shrewd, subtle and devious, as well as having a certain fascination. When somebody commented upon the importance attached by the Nazis to being 'Nordic', he tapped his nose, remarking that it was not a Nordic nose. He was reserved when speaking about the Nazi leaders, although he did cause some amusement by mimicking Ribbentrop being jealous of the other

Nazi leaders, on the grounds that some of them had belonged to the Nazi Party longer than he. But when the name of Goebbels was mentioned he looked round to see whether anyone was listening, and whispered with a hiss, 'Goebbels is a poisonous little man, who will give you dinner one night and sign your death warrant the next morning'. This was no doubt an indirect reference to Goebbels' attempt to have the Haushofer sons categorised as Jews in 1933, before Hess's protection.

Albrecht Haushofer was told that the important question for the British was whether Germany was bent on a course which would plunge Europe into war, or whether there was yet an alternative prospect. He argued that with modifications to the Treaty of Versailles, Hitler would mellow and would tone down his programme. He mentioned that as well as being a university lecturer, he worked for the German Foreign Office and that he had the ear of Rudolf Hess, who as Deputy to Hitler had a certain influence. As far as he was concerned he would do everything humanly possible to moderate German foreign policy.

Clydesdale expressed a desire to see the Luftwaffe and on 13 August, at a party given by Goering, Albrecht Haushofer introduced him to Goering, who summoned General Milch, Chief of Staff of the German Air Force, and instructed him to arrange a tour of Luftwaffe stations. Milch agreed and surprised Clydesdale by saying to him with intensity 'I feel we have a common enemy in Bolshevism'. Apart from expressing hatred of the Russians, Milch gave away certain information which was in due course passed back to Wing Commander Don, Air Attaché at the British Embassy in Berlin. Milch said that Germany was suffering from overproduction of aircraft and that the training of personnel was being so rushed that many pilots had been lost through accidents. The next day Clydesdale went to the Staaken and Döberitz airfields, at the first of which he saw the resuscitated Richthofen Squadron whose members were treated as a corps d'élite. He later visited Lechfeld, but was not allowed to see German bombing units. The Luftwaffe officers treated him with suspicion, but made it clear that they regarded the Russians as their primary enemy. The fact of most importance was that the Germans were rapidly rearming.

In January 1937 Clydesdale was skiing in Austria and wrote to Albrecht Haushofer, suggesting a meeting, in case he might glean any further information of interest. He received a reply on 7 January.

Dear Lord Clydesdale,
    Your letter was a friendly surprise. Thank you for your kind wishes! My own greeting to you is probably waiting for you in Scotland: I had no idea of your being so near my Bavarian home. I am looking forward indeed to the possibility of meeting you when you pass through Germany. Our long talk in August is perhaps the most pleasant of all my 'Olympic Visitors' memories! . . .
                                        Yours sincerely,
                                        A. Haushofer.[6]

On 23 January 1937 Clydesdale met him in Munich and was driven to Hartschimmelhof, the house of Karl Haushofer. The General Professor appeared as a formidable old man, who spoke English fluently, and treated Clydesdale with the most rigid politeness. In the background was the small and quiet figure of Albrecht Haushofer's mother. Geopolitics was not discussed. It would not have been courteous, considering that one of the purposes of German geopolitics was to deprive Britain of large parts of the British Empire in the interests of German Lebensraum. Afterwards Clydesdale sent Karl Haushofer *The Pilot's Book of Everest* which he had written with Wing Commander McIntyre, and Karl Haushofer replied thanking him.

Not long after his return to Britain, Clydesdale wrote to Albrecht Haushofer mentioning that he had recommended his name to the Royal Institute of International Affairs, Chatham House, so that they should invite him to speak on the economic position of Germany. Albrecht replied that he would be glad to accept an invitation, provided that he could speak about the German outlook on the problem of 'raw materials and colonies' or on 'East-Central Europe'. He also mentioned that he hoped to see Clydesdale in March 1937 when he would be in London. When he arrived Albrecht told Clydesdale that he had been sent over to Britain because Ribbentrop was in a mess, and it was his job to get him out of it.

Ribbentrop had certainly made himself an object of contempt. On arrival in Britain as Ambassador he had told the Press that he had come to warn the British about the Bolshevik menace, and that it was his intention to further an Anglo–German alliance against

Russia. And further, Ribbentrop, while presenting his credentials
to the King, gave the Nazi salute; and from that moment he was
heartily disliked. By his behaviour he had given the British to
understand that he did not expect Britain to stand in the way of
German aspirations. Furthermore Ribbentrop, while Ambassador
in Britain, made a special point of flying to Berlin in early November 1936 in order to sign the Anti-Comintern Pact between
Germany, Italy and Japan, whose very existence implied hostility
to Britain. Ribbentrop was always unpopular in Britain and was
even scornfully nicknamed 'Herr von Brick and Drop'.

At least some of his unpopularity had reached Germany, and it
seems that Hess sent Albrecht Haushofer to Britain in order to
keep an eye on him and prevent him from becoming a laughing
stock. It also appears that Ribbentrop's dislike of Albrecht dated
from this time. Albrecht complained to Clydesdale that it was
ironical that while von Hoesch had been popular in Britain he had
been without influence in Germany, and now that Germany had
sent an influential Nazi in the form of Ribbentrop the British
found him thoroughly objectionable. He also said that 'Hitler
understands Churchill, but he will never understand Chamberlain'.

On 29 April 1937 Albrecht gave his lecture to Chatham House
in London on 'Raw Materials and Colonies: A German Point of
View'. Lord Allen of Hurtwood was in the chair and introduced
him with words which signified that Chatham House very much
wanted to avoid the possibility of another World War. Lord Allen
was quoted as saying 'They were fortunate in having before them
a very distinguished representative of the great German people,
Dr Haushofer. The Institute of International Affairs was not
permitted to have a corporate opinion, but it had an unanimous
opinion which was that it longed to find the way to a cordial
friendship with an understanding of the great people from whom
the speaker came.'

Albrecht Haushofer then delivered a clever speech, without a
note, and it is worth reproducing the allegory he used to depict
the hatred felt by Germans for the Treaty of Versailles and for the
way in which German colonies had been confiscated after the First
World War:

We have had a terrible row in the school-yard, and one of the
bigger boys, with his following of smaller boys, has got a very

sound thrashing, after a prolonged struggle. And the boys were angry about him. Finally he got kicked down (his enemies had been much more numerous than his friends). Lastly one boy came from another school-yard across the big water to deliver the final kick, and suddenly dashed away again, saying he did not want to have anything more to do with it.

So they were going to punish the boy who had been knocked down. . . . His exotic toys, if I may use the expression, were taken away from him partly because they really did want to punish him and thought he was a very bad fellow, and partly because they rather liked his exotic toys. And so they decided to take them away.

But the biggest of these boys, perhaps the toughest of them, having at least partly grown up mentally . . . and possessing quite a lot of the good things of this earth, changing from the bold buccaneer into the hereditary possessor of nice things, developed a conscience. And he thought it would be a very good method of proceeding to say that the defeated boy's possessions were not taken away from him because the other boys wanted them, or because he ought to be punished, but because he was not fit to play with these toys. And so the solution was that they forced him to sign a declaration that he did not lose his nice exotic toys because he was to be punished or because the others wanted them but because he had treated them badly and was not fit to play with them.

Now you see, this – for a boy – is very humiliating and he does not tend to forget such an experience.[7]

His audience were very suspicious and were not altogether relieved when Haushofer said that 'nothing would be so fantastic as the results of another war'. After the lecture he stayed at Clydesdale's house, where he remarked that Ribbentrop was behaving with great stupidity and was becoming increasingly intransigent and unwilling to accept advice.

On 14 June 1937 Albrecht returned to London for a few days, no doubt to be briefed by Ribbentrop before leaving on his mission for Japan. In speaking to Clydesdale he left the impression of being a very worried man, as Germany was abandoning all self-restraint in her foreign policy. On 29 May Spanish Government aircraft bombed the German battleship *Deutschland* and by

way of retaliation on 31 May a German naval force bombarded the
Spanish town of Almeria, killing numerous civilians.

Previously the Non-Intervention Committee had been set up
by the League of Nations, and a system of naval patrolling established in order to prevent acts of piracy on the high seas. A few
weeks after the Almeria affair, Germany withdrew from participation in the naval patrol. These events caused much disquiet to
Albrecht Haushofer, who believed that Germany was advancing
steadily towards war. On 30 June 1937 he wrote from the ship
Europa, bound for the U.S.A., a very friendly letter to Clydesdale,
and this time a political note crept into it.

> My dear Douglo,
>   . . . I am not leaving Europe with an untroubled mind. Our
> big man had been brought into the 'experiment' of collective
> action (and deliberation before action) not without difficulties.
> The breakdown may have far-reaching consequences – first
> psychological, then practical.
>   But that can't be helped now. . . .
>
> Yours ever,
Albrecht.[8]

After arriving in America he wrote a report in the *Zeitschrift für
Geopolitik* in August 1937. He was firmly convinced that in the
event of conflict in Europe, Britain and the U.S.A. would work
very closely together.

> Whether you are in San Francisco or Washington – you are
> aware that a fight for existence by Britain would not leave the
> United States in the role of impartial observers. The British
> Empire is just as important for America's security as the other
> way round. There is no alliance between the two powers, but
> there exists such a profound community of interest that both
> sides can pursue a policy which resembles an indissoluble
> alliance. Whoever gets into conflict with Britain should know
> that America too will be among his opponents, in spite of all
> neutrality laws.[9]

At the end of 1937 he wrote for the *Zeitschrift für Geopolitik*,
noting that the British were becoming increasingly hostile to Nazi
Germany:

If one has visited England in the spring of 1937, one cannot avoid the conclusion that neither Italy nor Japan (nor even the Soviet Union!) are considered as Public Enemy No. 1. They (the British) are once again staring across the North Sea.[10]

During the last week of April 1938 Haushofer visited Britain again and stayed with Clydesdale at his home Dungavel in Scotland. He confessed that he was extremely concerned and the tenor of everything he had to say was gloomy. He said that Ribbentrop had left Britain (to become German Foreign Minister) an extremely bitter man, because he thought that the British had rejected him. He caused horror amongst those present by taking out an atlas of Europe, and, with two deft strokes of the pencil striking off the Sudetenland from the rest of Czechoslovakia, quietly commenting 'Those are the German demands'. When he was told that if Germany invaded Czechoslovakia it was very likely that there would be war, he made no reply.

Clydesdale wrote to Lord Halifax, the British Foreign Secretary, mentioning that Haushofer would be in London for the first week of May 1938 and might have interesting information to impart. Halifax replied, on 3 May 1938.

My dear Clydesdale,
Thank you very much for your letter of yesterday in which you were good enough to let me know that Dr Albrecht Haushofer is in London until next Thursday evening. I should very much like to have been able to see Dr Haushofer but unfortunately I have no free time left. I am glad to say, however, that Dr Haushofer is in touch with the Foreign Office and I shall have an opportunity of hearing his views.
Yours ever,
Halifax.[11]

On 6 May Haushofer wrote to Clydesdale from Paris:

In London Lord H. [Halifax] could not find time to see me, but I had long and I hope positive talks with two of his next collaborators. On the whole I leave England rather hopeful. If there are no real blunders made, we ought to be able to build up some sort of European stability.[12]

On 28 May he wrote again to Clydesdale:

Having spoiled your atlas by drawing an ethnological boundary from my memory, I want to make amends. Under separate cover I am sending the most up-to-date map of German settlements in Czechoslovakia that we possess. It is based upon the official Czech census figures, therefore slightly unfavourable to the German side.[13]

About ten days after Albrecht Haushofer had seen Clydesdale for the last time, he drew up the most important report that he ever submitted to Ribbentrop on Anglo-German relations, dated 26 June 1938:

Britain has still not abandoned her search for chances of a settlement with Germany (perhaps on the basis of German leadership, but not conquest, in South-east Europe, frontier revisions through plebiscites, West African colonies, four-power pact, armaments restriction).

A certain measure of pro-German sentiment has not yet disappeared among the British people; the Chamberlain–Halifax government sees its own future strongly tied to the achievement of a true settlement with Rome and Berlin (with a displacement of Soviet influence in Europe).

Then Albrecht came to the vital part of his report, which showed that he understood the British outlook and foresaw with great clarity the fate which Germany was approaching.

But the belief in the possibility of an understanding between Britain and Germany is dwindling fast. A new imperialism is suspected behind the pan-German programme of National Socialism (with which one has become more or less reconciled). Here the Czech question assumes the significance of a decisive test case. A German attempt to solve the Bohemian–Moravian question by a military attack would under present circumstances present for Britain (and in British opinion also for France) a *casus belli*.

In such a war the British Government would have the whole nation behind it. It would be conducted as a crusade for the liberation of Europe from German militarism. London is convinced that such a war would be won with the help of the U.S.A. (whose full participation, within days, not weeks, is anticipated) at the cost, of course, of an incalculable expansion of Bolshevism outside the Anglo-Saxon world.[14]

He was saying that Germany could achieve and gain all that she required but not at the cost of war, and if Albrecht's views had been accepted, and if his suggestions had become official German policy, there would not have been a Second World War.

However, Ribbentrop was no longer interested in such arguments. He was being told facts that he did not want to hear. It appears that even now, before the Munich Agreement, neither Ribbentrop nor Hitler were prepared to understand that in the event of German armed aggression, sooner or later the British would fight in earnest, and without looking back.

Ribbentrop passed on Albrecht Haushofer's report to Hitler, and contemptuously dismissed it by adding the marginal note – 'Secret Service Propaganda'.[15]

6 Munich and Decline: 1938

ALBRECHT Haushofer remained working for Ribbentrop up to the time of Munich. On 4 February 1938 Hitler brought Foreign Office policy more directly under his own control by appointing Ribbentrop Nazi Foreign Minister. Meanwhile Austria was being threatened by military invasion. On 12 February Chancellor Schuschnigg of Austria travelled to Obersalzberg, Berchtesgaden, for his famous interview with Hitler. There Schuschnigg was battered into submission and accepted Hitler's ultimatum, which spelt the beginning of the end for Austria. The news of what had happened had not reached Albrecht Haushofer, but he knew that Germany's armoured divisions were poised to strike. He wrote to his father on 13 February:

> In the meantime the meeting at Obersalzberg has taken place without my being informed as yet of the progress. . . .
> The individual operations in the military sphere are too delicate to be confided to paper. The external form of the solution – here I completely agree with you – is masterly on the face of it. The tensions in the structure are not, however, thereby eliminated. Only the facade is really sound. . . .
> To use a medical comparison: the disease of the democracies is leprosy – that of the dictatorships is cancer.

He also included a more personal note:

> Many people send you their regards, very cordial ones from Ribbentrop, who made a calm and collected impression on me. I am very curious what effect the new facts will have on his character. . . . A man of great ambition, who has achieved the highest aim attainable, usually looks different from the way he looked at the time of his rise. . . .[1]

Like most patriotic Germans Albrecht Haushofer supported the

Anschluss but he wanted it to be realised by peaceful means and not by military invasion. During the night of 11–12 March 1938 he was in the room in the Foreign Ministry in which foreign broadcasts could be heard, along with Dr Wehofsich, the head of the Austrian section of the V.D.A. They heard that the Government of the Nazi Seyss-Inquart was in control, and it struck them that military intervention was unnecessary and undesirable. Albrecht then went to see Hess in order to ask him to persuade Hitler to countermand orders for marching into Austria on the next day, but to no avail.[2] On 12 March the German Wehrmacht streamed into Austria.

It was Albrecht Haushofer's opinion that the Anschluss was the last step that the British were prepared to accept without serious resistance, and he viewed with concern German threats to Czechoslovakia. He knew that there were plans to use the Sudeten Germans as a springboard for ripping Czechoslovakia apart by force. On 29 March 1938 he was present as a representative of the Volksdeutsch Centre along with Ribbentrop, Weizsacker and S.S. Obergruppenführer Lorenz of the Volksdeutsch Mittelstelle at the meeting in the Reich Chancellery, at which Henlein and the Sudeten Germans received instructions for future movements in the Sudetenland.[3] Henlein was proving a useful puppet for Hitler's plans and the crisis between the Third Reich and Czechoslovakia loomed up, as the summer weeks passed.

Albrecht had always wanted a peaceful German–Czech settlement whereby the Sudeten Germans would be given a large measure of autonomy. He was utterly opposed to war or forcible subjugation, if only because he was convinced that Britain would fight rather than watch the growth of a threatening superpower on her doorstep. During the spring of 1938 Ribbentrop, with Albrecht, had a discussion with Nevile Henderson, the British Ambassador in Berlin. Henderson said that his Government was in principle ready to make colonial concessions in Africa and he actually laid out a map. Ribbentrop however made excessive territorial demands in such offensive language that Henderson pocketed the map and terminated the conversation. Afterwards Ribbentrop drew up a false statement on the discussion and Albrecht refused to sign it.[4] By mid-1938 Albrecht had come to the conclusion that he had lost what influence he had ever had with Ribbentrop, that Germany had lost all hope of Britain's goodwill and that war against Czechoslovakia was very close.

On 18 August he wrote to his parents about the deterioration in Anglo-German relations:

A wise Englishman complained to me that one no longer knew in which voice to speak in Berlin; if one talked in a low voice one would be laughed at as being weak; talking in a loud voice however would be resented as intimidation. One would never be understood. Conversely one can rightly say that London's understanding for our rights lessens week by week. Correspondingly the attitude of Beneš, who believes he holds reliable trumps, stiffens. In short: everything is rapidly approaching the point at which one will no longer be master of one's decisions, but where one will be hurled down as surely as the stone which tried to roll from Partnach-Alm to Graseck without touching Partnach ravine.[5]

Albrecht was certain that Hitler intended to go to war against the Czechs that autumn, unless he was deterred by the British Government, which he thought unlikely. A letter he wrote on 22 August 1938 to his mother explained the nature of his dilemma:

Of course I know the possibility exists that London will yet find ways to make Berlin understand the full seriousness – but our chance of reaching winter without war appears to me at best to be one to four. Once one sees matters in this light one cannot very well avoid preparing for them internally and externally I am therefore striking a balance.

Albrecht then examined the possibility of leaving Nazi Germany, but rejected this thought primarily because his mother, to whom he was deeply attached, was going to stay. There was also a subsidiary reason for not leaving. His father was in a position to protect the family from anti-Semitic outbursts through his friendship with Hess.

As long as you are still alive – and you are, after all, bound by the fact that you put into the world a second son as well, who enjoys life more than I do . . . and there is no point in fooling oneself that father's presence would not still have a high value for the further existence of this family – during that time therefore, I must not permit myself to consider a voluntary departure.

He wrote that in the case of war he could only survive if he closed his mind to even the most atrocious events.

I must, therefore, make the effort to carry on life until it is taken from me by external forces, even in conditions which would be abominable for me. I know exactly that I could survive a war in the attitude demanded from me only on one condition; that my own life has become completely indifferent to me, that no event, be it the most atrocious, could produce in me a spark of emotion. Such a transformation with the necessary speed can only take place when one prepares oneself accordingly. And I am now engaged in this internal preparation.

He finished his letter with the despairing words that the leaders of the Third Reich were determined to launch Germany into war, there being no question of any other country sparking off the conflagration.

If nothing surprising happens from the opposite side, the next four or five weeks may well still pass without an eruption. For the late autumn we have to reckon, however, with the Bohemian boiler being brought to an explosion. . . .

I no longer believe that anybody or anything can stop the lighting of the fuse. And the possibility of the Bohemian conflict being localised seems to have one chance in ten. The Czechs would have to commit stupendous blunders in the next few months, or Lord Runciman would have to muster an amazing measure of power of judgement and determination.[6]

He saw virtually no chance of war being avoided through the efforts of the Runciman Mission which had been despatched by the British Premier Neville Chamberlain to Czechoslovakia on 3 August 1938. At that time Albrecht had another conversation with Nevile Henderson, without Ribbentrop. Henderson asked him if Hitler would be satisfied if he received the Sudetenland and Albrecht told him that Hitler knew no bounds.[7]

Haushofer thought that nothing would restrain the Nazi leaders from going to war with Czechoslovakia, unless Britain made a firm and vigorous stand, and even that would almost certainly not prevent war. At the beginning of the ensuing Munich Conference he travelled in Hitler's train, which had been sent to meet Mussolini, and later claimed that he had asked Mussolini to try to moderate Hitler.[8] During the conference he prepared geographical maps of the proposed German–Czech frontier for Ribbentrop, and as he saw it the Munich agreement merely postponed war. He told his brother Heinz that at the end of the Conference, just after the statesmen of France and Britain had left the room, Hitler turned to his entourage and remarked 'I am still going on to Prague'.⁹ Hardly had the ink dried on the paper of the Munich Agreement, long before Chamberlain had arrived back in England supposedly bringing Peace in our Time, than that Treaty had been broken in all but name.

Albrecht Haushofer knew that any future war would not remain localised and viewed with pessimism the onward march of events. He had made his bid for peace in his report of 26 June 1938, and his report had been dismissed. His influence with Ribbentrop had come to an end and shortly after the Munich Conference he stopped working for him.¹⁰ Ribbentrop consistently told Hitler that he could base his plans for aggrandisement of the Reich on the use of military force without risking a general war, and it greatly annoyed him when Albrecht Haushofer flatly contradicted this line of thought. He resented the fact that Albrecht was primarily an agent of Hess, and only secondarily an assistant of the Ribbentrop Bureau, and the fact of Albrecht's part-Jewish ancestry rendered him untrustworthy to the Nazi apparatus.

On 28 September 1938, the date which had been chosen by Hitler for the military invasion of Czechoslovakia prior to Neville Chamberlain's intercessions, Ribbentrop ordered two of his collaborators to check up on Albrecht Haushofer and write a report on him, indicating that if the matter had been solely in Ribbentrop's hands Albrecht might have been slipped into a concentration camp as a deviationist. It is no coincidence that amongst Albrecht's letters is a handwritten draft with numerous amendments and deletions, almost certainly intended as an excuse for Hess, who always extended his protection in such circumstances.

Regarding the occurrence of 28/9/1938, I have to say the following:

It is not quite easy to comment after five months on a conversation, the fixing of which in my memory did not appear urgent in proportion to the other duties of those days. The conversation commenced when I . . . was stopped in the passage by two gentlemen of the office with the worried question: 'What will happen?' The contrast between the former standing to attention of these gentlemen and the tone of this question provoked me to the ironic answer: 'Have you already got your steel helmets and gas masks ready?' To the counter remark: 'But surely there will be no war! That would be insanity!' I retorted: 'Do not say that. History is sometimes written in blood. Do you know then what the Chief really wants?'

From that moment onwards, I had the impression that in the further course of conversation it was intended to commit me to statements which were suitable for a report on me, and I confined myself to a few remarks, which left no doubt, however, that I considered a peaceful solution attainable . . . I then added that very many people now grumbled secretly, who would never have had the courage to express anxiety and deviating opinions directly. I myself had always stated my opinion to the Minister, especially relating to Britain (this being the first duty of an assistant): I therefore did not have a bad conscience. What the leadership would then decide was just whether it was to be gas masks or pipes of peace.

Albrecht stated that it had not been his intention to express contempt for Ribbentrop:

> After a lapse of five months I cannot with certainty give further particulars on wording. It was decidedly not my intention to ridicule or scorn the politics of the Reich Minister. It was equally not my intention 'to cause pessimism'. Of course apart from the seriousness, the anxiety and willingness, which was no doubt felt by every German in those September days – the conversation contained indeed an element of irony, but of an irony which was directed less against the great foreign policy than against the 'attitude' of some of my interlocutors.[11]

In such circumstances Albrecht was in despair, especially as he believed that Hitler would never keep his word. Hitler said as much in a speech on 9 October 1938 at Saarbrucken. Nonetheless in his report for the *Zeitschrift für Geopolitik*, written in October, Albrecht inferred that in the interests of peace it was vital that Hitler should not break the Munich Agreement:

> One may perhaps consider as the most important gift to the future that strip of paper which Neville Chamberlain held in his

hand on alighting from the aircraft at London: the Anglo-
German peace proclamation, signed on the basis of a personal
trust between the Fuehrer and Chamberlain contains more than
its wording betrays, especially if one remembers that in his
Berlin speech the Fuehrer clearly said that the Sudeten German
territories are the last territorial claim in Europe. . . .

Chamberlain with the full support of the entire Empire
would have gone to war if this had become necessary. And
nobody can foresee how much would have been left of the white
race and of its nordic leadership if another world war had been
started within European frontiers.[12]

The Nazi leadership disregarded this warning, and it did not
help Albrecht Haushofer when his father had a mild altercation
with Hitler in November 1938. His father had recently attended
the Convegno Volta African Congress at which colonial problems
had been discussed. Afterwards, he asked Hess to arrange a
meeting between himself and Hitler, and at the baptism of Hess's
son Wolf Rudiger, Hitler and the Professor General were left
together in Hess's house on the hearth before the fire. He told
Hitler that further territorial demands in Europe would produce
great hostility in the Western Powers. Germany should, he argued,
make an offer to Britain guaranteeing the lands alongside the Reich,
promising to waive all right to Poland, provided that Britain
recognised the *status quo* and returned the lost German colonies in
Africa. It would be wise for Hitler to visit England, as according
to his information there were circles in Britain around Chamberlain
and Halifax who would be willing to consider such proposals.

Hitler eyed him stonily as though to say 'You foolish old man,
you have never understood me', turned on his heel and walked out
of the room without a word.[13] Hitler was not thinking in terms of
colonies in Africa. He was thinking of the eastern steppes and
plains of eastern Europe and Russia, and he was prepared to risk
incurring the enmity of Britain. His successes had whetted his
appetite for more.

On 16 November 1938 Albrecht Haushofer wrote a letter of
hopelessness to his mother.

> Today is the Day of Repentance and of Prayer here. This
> appears to me very appropriate for writing the letter requested
> by you. Dear Mother, why do you always so press for letters!

That I am alive is evident from our telephone conversations. If I were physically ill, I would let you know. Should there be essential changes in the external order of my existence or should such be in the immediate offing, I would write about it, although such changes nowadays occur so quickly that often there remains no time for thinking or even for writing.

But on what else should I otherwise write? I no longer have a private life, and if I had I would not write about it. One never knows, after all, who else reads one's letters. One cannot write about things which move one. And when one can write about them once in a while like today, when I can send the letter by my brother – what is the point of making life even more difficult for each other?

He left his mother in no doubt that it had been the intention of Hitler and Ribbentrop to destroy Czechoslovakia by having 'a nice little war' and that they no longer cared what the British would do.

You know very well yourselves that we live in medieval circumstances, which are an insult to the gallantry of our Middle Ages; that our spiritually possessed great leaders are enraged over their failure with their nice little war (with the result that all those who in the last minute pleaded for settlement and peace are now highly unpopular), that they endeavour as far as possible to frustrate a German–English settlement. And if you do not know it, it is perhaps better for Father's peace of mind.

He went on to deal with a subject which must have been very painful for him, since he was in the category of 'protected Jew'. On 7 November a Jewish refugee from Germany had mortally wounded Ernst vom Rath, the third Secretary of the German Embassy in Paris. On 9–10 November, with the encouragement of Hitler, Goebbels and the other Nazi leaders, Heydrich at the head of the S.D., during the Crystalnacht, organised the looting of Jewish property throughout Germany, and the sending of Jews to prison and concentration camps. The Government of the Third Reich imposed a fine of one billion marks upon the Jewish community, making it obvious that it wanted to expel all Jews from Germany. This naturally affected the family of Albrecht's mother. He continued:

It will be soon enough to realise what is going on, when we are all robbed or hanged. The disappointed fury over the missed war is now raging internally. Today it is the Jews. Tomorrow it will be other groups and classes.

The financial advice I gave to you yesterday is based on the contingency that perhaps as early as next Saturday, but perhaps only later, a partial capital levy will be imposed also for Aryans the financial consequences of which cannot be assessed, but which can very easily lead to a lowering of purchase power so that one may suddenly become non-liquid. The exact amount of the confiscation, which is to go by the name of 'Thank Offering' is not yet known. It will be unavoidable because public coffers are empty.

He said that all his knowledge of Britain was useless, because he had hopelessly compromised himself in British eyes by collaborating with Ribbentrop. He described a conversation, probably with Nevile Henderson.

A conversation with the British Embassy Counsellor and with a confidant of Chamberlain, who was here during these last few days, has convinced me that my personal credit and thereby my usefulness in the West in foreign political matters is now exhausted. You will, therefore, have to be prepared for the gradual ending of my chances for action. This coincides also with an inner necessity. He who constantly spits at himself becomes worthless.[14]

About this time, just after the Crystalnacht, on 9–10 November 1938, Fritz Hesse had a meeting with Albrecht Haushofer and wrote:

I found him as pessimistic as I was myself. He told me that he had fallen into the deepest disfavour because of his warnings and that hubris ruled in Germany. 'Hitler', he said, 'is now convinced that he can afford to do anything. Formerly he believed that we must have the maximum armaments because of the warlike menaces of the Powers striving to encircle us, but now he thinks that these Powers will crawl on all fours before him!'

Hitler had told Haushofer: 'This fellow Chamberlain shook with fear when I uttered the word war. Don't tell me he is dangerous!'

Haushofer ended by saying: 'We shall probably slither into the catastrophe we thought we had averted. I am more pessimistic than ever. It's true that Hitler does not want war, but he is ready to risk it, and this, in my opinion, is a guarantee of disaster.'[15]

Later Albrecht again told Fritz Hesse that Hitler was certain that the British would give way. At Godesberg he had threatened Chamberlain with war and Chamberlain had made concessions. Hitler simply was not prepared to believe that Chamberlain would act differently on the next occasion. Although Albrecht was in the political wilderness for giving unwelcome advice he did not stop warning, and he wrote in the 1939 January issue of the *Zeitschrift für Geopolitik*:

> The whole of British history, the whole grim history of its conflicts with rival powers, from Spain, via Holland and France to Germany and Russia would have to be rewritten if one wanted to believe that present-day British armaments are merely bluff or that the Anglo-Saxon world could be bluffed forever. There are still political issues for which Britain (and France with her) would fight.
>
> No world power which is not in a condition of extreme decay would allow itself to be dismembered without resistance. The methods of resistance vary of course. Countries which have a long financial and economic breath are sometimes inclined to postpone military involvement for longer than other States; sometimes further than is considered right in later days by their own historians.[16]

As Albrecht had feared, the German Army in blatant violation of the Munich Agreement occupied Bohemia and Moravia on 15 March 1939. It was now manifest to the British Parliament and public that Hitler had lied at the Munich Conference, and had played with Neville Chamberlain as a skilled fisherman plays with a salmon on a line. It brought home to British M.P.s that Hitler's dishonesty was so fundamental and endemic that never again could any meaningful negotiations be held with him or with any Germans serving under him.

On 31 March the British Government pledged Anglo-French aid to the Polish people in the event of German intervention in Poland. Albrecht knew with certainty that he could not prevent the attack on Poland. His failure was complete.

7 A Message of Despair: July 1939

DURING 1939 Albrecht Haushofer repeated in his articles on the Atlantic World for the *Zeitschrift für Geopolitik* the warnings which he had given to the Nazi leadership. In mid-1939 he wrote that Chamberlain 'had for some months been completely cured of his Munich illusions' and that 'the final conflict between Napoleon and the other European powers was not caused by the incompatibility of real interests but by both sides looking at all treaties as scraps of paper'.[1]

He was convinced that in any world war Germany could not defeat Great Britain, aided by the U.S.A. and Canada. He wrote, in the July issue of the *Zeitschrift für Geopolitik*:

> From watching American sources too, one reaches the conclusion that the danger of a world war is greater in Europe than in East Asia, and that one can only regard with misgivings the rapid advances in the Anglo-Saxon community. One of the pillars of this armaments community is the development of Canada into a spare part store for the British aeronautical industry. One has only to imagine what it would mean in a European war if British bombers have every European aeroplane factory within their reach, while American and Canadian factories remain immune from European or Asian attack, in order to realise the enormous advantages in the military field which Anglo-Saxon co-operation would offer to Britain in case of war.[2]

As usual his writings were to a large extent disregarded by the Nazi leadership. Albrecht had cause for concern: his country was drifting inexorably towards war in spite of all his efforts; he was now looked upon with disfavour by Hitler and Ribbentrop, and his father was infuriating Hitler by suggesting possibilities of a better future for the Germans in the South Tyrol.

Hitler had been ready to exploit the alleged grievances of the

Germans in the Czech Sudetenland and in Poland, but it was different with the South Tyrol. Since the Treaty of St Germain in 1919 the South Tyrol had come under the sovereignty of Italy, in spite of the fact that the overwhelming majority of Tyrolese were German-speaking, and would have preferred the South Tyrol to remain part of Austria. Hitler hastily disowned the Tyrolese Germans, for Mussolini's friendly attitude towards him had become evident during the formation of the Anti-Comintern Pact, and at the time of the Anschluss and Munich. Wishing to make sure of Mussolini's support, Hitler encouraged Himmler, in control of the Volksdeutsche Mittelstelle, to make plans for transplanting 80,000 Germans from the South Tyrol to Southern Bavaria, where they could be held in readiness for colonising the Crimea at a later stage. Hitler also ordered Goebbels, Reich Minister of Propaganda, to ban any written material in Germany which highlighted the attempts made by Mussolini's Fascists to Italianise the Germans in the South Tyrol.

Karl Haushofer, being unable to fathom the workings of Hitler's mind, recommended in his book *Frontiers* that many European boundaries should be redrawn, and that the South Tyrol more properly belonged to Germany than to Italy. On 12 July 1939 Albrecht wrote to his mother from Berlin:

> ... because of a matter, which affects Father personally and which can have far-reaching consequences in view of his tendency only to feel injustice in its full impact when it concerns a sphere which is emotionally near him. Father will one of these days be informed by the publishers that the Ministry of Propaganda has prohibited *Frontiers* since, because of its treatment of the South Tyrol, it endangers Reich politics. . . .

He advised that his father should ask Hess to intercede with Hitler, making it clear that he was prepared to make a tactful withdrawal from public activity.

> I must add, however, that I am very doubtful whether Tomodachi [Hess] will achieve anything against Dr. G. [Goebbels], not perhaps because of the latter's special malice, but because O'Daijin is at this moment in such an over excited state . . . that he immediately sees red at the word South Tyrol and starts to rage. . . .

Here now my analysis of the general situation, which is based
on the innermost information (just as last year, when I after all
knew, not only 'assumed', since the beginning of June, that
October had been fixed by the highest authority as the deadline by which the Czechs question must be 'settled' with all,
including military, means).

Until the middle of August nothing will happen. From the
middle of August onwards everything is to be prepared for a
sudden war. Now as before O'Daijin wants only a local war and
he is wavering as last year since he is not sure whether the West
will remain quiet.

The difference compared to last year is only that this time the
West is taken more seriously, and that the deadline has not been
fixed with the same determination as last year. Instead the will
to fight on the opposite side is stronger, our own economic
situation worse and the prospect of finding more favourable
conditions, perhaps next year, is diminished. The state of
danger is, therefore, at least just as acute.

He felt that he had to escape from the Berlin atmosphere at
least temporarily, taking with him some of his students on a
journey abroad.

I have very seriously considered whether to go on my
excursion. But it is perhaps a last chance and I have to get out
of this asphyxiating atmosphere once again, otherwise I shall
burst. . . .[3]

On the same day, 12 July, he wrote another letter to his father
pleading with him to be careful:

Matters are bad – but I must tell you that O'Daijin sees red
in this matter. . . . Opposition on the south alpine question is,
therefore, at present dangerous in the extreme.[4]

He then made a comment of dissatisfaction about Britain in
general and Clydesdale in particular, saying that English reactions
were making themselves felt in a 'very painful form',[5] which
showed that he must have been watching developments in Britain
closely. It is easy to understand what Albrecht Haushofer meant
by looking at Hansard for 10 July 1939, when Clydesdale asked
the Prime Minister two questions concerning the South Tyrol. In

view of the fact that Hitler had removed the Germans from the South Tyrol to Germany, Clydesdale wanted a recommendation to be made by the Prime Minister to Hitler, that he should remove the Germans from Danzig to Germany, and thereby avoid the expectation of war. Clydesdale also asked the Prime Minister whether he would remind Hitler and Mussolini 'that by their settlement of the South Tyrol, where alone in Europe a simple frontier revision is possible, they have not got a leg to stand on in demanding territory elsewhere'. R. A. Butler, Under Secretary of State for Foreign Affairs, replied evasively on behalf of the Prime Minister.[6]

Albrecht knew that the tone of these remarks meant that there would be general war if Germany invaded Poland, and while on holiday with his students he sent Clydesdale the following letter which is worth quoting in full since it reveals so clearly his attitude to the world situation.

> Cruising the Coast of Western Norway.
> July 16th, 1939.

My Dear Douglo,

I have been silent for a very long time – partly from outside, partly from inside reasons. The outside reasons are easily and quickly stated: having told some very unpopular truths after my last return from England, and having pulled my full weight with the forces of moderation on our side during the weeks before Munich, I had to move very carefully afterwards. I did not want to find myself waking up one morning with an appointment as Consul General to Paramaribo (I dare say such a place exists somewhere in South America).

The inside reasons are less easily put down. But I think I can make them clear at least to you. We have had more than one talk on the Versailles Treaty and its aftermath. You know how I feel about it. I have always regarded it as a failure on the side side of British farsightedness – to put it mildly – (but you may blame the French!) that concessions and revisions mostly came too late. I fully admit that the critical years were 1931/32. One third of the concessions to Germany that you allowed to be taken later on without agreement, offered in 1932 – and Germany would never have taken the revolutionary plunge she took in 1933. But that is old history.

After the National-Socialist advent to power there remained
one hope: that – after having done away with most (if not all)
of the Versailles grievances by rather violent and one-sided
methods – the great man of the regime would be prepared to
slow down, to accept an important (though not an all-
dominating) position in 'the Concert of Europe'. It may have
been an unreasonable hope – knowing the man as we know
him – but – realities being what they were – it was the only
hope one could act upon. Now – I cannot entertain that hope
any longer; and that is my reason for writing and posting this
letter somewhere on the coast of Western Norway, where I am
taking a few short weeks of rest.

I just want to give you a sign of personal friendship – I do
hope that you will survive whatever may happen in Europe –
and I want to send you a word of warning. To the best of my
knowledge there is not yet a definite time-table for the actual
explosion, but any date after the middle of August may prove
to be the fatal one. So far they want to avoid the 'big war'. But
the one man on whom everything depends is still hoping that
he may be able to get away with an isolated 'local war'. He still
thinks in terms of British bluff, although the Prime Minister's
and Lord H's [Halifax's] last speeches have made him doubt – at
least temporarily; the most dangerous thing is that he is racing
against time: in more than one sense.

Economic difficulties are growing, and his own feeling (a very
curious and remarkable one) that he has not a very long time of
life ahead of him, is a most important factor. I could never adapt
myself to the idea that any war might be inevitable; but one
would have to be blind not to realise that war may be very near.

So the question: what *can* be done? gets all the more important. But perhaps I should have added a few things about the
psychological position in the mind of the German people before
trying to answer that question. On the merits of their present
government, the Germans are less united than at any date since
1934. But if war breaks out on the Corridor question, they will
be more solidly behind their present leader than over any case
that might have led to war in these last years. The territorial
solutions in the East (Corridor and Upper Silesia) have never
been accepted by the German nation, and you will find many
and most important Englishmen, who never thought them to be

acceptable – and said so! A war against Poland would be not unpopular.

World war of course is quite another thing: but few people in Germany realise that they would be up against a world war. I should just mention one more point: 'encirclement' has proved to be a most efficient weapon of inside propaganda. Pre-war memories (and war-blockade experiences) have risen in many minds – and the idea that England wants to 'hem in' Germany on every side has got very deep into the German mind (even there, where it is *not* 'Nazi'). Of course there are difficulties. That hateful South Alpine deal is making a big, though naturally subterranean, stir.

But war against Poland would – for the first weeks at least – unite, not disintegrate the German nation. And that is – at least to my feeling – all-important; not because I might hope that an united German nation might win the war: I am very much convinced that Germany cannot win a short war and that she cannot stand a long one – but I am thoroughly afraid that the terrific forms of modern war will make any reasonable peace impossible if they are allowed to go on for even a few months. Therefore we simply have to stop the explosion. Another European war, another Treaty of Versailles, another total revolution all over Europe – well – I need not say what it would mean for Europe as a whole.

Now to the core of the question: what can be done? Very little from inside Germany. Even now at least something from England.

Something on the tactical side: Your 'inside' people know how to put a certain amount of pressure on the big man in Rome: they ought to start that pressure fairly soon. Something of the more general type: It is not enough for England to advertise herself as the big boss in the fire brigade, or to organise a fire insurance company with other nations (some of them – viz. Poland – not quite above playing with fire themselves): What Europe needs is a real British peace plan on the basis of full equality and with considerable (but strictly mutual) safeguards on the military side. I realise to the full that a strong system of safeguards will be necessary if your people are to be persuaded to meet even the slightest German wishes regarding European or colonial territory. But as long as your Government has not lost sight of the second part of their original programme – full security and peaceful change through negotiation – they might be able to test the second part early enough to secure a positive effect. I cannot outline what might be an acceptable compromise in detail.

I cannot imagine even a short-range settlement without a change in the status of Danzig and without some sort of change in the Corridor. Possibly a long-range settlement between Germany and Poland would have to be based upon considerable territorial changes combined with population exchanges on the Greek–Turkish model (people in England mostly do not know that there are some 600,000–700,000 Germans scattered through the inner (formerly Russian) parts of Poland!) – but if there is to be a peaceful solution at all, it can only come from England and it must appear to be fair to the German public as a whole.

Even now – after the present rulers of Germany have given ample provocation – your people would be wise not to forget that they refused a plebiscitarian solution in the Corridor (and that subsequently the Poles drove some 900,000 Germans out of their former German provinces!) and that they prevented one in Upper Silesia.

Last September Mr Neville [Chamberlain] had the trust of the majority of Germans. If you want to win a peace without – or even after – a war, you need to be regarded as trustees of Justice, not as partisans. Therefore – once more – if you can do anything to promote a general British peace and armaments control plan – I am sure you would do something useful. . . .

I am rereading this letter and should like to add something of a personal kind. You will realise that I have written this letter with the utmost frankness because I know that you realise the risk I should be running if the existence of this letter should become known. . . . Therefore, I wanted to add what may seem very curious to you: please destroy this letter after reading it – and destroy it most carefully. But perhaps this is unfair: so I give you freedom for your own discretion to show this letter personally either to Lord H [Halifax] or to his Under Secretary Mr B [Butler] – if you see fit of course – under one condition: that no notes should be taken, my name never be mentioned, and the letter be destroyed immediately afterwards.

As a sign that you have received this letter I only ask for some non-committal picture-postcard (to my normal address) telling me that you are well. If you have seen fit to show the letter you might add something about your family. . . . I do hope we may meet again.

Yours very sincerely,

A.[7]

After returning to Berlin he wrote to his parents on 13 August: 'One differs from the scoundrels and fools by the lack of present-day joy – from the others by the lack of hope for the time beyond the cataclysm. . . .'[8] His despair was apparent and Carl von Weizsaecker, a friend, wrote of him:

> When it proved impossible to prevent Hitler's war, the outcome of which he foresaw, he sank into a year-long bitterness and pessimism which lay like lead on him and his friends.
>
> He omitted no single step which seemed to offer hope, although he entertained no hope. When we younger people told him that we believed in the future and in present events being perhaps a means of purification, all he could say was that he saw nothing but senseless destruction, that perhaps we might live in such a future but for him there was no place in it.[9]

On 22 August 1939 the news came through that the Nazi–Soviet Pact had been signed, and Walter Stubbe, Albrecht's assistant, recorded that Albrecht was standing against a desk, with two young students beside him and the *Times Atlas* page of the Soviet Union open in front of him:

> I just heard Haushofer say: 'Now they have concluded a friendship, but in four weeks at the latest we shall have a war. Then the madman in his drunkenness will overrun the West and Alfred Rosenberg will get what he wants: he will gorge himself in the Sarmatian steppes and it will be the end of Europe.'
>
> Then something unexpected happened: with a cry of despair at such sombre visions, Wolfgang Hoffman [one of his favourite students] shouted, 'You damned pessimist!' Haushofer seemed to collapse: he left the room and uttered a moan, 'You know best, of course'.[10]

Meanwhile in Britain Albrecht Haushofer's letter had arrived
just after Clydesdale had been asking further questions in the
House of Commons as to whether the German population in
Poland could be removed to Germany in the same way as the
German population in the South Tyrol had been transplanted to
Bavaria. He asked whether Hitler was 'acting as treacherously to
his own people as he acted to the Prime Minister at Munich'
merely for the sake of expediency, and Butler again replied
evasively on behalf of the Prime Minister.[11]

On his return from the House of Commons Clydesdale found
Albrecht Haushofer's letter waiting for him. The first half of it
was of interest because it confirmed his suspicions that Hitler was
determined to have war. As for the second half of the letter
containing proposals as to what Britain might do, he considered it
to be quite useless. Clydesdale saw Albrecht Haushofer as a very
able man who was trying to reconcile his patriotism with his
hatred of war, but was finding it impossible. He interpreted this
letter as a message of despair.

Shortly after, in late July 1939, Clydesdale approached Winston
Churchill after Question Time in the House of Commons and
asked to see him alone, whereupon Churchill asked him round to
his flat that evening. Churchill, being a backbencher, was still in
the political wilderness, but he always had time to listen. Clydesdale arrived at his house while Churchill was in the bath, and
Churchill emerged wrapped in a large bath towel. Clydesdale
handed him Albrecht Haushofer's letter. Churchill sat down and
read it very slowly with so much concentration that his cigar went
out. Eventually he thrust the letter aside and sighed: 'There is
going to be war very soon', to which Clydesdale replied, 'In that
case I very much hope that you will be Prime Minister.' Churchill
did not deny that this would happen and merely shook his head
saying, 'What a hell of a time to become Prime Minister.'

After this interview Clydesdale showed the letter to the Foreign
Minister, Lord Halifax, whose comment was 'Hitler is out for
world hegemony', and via Lord Dunglass (who as Sir Alec
Douglas-Home would be a future Prime Minister), to Nevile
Chamberlain, as he thought it important to let him know that war
against Poland was imminent. Having done this Clydesdale re-
claimed the letter, and sent a non-committal postcard about his
family to Albrecht Haushofer.

Albrecht Haushofer's parents

Professor Karl Haushofer, the originator of German Geopolitik

Martha Haushofer

One of the few pictures of Albrecht Haushofer (above left) in existence. Here, as Secretary-General of the Berlin Society for Geography, he welcomes the Swedish author and explorer Sven Hedin at the station

Above: *25 March 1935, Berlin; Hitler gives his portrait to Lord Simon;*
Albrecht Haushofer stands behind Hitler and the interpreter Schmidt
Below: *29 August 1938, Stuttgart; Hess addresses the Ausland Organisations*

Please destroy this letter after reading it —
and destroy it most carefully. But perhaps
this is unfair: So I give you freedom
for your own discretion to show this letter
personally either to Lord H. or to his
Under-Secretary Mr. B. — if you see fit
of course — under one condition: That
no notes should be taken, my name
never be mentioned, and the letter be
destroyed immediately afterwards. — As
a sign that you have received this
letter I only ask for some non-committal
picture-postcard (to my usual adress)
telling me that you are well. If you
have seen fit to show the letter you
might add something about your family...
I do hope we may meet again —

Yours ever sincerely

A.

Albrecht Haushofer's letter to Clydesdale on 16 July 1939. It was also read by Churchill, Halifax and Chamberlain

Above: *19 July 1940, Berlin; Hitler has made his Reichstag peace offer to Britain.* Left to right: *Hess, Hitler, von Neurath and Goebbels*

Below: *10 May 1941, the start of Hess's peace mission!*

Uneasy partnership! 13 November 1940, Berlin; Hess with Molotov, the Soviet Foreign Minister

*Wing-Commander
Duke of Hamilton*

*Ivone
Kirkpatrick, the
Foreign Office
expert on
German affairs*

Russian soldiers guarding Hess, the only remaining prisoner in Spandau

A month later, on 1 September 1939, German armed forces swamped Poland and after the expiry of the British ultimatum to Germany, Neville Chamberlain committed Britain to war against Nazi Germany on 3 September. Afterwards Churchill was asked in the Lobby of the House of Commons by Clydesdale how long he thought the war would last, and Churchill replied several times, 'Until the end of Hitler.'

The conquest of Poland followed within a few weeks, and many in Britain were surprised at the relative lack of activity in the first months of what came to be known as the 'Phoney War'. There was immediate demand for a statement of British War Aims, on the grounds that every attempt should be made at the outset of the war, in so far as it was possible, to separate the German people from Hitler. This demand came from a variety of different men, including William Temple, Archbishop of York and later Archbishop of Canterbury, Clydesdale, A. D. Lindsay, the Master of Balliol, and Arthur Salter.[12] Their hope was to encourage any potential German Resistance to Hitler in Germany, by announcing that as soon as Hitler and the Nazi leadership had been destroyed there would be room for negotiation.

On 2 October 1939 the Archbishop of York broadcast on the B.B.C. on 'The Spirit and Aims of Great Britain in War', and expressed this point of view:

> Men are taking up a hateful duty: the very fact that they hate it throws into greater relief their conviction that it is a duty. . . . Our purpose is to check aggression, and bring to an end the perpetual insecurity and menace which hang over Europe spoiling the life of millions as a result of the Nazi tyranny in Germany. . . .
>
> It seems to me that the achievement of our purpose is possible only if two conditions are fulfilled. The first is that we should make no terms with Herr Hitler or his Government not because it is undemocratic, which is Germany's concern and not ours, but because it is utterly untrustworthy. The second is that the terms which we make with an honourable German Government shall be arrived at in such a way as to show that we have sought no kind of advantage for ourselves and no humiliation for the German people. . . .[13]

Clydesdale wrote a letter on the same theme to *The Times* which

D

was published on 6 October 1939, and which had been written for
the purpose of encouraging men in the position of Albrecht
Haushofer who might form a potential German Resistance to
Hitler:

Sir, Many like yourself, have had the opportunity of hearing
a good deal of what the men and women of my generation are
thinking. There is no doubt in any quarter, irrespective of party,
that this country had no choice but to accept the challenge of
Hitler's aggression against one country in Europe after another.
If Hitler is right when he claims that the whole of the German
nation is with him in his cruelties and treacheries, both within
Germany and without, then this war must be fought to the bitter
end. It may well last for many years, but the people of the British
Empire will not falter in their determination to see it through.

But I believe that the moment the menace of aggression and
bad faith has been removed, war against Germany becomes
wrong and meaningless. This generation is conscious that injustices were done to the German people in the era after the last
War. There must be no repetition of that. To seek anything but
a just and comprehensive peace to lay at rest the fears and dis-
cords in Europe would be a betrayal of our fallen.

I look forward to the day when a trusted Germany will again
come into her own, and believe that there is such a Germany,
which would be loth to inflict wrongs on other nations such as
she would not like to suffer herself. That day may be far off, but
when it comes, then hostilities could and should cease, and all
efforts be concentrated on righting the wrongs in Europe by free
negotiations between the disputing parties, all parties binding
themselves to submit their disputes to an impartial equity
tribunal in case they cannot reach agreement.

We do not grudge Germany Lebensraum, provided that
Lebensraum is not made the grave of other nations. We should
be ready to search for and find a just colonial settlement, just to
all peoples concerned, as soon as there exist effective guarantees
that no race will be exposed to being treated as Hitler treated
the Jews on November 9th last year. We shall, I trust, live to
see the day when such a healing peace is negotiated between
honourable men, and the bitter memories of twenty-five
years of unhappy tension between Germany and the Western

democracies are wiped away in their responsible co-operation
for building a better Europe.

> Yours truly,
> Clydesdale
> House of Commons.[14]

Similar letters and publications followed. It was thought that
at the beginning of the war a statement of British War Aims urging
Germans to destroy Hitler might have been accepted as an incentive to moderate Germans. It was believed that such a statement
would have meant no more than the taking out of an insurance
policy against an event which might never happen. No emphatic
statement of War Aims however was ever made by Neville
Chamberlain's Government. Clydesdale's letter, along with the
other letters and articles, had no effect on British Government
policy but it does provide one of the connecting links in this story.

It came to the notice of Sir Frederick Ogilvie, the Director-
General of the B.B.C., that on the 10.15 p.m. German News on
6 October 1939, Clydesdale's letter had been quoted.[15] It is very
likely that one of the Haushofers or Hess learnt about it, and that
a sentence in that letter appealed to Hess, namely 'We shall I trust
live to see the day when such a healing peace is negotiated between
honourable men'. To the Nazis honour implied loyalty. It was not
for nothing that the motto of the S.S. was 'Our honour is our
loyalty' and Hess's loyalty to Hitler was beyond doubt. Hess would
have been the first to have considered himself an 'honourable
man', and would not have paid attention to the rest of Clydesdale's
letter, which he would not have liked.

Albrecht Haushofer, on the other hand, would have understood
Clydesdale's letter and would have appreciated that war beween
Britain and Germany would be waged until Hitler and all that he
represented had been destroyed – with or without the help of the
German people. The issue was a clear-cut one for Clydesdale and
the British, but it was not so simple for Albrecht who was a man
writhing within himself, torn and tormented.

8 A Bitter Dilemma: December 1939

AFTER Munich and even after the outbreak of war Albrecht Haushofer had several options open to him. He could have attempted to assassinate Hitler or to oppose him openly, but he well appreciated that in a State controlled by the S.S. and Gestapo any such course would have been difficult to put into practice and would almost inevitably have been suicidal. He did not consider open hostility to Nazism within the Reich as a practicable possibility for himself in 1939, and few – if any – Germans did.

This left him with the same basic choice which he had faced in 1933, that of staying in Germany or of emigrating. He could still have fled the country to Britain or the U.S.A., and could have opposed Nazism from without. However, it was unlikely that he would leave without his mother, to whom he was very close. Besides, his father in all likelihood would not, in any circumstances, have countenanced his son and his wife leaving their country in its hour of need. In any case Martha had rejected emigration in 1933, and she did not want to leave her husband.

Consequently Albrecht Haushofer may have felt that the easiest course would be to stay in Germany. But if he stayed his would be a bitter dilemma. He could passively resign himself to the most atrocious events, but that would be the attitude of a coward or even of an accomplice. The only other possibility was to pretend to be a loyal supporter of the regime in public, whilst collaborating with those who wished to form a secret German Resistance to Hitler. Such was his predicament, and as long as he remained in Germany there was no way out. It would have been possible for him to leave. He chose to remain.

At the beginning of September 1939 Ribbentrop called Albrecht Haushofer to the Foreign Ministry and asked him to resume work.[1] Haushofer accepted and occupied a position in the Information Section, partly because he feared the isolation which would have accompanied inactivity and partly because he wanted to have a job which would enable him to observe closely the course of events.

He now found the writing of geopolitical reports so distasteful that he could not go through with them any longer. On 5 October 1939 he wrote to Kurt Vowinckel, the publisher of the *Zeitschrift für Geopolitik*, that he could not write the Atlantic Report for the following reasons:

> Should the Journal decide to continue the report, the following will be essential: abandonment of the present prevailing topicality and relative objectivity of the report. Systematic suppression of important facts. . . . Conclusion: the present author cannot do this. . . .[2]

He sensed the lack of permanency of the Third Reich and the approach of disaster. On 8 October Albrecht wrote to one of the geopolitical writers, Hans Zehrer:

> It has to be said that those, who have the power and who make revolution in their own way . . . are lacking the ear for spiritual language – and that the few, who had it and who as advisers and experts are still tolerated in the proximity of power for the sake of their practical usefulness, have lost all faith in their own effectiveness. . . .
>
> I have doubts. These doubts revolve around two central points: on the one hand around the relative position of the German and Italian revolutions in relation to the Russian revolution and on the other hand around the liveliness of what you call the West.
>
> To begin with I will consider the first point. . . . At the present there is only one great revolution and that is the Russian one. The German and especially the Italian ones are only derivatives. You are entitled to demand a substantiation of these theses. In doing this, I can, I hope, be brief. Two allegories may serve here, one of which is completely objective, the other has a malicious tinge.

The first allegory he used depicted the desire of German officialdom to contain Bolshevism and the hope of men such as himself who were trying to check a fire and the methods employed to do so.

In prairie areas there are sometimes huge grass fires, which are carried forward by strong steady winds and which seize vast areas: When herdsmen and herds are threatened by such fires experienced herdsmen kindle their own fire, which moves ahead of the primary fire. Behind the second fire there is safety on the already charred ground. A part of the herd usually starves and dies of thirst in the process; another part, however, is usually rescued; the herdsmen usually stay alive.

He then used a very different allegory, painting a picture of a man or group of men, who had become so innoculated to what was happening that it was hard to avoid the road to suicide.

The other example is a medical one: the vaccination illness, which usually takes a light course, sometimes causes death. The physicians, however, only admit this when one is already dead – you will not ask me for further interpretation.

He was sure that the Nazi revolution was not a lasting revolution with deep roots.

There appear to me to be at present only two primary revolutionary fires in this world; the Chinese revolution, which commenced in 1911 and will perhaps be finished in the year 2100, and the Russian one of 1917. Both are the long-distance effects of Europe, but on non-European soil. A third revolution will probably come one day, that of the Western colonial world in North America. This will still take some time. Everything else appears to me to be secondary.

He argued that the Nazi revolution, coming after the Russian revolution, was following the same pattern as the Napoleonic Wars after the French Revolution.

What takes place today in Germany and in Italy appears to me to bear the same relation to the Russian revolution as the various European revolutions of the first half of the nineteenth century bore to that in France in 1789 – secondary also there where they were immediately directed against France in various forms – from the Prussian Reform to the Spanish Guerilla – from this results, of course, a totally changed general picture.

I do not know whether we may assert schematically that in every nation there is only one revolution. But if that is so, then Germany and Italy had theirs in the fifteenth and in the sixteenth centuries, and the Thirty Years War was the termination of that of Germany.

What is at present taking place in these countries appears to me to be adaptation and resistance processes of some violence, rather than events of depth of a spiritual religious character.

The Spanish Civil War struck him as a struggle of great significance.

The most significant European individual process of the last few years appears to me to be the Spanish one: there waves of 1789 and 1917 met and were absorbed in a very remarkable way.

He was building up to the conclusion that the war would bring the Russians and Americans into the heart of Europe.

You will perhaps say: these details do not matter. I fear the contrary. Because if it is as I believe it is, then this means (from the external level) that there are only two ways for Europe; the Russian one and the American one.

He came to his second thesis that war was going to lead to untold death and destruction as well as to the abolition of all moral values:

The body of the West is already dead, even when the garment of its external culture is still preserved. The war into which we now enter will also tear this garment to pieces. I fear that in the end this war will convince us with a harshness which is as yet unimaginable for most, that there is no longer a Europe, nor a West. . . . We know that such a destruction is mechanically possible. The postulate for it being wanted and thereby that it may occur is, however, just the extinction of the fundamental spiritual, ethical and religious powers of the western world. . . .

Let us now take a look at our time and let us be honest: is there still an ethical or spiritual order in the 'West' today? Is there still a generally binding religious basis in the ethical foundation or in the metaphysical hope? I say No![3]

After portraying the New Dark Age which was going to con-
vulse Germany and Europe, Albrecht Haushofer gave a picture of
himself, of what he was, and of what he was trying to do, in a long
letter to his mother on 23 December 1939. No clearer or more
terrible description could be given of the hateful dilemma which
confronted intelligent German patriots early on in the Second
World War.

I wish to send a few personal lines by Father, who is returning
home. I do not know how far I am able to express myself
properly in writing. I find all talk about personal things much
harder at the present than ever before. . . .

I do not want to analyse past matters, whatever unintentional
damage could occur or has perhaps already occurred in my
present 'chrysalis' state. As regards my relationship to most
people, the occurrence or non-occurrence of such damage is
indifferent to me.

I need not assure you that it is different in regard to you. I was
all the more shocked by the fact that an incident, the details of
which I can hardly remember even by sharp concentration, has
left upon you deep and painful effects. . . . When a son really
deeply hurts his mother something deep-seated has to be
examined, revealed and put in order, lest harm be done. I will
not try to clarify what is apparent and perceptible to myself.

You will perhaps remember a letter, which I wrote to you in
the summer of 1938, at that time premature by one year, when
I tried to prepare myself internally for the coming war and the
approaching collapse of an entire cultural world. I must refer
to this letter and add an explanation.

He explained that if his behaviour was odd, it was because what
was happening in the Third Reich was so revolting that he
required to build a hard and cold shell around his exterior self,
which was devoid of emotion, so that he could survive.

There may be defects in my character, defects in my spiritual
structure, which I may carry from my ancestors: I may be
responsible for them myself – in any case, there is in me a group
of qualities, which causes me a great deal of trouble in times of
great turbulence and forces me to behaviour, which is very
difficult for other people to understand, to the cold sleep, to the
long-term anaesthesia of the emotional world.

He needed to destroy all spontaneous sentiments, because he hated all forms of physical violence.

The leading types of human unreasonableness and violence are so deeply loathed by me in all their manifestations, and the constant pressure to serve which this war brings to bear on everybody who is officially active, even on those who do not themselves shoot, creates in me such destructive effects that I am in need of mental anaesthesia in order to escape an explosive conclusion.

He wrote that one day he would recover his natural self, because if he could not, it would be because he was going to be killed.

This state of anaesthesia cannot of course be a permanent condition for one's entire future life. Either there will once again be an air, which one can breathe, or the realisation will come that it is futile to save oneself for a time in which one will raise a spark of faith in what one does, because such a time cannot come again – and then it is time for the end.

He considered leaving Germany, but he sheered his mind away, perhaps because he was deceiving himself by imagining that he would be running away. He argued that it would be better for him to stay in case he might be able to salvage something from the wreck of the German ship of state. Yet underlying his words was the fear that the ship would be so dashed to fragments by the 'fools and criminals' in charge of the Third Reich, that it would be impossible to pick up the broken pieces, let alone put them together again.

Meanwhile it appears to me premature to depart voluntarily – partly because I still have some human ties, both hereditary and voluntarily accepted, partly because I can still see a tiny ray of hope that some of the values for which it is rewarding to act will be preserved. The decision not to jump into the water – where one would quickly submerge – from a damaged ship, which is already burning in some places and which is predominantly commanded and steered by fools and criminals, but to make the attempt to watch, to put one's hands on a hose and perhaps to seize an important lever, all this demands such mental concentration that there remains no capacity of expression concerning many things of inherent value.

He had to give himself a mental anaesthetic, because the men
for whom he was working were murderers. He described a meeting, possibly with Himmler or Heydrich.

> An example: I sit at a table with a man whose duty it will be,
> in the Jewish Ghetto of Lublin, to let a great part of the German
> Jews deported there freeze to death and starve according to
> programme. By one frivolous sentence – whether he had proper-
> ly considered that for the 60- and 70-year-old people the costs
> of transport would no longer be worthwhile – I can perhaps
> achieve that at least the old ones will be spared – but in such a
> case I quite plainly could not endure an emotional observation
> of the whole process from a personal angle. Similar considera-
> tions are valid for many spheres of life.

He could only work in the German Foreign Office if he trans-
formed himself into an automaton, crushing all feelings of
humanity, and only to his mother and a few others could he be
honest:

> I am lacking – and, by God, I did not steal it – the ability of
> quick adaptation in the emotional sphere. Sometimes I envy
> Father this ability, which has enabled him to hold out through-
> out the war: to enjoy a sunset even in the Battle of the Somme,
> or to feel a friendship. I cannot do this. For me there is only one
> security; the ataraxia, the torpidness of grief and joy, of hope
> and despair. When I regard everything as dead and as destroyed,
> with the killing and with the destruction of which I have to
> count in these times, then it no longer affects me when it
> occurs.

The price he had to pay for working for the German Foreign
Office was great:

> I can cope with the foreseeable. The price I pay for this
> tranquillity is, of course, high; the renunciation of all emotional
> expression, which would lead to relaxation. For general practice
> I have prepared a formula for myself, which is partly false (in
> the part which pretends personal interest), partly genuine but
> impersonal; a matter-of-fact readiness to help the beetle, which
> has fallen on its back, as long as mechanical help suffices. Some
> are taken in by this, some are not; I am lacking the courage to lie
> to a select few people, and you are among them.

But when he thought of the Germany which he cared for and
the ways of life which he loved, he could not bear it:

> It is simply like this: when I permit myself in this time even
> to think of the native place and of the parental home, of the
> many pleasant recollections, of the living persons and of the
> things dear to one, of the Alpine cottage and of the chapel, then
> a wave of hatred and of anger against the destroyers rises at the
> same time in me, which could completely unbalance me, if I am
> not careful.

He dismissed the possibility of withdrawal as a hermit.

> I know that there would be, theoretically, another alternative,
> the way to contemplative wisdom without action. But this way
> is in our world completely barred for a man of my age.

He knew that he was no longer fighting to contain evil. He had
become part of it, and he admitted that which few Germans
admitted:

> I can only live in two different forms; as a mind in the service
> of lying, or as a body in the service of murder. Both can be
> endured, but only when one no longer feels it.

Because of this he shrank instinctively from all affection and
warmth. He feared that, if he responded to human kindness and
generosity, life as a part-time Foreign Office official would become
insufferable, and he would kick over the traces, thereby causing his
own destruction. He wrote that when he last saw his mother his
coldness and insensitivity to her was caused by the fact that he was
preparing to go to Headquarters, presumably to meet Ribbentrop.

> And now I return to the personal matter between us. From
> what father has told me, I am afraid that I gave myself the
> anaesthetic injection which I urgently needed on my trip to
> Headquarters an hour too early, and that I have thereby un-
> neccessarily hurt you. When I have been hard I have been so in
> anticipation. When I have been impatient against loving care,
> when I shrink from the exchange of personal warmth then it is
> only the instinct of self-preservation, of a hibernating animal
> which survives only by reducing its body temperature. If one
> wakens it and if then it is unable to warm itself artificially, it will
> perish.

All comparisons are inadequate. I hope that I have succeeded in exposing some roots. Perhaps understanding will make it possible to forgive. . . .[4]

This must have been poignant reading for his mother. In 1933 her son Albrecht, to use his own allegory, had decided to try to control the fire raging in Germany as prairie herdsmen fight to contain prairie fires, and in spite of all efforts he had never been rewarded by success. He had been fascinated by the heat and had rather enjoyed tampering with the furnace, however precarious his position as a firefighter had been. In 1939 he found that he had been overtaken by the flames, which surrounded him and were beginning to hurt. Now the blaze gave him no enjoyment, and the harshest reality of all was that he was no longer a fireman. By his own decision he had joined the millions of swarming stokers behind the inferno.

Haushofer knew that if he left Germany himself matters would be hard for his parents, and they would have to face the consequences arising out of his defection. He cared in particular for his mother and knew that as a 'half-Jew' she was going to have enough problems in Nazi Germany. He did not want to create any more for her. He had decided to stay. Even so, with the sole exception of Rudolf Hess, he loathed his leaders, and he despised himself for his own hypocrisy, and all the time he was looking and searching for an opportunity to doublecross those who had plunged Europe into such appalling misery.

9 The Double Game: 1940

IN 1940 Albrecht Haushofer was in a state of deep depression. After giving up his job as Secretary-General of the Berlin Society for Geography, his public work involved teaching at the University of Berlin or working part-time for the Foreign Office under Ribbentrop. During the same year in a very secretive and cautious manner he began to work with three men who were to become prominent in the German Resistance to Hitler – Johannes Popitz, Karl Langbehn and Ulrich von Hassell.

On 24 July 1940 he wrote to his father, sarcastically commenting on Hitler's peace offer to Britain made some five days before, and on the fact that Ribbentrop was quite as inconsiderate as he was stupid.

> Today there is a change of weather – on the large as well as on the small scale. Until yesterday 'One' had – for reasons difficult to understand for me (and for all experts on English pigheadedness) – the real hope that the people in London would give in before one has tried a landing or total aerial warfare. Now this seems to be over. . . .
>
> The Ministry for Foreign Affairs just telephoned. Its head demands within twenty-four hours to be supplied with maps, for the making of which one needs at least four weeks. Four months ago I offered to have them made for him. At that time he did not want them. . . . Now he says: Money and people are no consideration. . . . Governing is an art. . . .[1]

On 4 August 1940 he wrote to his mother saying that he had done what he could to resign himself to his environment, that all enthusiasm within him was dead and that he could not make meaningful contact with those around him. As he wrote:

> Any outsider would, of course, be entitled to say: what is the

matter with you? You are surely doing splendidly: you have
really achieved everything you could wish for at your age;
Berlin University arranged a professorship for you: you have
asserted yourself; you can still achieve infinitely more: you have
sailed through the war in a most comfortable way. All this is
correct. I tell myself so almost every day.

And yet: you know that this is not the decisive factor. All
this seems to me like a dish full of good things, but dressed with
vinegar instead of oil.[2]

He admitted that he was not struggling particularly hard for or
against the Third Reich. Yet his services were considered to be
technically useful and his presence was required at Vienna on
27 August. There Ribbentrop and Ciano having conferred with
Hitler, told the Foreign Ministers of Romania and Hungary that
they must accept their frontiers as Ribbentrop and Ciano had
chosen to redraw them. On 29 August Albrecht Haushofer wrote
to his mother in Vienna:

> The day before yesterday I was required again in the great
> theatre. Head over heels I was called here – yesterday bundled
> off in an aeroplane to Salzburg and back again – merely to find
> that the decisions had already been made – decisions for which
> I would not like to bear the slightest responsibility in the face of
> history. Two years ago the political contents of such a conference
> would still have moved me; a year ago the curious game, the
> strange behaviour of the main participants would still have
> interested me. Now it hardly affects me. Turkeys gobble . . .
> peacocks rustle with their tail – and professional jealousy is
> everywhere. It was very useful to have seen all this. But now it
> is enough.

He had not forgotten the techniques of personal advancement,
but he felt no incentive to engage in them and sat dreaming about
the plays he had written:

> Now I should really sit downstairs in the hall, I guess, conduct
> anxious conversations with ambassadors and envoys, rush with
> important face past curious journalists, book as a gain in prestige
> friendly handshakes from Ribbentrop and from Ciano – gather
> greetings for Father – instead I sit quietly in my pleasant room –
> if they need me, they can send for me – dream about my Chinese

Legend, in this dream world one can for a change let the just
men survive and let the unjust perish – which does not usually
happen otherwise – and write this letter.[3]

His views were accurately described by his colleague Fritz Hesse
who recalled a visit from him shortly after the outbreak of war:

> He greeted me like an old fellow plotter. . . . Haushofer called
> Hitler and his circle scum, his collaborators gangsters, and with
> an unsurpassed sharpness and malice enumerated the personal
> weaknesses of individuals. Since Haushofer himself had, at
> least for some time, had the role of adviser and was then, as was
> usual, dropped by Hitler, his remarks bore the stamp of
> authenticity.
>
> Haushofer entirely agreed with me that once the die was cast
> the war with Britain would be fought to the bitter end and that
> there was no chance of an agreement with Hitler. In his view of
> Germany's inner political situation, Haushofer also agreed with
> me that the patriotic pressure exerted on all Germans, the
> Gestapo terror and the indecision of political generals made it
> appear impossible that any internal action for the removal of
> the Hitler regime could succeed during the war. Thus we fully
> agreed, already at the beginning of the great struggle, that
> Germany's chances of an understanding with the opponents
> would only present themselves after Hitler's downfall.[4]

As it happened, at the same time as Albrecht was occasionally
working for Ribbentrop he was also doing something very different,
which his parents did not know about. He was working for a
pocket of the embryonic Resistance. We know this from one of his
students, Rainer Hildebrandt, who wrote an account of Albrecht
Haushofer entitled *Wir Sind die Letzten* ('We are the Last'). Many
of the opinions given by Hildebrandt are emotional assertions
unsupported by evidence, and as Gerald Reitlinger wrote 'the
tortuous mind of Albrecht Haushofer will not be found in the
pious tract of a hero-worshipping disciple'.[5] Yet Hildebrandt does
give many of the facts which he was in as good a position to know
as anybody.

In the University of Berlin Albrecht Haushofer had a high
reputation and it was said that his assistants carefully creamed off
advanced students who wished to work under him. His courses

were popular because his students knew that under the guise of discussing the historical characters of Ancient Greece and Rome, Albrecht would elaborate upon the shortcomings of the Nazi leadership. He used to take his students on travels throughout Europe, frequently into the mountains of the Bavarian Alps, and he would help by giving them letters of introduction, and by placing them in positions in the Foreign Ministry. He was respected by his students, and was friendly with several of them, including Rainer Hildebrandt, whom he occasionally sent on errands.[6]

He told Hildebrandt that there were three types of men surrounding Hitler. In the first group were people like Hess and Ribbentrop who acted as though they were completely mesmerised. In the second group there were many variations including Goering and many senior army officers who saw through Hitler, but at decisive moments always succumbed to his will. In the third group, which might have included himself, Albrecht said there were men who failed to find anything 'electrifying' in a man whose 'mental limitations must cause an evergrowing sense of distance'.[7]

With such an outlook his easiest outlet was to co-operate with persons who might fit into this third category and who wanted to save what they could of the Germany which Hitler was plunging into ever-expanding war. In 1937, on his way back from Japan through the Mediterranean, Albrecht met Karl Langbehn, a lawyer, with whom he had formed a friendly acquaintance. In the spring of 1940 Langbehn introduced him to Johannes Popitz at the latter's home at 50, Brentano Strasse, Berlin.[8]

Popitz, like Albrecht Haushofer, had been on good terms with Bruening in the last days of the Weimar Republic. In December 1932 he had become Prussian Minister of Finance, and after Goering became Premier of Prussia had tried to influence the latter, with as much lack of success as Albrecht Haushofer had with Ribbentrop. Popitz belonged to the circle of men who comprised the Wednesday Society in Berlin, which included some fifteen persons who had made outstanding contributions in the academic and scientific field. Three of its members whom Popitz knew well were Ulrich von Hassell, the former German Ambassador in Italy, Professor Dr Jessen who held a command under Quartermaster-General Wagner, and General Beck who had resigned as Chief of Staff of the German Army in 1938. Associated with these men was Dr Carl Goerdeler, the ex-Mayor of Leipzig,

General Oster of Admiral Canaris's Abwehr (the German counter
espionage service), Erwin Planck, director of the Otto Wolf
Foundation, and a number of high ranking officers, including
Witzleben and von Tresckow.[9]

Albrecht and Popitz became friends and through Popitz
Albrecht became acquainted with the Wednesday Society, which
under the pretence of discussing scientific matters offered its
members the opportunity to consider more pressing problems.
Opposition to Hitler in the Wednesday Society was only in
embryonic form: Hitler was winning battles, and while victory
pervaded the air the generals were unable to revolt successfully
against him, even if they had so wished. And generals like
Brauchitsch, Kluge, Manstein, Guderian and Rundstedt did not
so wish. Their outlook can be summarised in the words of
Rundstedt: 'In my position I cannot of course have any part in
such a plan. Should it succeed, however, I want you to remember
that I am senior among the generals.'[10]

Even those generals who were opponents of Hitler, such as Beck,
Witzleben and Tresckow, believed in General Halder's 'Set-Back
Theory', that only a severe military disaster or a deterioration in
the war situation would induce the German soldiers and generals
to act against Hitler. Therefore little or nothing could be done for
the time being to remove the Nazi regime.[11]

Yet Albrecht did make certain suggestions. After the fall of
France in June 1940 he knew that Hitler wanted to attack Russia
in the May of the following year, and that if two million or more
German troops invaded the only likely result would be a Russian
advance into the heart of Europe and a German capitulation. A
war on two fronts would be disastrous. He believed that it would be
easier to encourage the generals to act against Hitler if an assurance
could be extracted from the British that they would be prepared to
negotiate with a non-Nazi German Government and would not
invade while Germany was in the throes of an internal upheaval.

As it happened, a number of attempts had been made by various
groups of the embryonic Resistance to obtain similar guarantees
from Britain. Theo Kordt and Adam von Trott zu Solz, two German Foreign Office officials, had made overtures late in 1939, and
more important to Haushofer, Ulrich von Hassell, whom he met
periodically at Popitz's house, had made contact with 'a so-called
English associate of Lord Halifax'. This Englishman was Lonsdale

Bryans, who had met Hassell at Arosa in Switzerland on 22 February 1940. Hassell told him that if a revolt against Hitler was to be successful it would have to be carried out only by Germans, and the British would have to promise not to attack a non-Nazi German Government. He argued that Germany should keep Austria and the Sudetenland, that the German–Polish Border should be as it was in 1914, and that there should be no negotiations on the subject of Germany's western frontiers. On 14 April, after German troops had attacked Norway, Hassell met Lonsdale Bryans again, but Bryans came empty handed as the British Government was communicating through another channel with the German Resistance, through Dr Josef Mueller and the Vatican.[12]

After Hassell's talks with Lonsdale Bryans had come to a dead end, Albrecht, as an expert on Britain, offered his services. He knew that German generals intensely disliked the thought of a German defeat, and he believed that they would only act against Hitler if the British Government gave an undertaking that it would not attack a Hitlerless Germany. With this in mind he wrote:

> For an understanding with Britain the evacuation of the Western and Northern territories under German occupation must be accepted as a basis.
>
> The German–French frontier, in the event of Alsace-Lorraine remaining within the German Reich's territory, should be moved further West than before 1914. . . . This problem should form the topic of a joint German–French discussion. . . .

The proposals offered to safeguard Britain's imperial interests and her supremacy over the seas. In return Britain would have to recognize Germany's interests in Central Europe. These suggestions differed from the Nazi line in that the Nazi leaders wanted control over Greater Europe, which included the whole of eastern and south-eastern Europe.

> Having regard to the fact that for Britain the way to India must be unconditionally secured, Britain's special interests in the Eastern Mediterranean and Near East would have to be recognised. . . .
>
> Germany would have to be guaranteed, on the other hand, her special interests in the south-east European sphere. . . .

The regulation of her eastern frontier is regarded by Germany as a special problem which should be settled by the states directly concerned alone. . . .

There should, however, be no doubt that the occasion of a peace conference must be used for a basic reorganisation of Europe since the proposals would otherwise offer no guarantee for a permanent solution.

His proposals were aimed at the formation of a European Common Market, and he threw out a sop to the British Navy:

It is proposed that Europe should be enlarged into one economic region in which her peoples are led to a joint economic co-operation under the control of an Economic Council to which all European nations would send their representatives. . . . Each state should declare its willingness to contribute towards the creation of an European police force which could carry out, jointly, all military and security measures.

The German navy, like all other European naval units, would be placed under British command for safeguarding Europe's military co-operation, and would be available for the protection of British interests in the Indian Ocean.

The proposals went on to recommend the foundation of a joint European colonial association, which amounted to a request for the return of the lost German colonies. This again differed from the position of Hitler, who wanted to colonise Eastern Europe and Western Russia, rather than to dissipate his efforts in remote parts of Africa.

. . . The foundation of a joint European colonial association would appear to be necessary. It would be the task of this association to ensure a joint and equitable distribution of all African economic goods in an all-European market and of the corresponding counter-supplies (exports).[13]

This peace plan, like the other peace plans of the German Resistance, would have been quite unacceptable to the Nazis. It would have involved handing back Norway to the Norwegians, Denmark to the Danes, Belgium to the Belgians, Holland to the Dutch and France to the French, and the Nazi High Command was not prepared to relinquish control over any territory which had been conquered. It was also quite unacceptable to the British, because in practice it involved clinging on to many of Hitler's gains, especially in Eastern Europe.

One of Albrecht's pupils, H. W. Stahmer, had acquired a Foreign Office job in the German Embassy in Spain, and he handed these peace proposals into the British Embassy in Madrid.[14] The memoirs of the British Ambassador, Sir Samuel Hoare, later Lord Templewood, recorded the reaction to such offers, when they were made:

> Throughout the summer individual Germans made several attempts to enter into relations with the British Embassy. Although their credentials seemed good, my staff and I were extremely cautious in our response. . . . All that we did was to refuse to enter into any discussions and in the meanwhile to collect any German information that might be useful to the Allies.[15]

Albrecht Haushofer's peace plan thus had no effect, but it does show what he was doing. Believing that Britain with the help of the U.S.A. and with the involuntary assistance of Russia would win the war, he wanted to bring about a peace settlement between Britain and Germany before Russia was attacked. He would have preferred to make contact with the British on behalf of the German Resistance to Hitler, but if that was impossible he wanted peace with Britain on any terms which were acceptable to Germany. With his hatred of all forms of violence he was in the position of a man who did not want to fight against Germany and did not want to fight for her. Indeed Albrecht Haushofer was a man who did not want to fight at all.

As an ambitious German patriot he had refused to leave Germany before the outbreak of war and he was now relying on the strength of his wits. He had one foot firmly planted in the German Resistance to Hitler, and the other firmly planted in the Nazi camp, both as assistant of Ribbentrop and as personal adviser to Rudolf Hess.

He talked about his dealings as 'sailing through troubled waters' and when questioned by friends as to the expected outcome of his hopes for peace he would say 'One can only foresee three or four moves in a game of chess with any degree of accuracy.'[16] His uncertainty was not without cause, for with Hitler there could be no half-measures. Those who were not with him were against him, and Albrecht was not with him. In 1940 Albrecht was playing a double game.

At this point it is appropriate to leave Albrecht Haushofer, and return more closely to the career and fortunes of Hitler's personal Deputy, Rudolf Hess.

11 | The Hess-Haushofer Peace Feelers

'I cannot imagine that cool, calculating England will run her neck into the Soviet noose instead of saving it by coming to an understanding with us.'

Rudolf Hess to Dr Kersten, *c*. 24 June 1940.

'It must be realised that, even in the Anglo-Saxon world, the Fuehrer was regarded as Satan's representative on earth and had to be fought. . . .

'As the final possibility I then mentioned that of a personal meeting on neutral soil with the closest of my English friends: the young Duke of Hamilton, who has access at all times to all important persons in London, even to Churchill and the King.'

Albrecht Haushofer's Tutorial to Hess: 8 September 1940.

'The whole thing is a fool's errand.'

Albrecht Haushofer to his parents: 19 September 1940.

'Do you mean to tell me that the Deputy Fuehrer of Germany is in our hands? . . . Well, Hess or no Hess I am going to see the Marx Brothers.'

Winston Churchill to Duke of Hamilton: 11 May 1941.

'England should give Germany a free hand in Europe, and Germany would give England a completely free hand in the Empire. . . . Germany had certain demands to make of Russia which would have to be satisfied, either by negotiation or as the result of a war.'

Rudolf Hess to Ivone Kirkpatrick: 1.30 a.m. 13 May 1941.

Hess's Decline and Hitler's Peace Offers

TOWARDS 1939 Hess's influence with Hitler was declining. It is sometimes said that Hess's character was different from that of Nazi leaders like Goering, Himmler and Goebbels. He was certainly more loyal and less intelligent. His loyalty to Hitler secured for him positions of great power, and his lack of intelligence led to his gradual decline, a process which became noticeable in 1937 with the rise of Himmler.

In the 1920s Hess had been Hitler's closest friend. Hitler had been an insignificant corporal in the Great War, while Hess had been an officer, and his unqualified admiration had given Hitler a certain self-confidence, for he felt that Hess's loyalty meant recognition by the German officer class. Hitler also believed that if his speeches passed Hess they would easily go down with a German mass audience, since, as Hitler said, a mass audience is apt to follow the lowest common denominator.[1]

Hess himself was a man longing for domination by a stronger will. His close friendship with Hitler made him into a hard and ruthless Fascist, prepared to do anything on Hitler's behalf, as he had shown during the Night of the Long Knives. Because his loyalty to Hitler was absolute he was quite unlike Himmler and Goering. Consequently, Hess had not sufficient imagination to be a prime mover of Nazism. He was the devoted follower, implementing Hitler's will in Hitler's wake. Content to reflect the lustre of his leader, diverting all light away from himself, he was a pale carbon copy of his Fuehrer. Inseparable from Hitler in the Reichstag and elsewhere, he had become almost an adjunct of Hitler's personality.

Hitler had a great affection for Hess as his closest and most devoted friend, and, as such, he wanted to reward him. He found administration tiresome and was glad to delegate. In April 1933 he appointed Hess as his Deputy with power to make decisions in his name in all matters of Party leadership.[2]

Hess in return helped to extend Hitler's power in many ways. He appointed a University Commission of the Party and on 18 July 1934 the Nazi League of German Students was directly subordinated to him. He also sent circulars for the Adolf Hitler Fund for German Industry to organisations such as Krupps, so that the necessary funds could be acquired 'for the unified execution of the tasks which fall to the lot of the S.A., S.S. and other political organisations'.[3]

In the early years after his accession to power Hitler found Hess's work satisfactory, and on 27 July 1934 he increased Hess's authority by compelling all Nazi leaders to present drafts of laws to Hess for his preliminary sanction. Through Hess he wished to keep a check on other Nazi leaders.[4]

It looked as though Hitler might make Hess his heir. However, in 1934, after visiting Hess's house near Munich, Hitler said that he had decided not to make him his successor because Hess's house had displayed a lack of taste for art and culture.[5] Consequently Goering was appointed Hitler's successor over Hess's head, Hess remaining Hitler's personal Deputy.

Hitler may not have felt until later that Hess was deficient in other respects, for his new job was more demanding than that of being simply Hitler's secretary. At the Brown House in Munich, Hess at the head of the Nazi Party had control over at least nineteen departments, his Chief of Staff being Martin Bormann. These departments included a Department of Racial Hygiene, which embraced sub-departments of Race Politics and Investigation of Kinship, a Department of Practical Technical Questions, a Department of Unemployment, Financial and Tax Policies, a Department for Schools, and a department which dealt with Nazified Art.

Three of the most important departments under Hess were in Berlin. Todt's Department for Technical and Organisation Questions had considerable control over German industry and was responsible for the construction of *autobahns*, so that panzer divisions could move with maximum speed throughout the Reich. Another was the Foreign Department dealing with the Nazi Party's Ausland Organisation under Hess's protegé, Gauleiter Bohle, and perhaps the most important department was the Dienststelle Ribbentrop.[6]

Hess, as the head of the Nazi Party, was responsible for bringing in vicious legislation against those who were anti-Nazi and those of Jewish, or of part-Jewish origin. On 20 December 1934 he signed a decree entitled 'Laws against Treacherous Acts towards the State and Party'. Article 1 imposed penalties upon anyone making utterances which harmed the prestige of the Nazi Party or Nazi State, and Article 2 made it illegal for anyone to make malicious statements about the Party or its leading personalities.[7] Hess and Himmler saw to it that this decree was rigorously enforced.

Hess brought in many of the Nuremberg Race Laws, along with Frick, the Reich Minister of the Interior, and Goering. On 14 November 1935 he signed the decree which deprived all Jews of their right to employment in government offices and of their right to vote. On 15 September he signed the Law for the Protection of Blood and Honour, and under that decree and under the Reich Citizenship Law he went on to issue the necessary legislation for the carrying out or the supplementing of those laws. Another decree signed by him forbade Jews to marry or to have extra-marital relations with Germans.[8]

In one of his speeches Hess quoted Treitschke's saying 'All justice is political'.[9] Hess certainly made it so. He had set in motion the wheels which culminated in the mass murder of Jews. In a speech in Berlin to the officers of the German Wehrmacht on 16 January 1937 he spoke proudly about Nazism as a forceful movement which had been 'enabled to obliterate Jewish poison in all spheres'.[10] The actual obliteration was carried out by Himmler and his men. Like Hitler, Hess was content to leave the matter to Himmler. On 9 June 1934 Hess decreed that the Nazi Party's Intelligence Service should be absorbed by the S.S., the Security Service of the Reichsführer S.S. being established as 'the sole political news and defence service of the party'. Again, on 14 December 1938 Hess issued a decree that control over the S.D. (the Secret Service of the S.S.) should be transferred to Himmler's S.S. To express solidarity with his accomplice Himmler, Hess accepted the honorary position of Obergruppenführer in the S.S.[11]

He was responsible as the head of the Nazi Party for the killing of many old people who were sick and were considered to be of no further use to the State, even if his Chief of Staff Martin Bormann took a greater interest in the use of this compulsory euthanasia.[12]

Hess encouraged Germans to look upon themselves as a master race, and in his speech on 16 January 1937 he declared:

> As at home, abroad too Germans are being instructed in National-Socialist ideology. . . . They are being re-educated to a proud sense of being German, to cohere among themselves, to respect one another, so as to make them realise that they stand higher than any other national group. . . .[13]

The methods which Hess used for encouraging Germans to 'cohere' to the Reich can be discerned in the events leading up to the Anschluss. Through the Ausland Organisation Hess had been in touch with the illegal Nazi Party in Austria from 1933 onwards. In the autumn of 1934 he appointed Reinthaler as leader of the peasants in the Austrian Nazi Party. In 1936, Hess and Goering had meetings with the Austrian Nazi Seyss-Inquart and on 25 January 1938 the Austrian Government discovered his underhand game. On that day the Austrian Police visited the Headquarters of the Committee of Seven in Vienna, which was in fact the head office of the illegal Nazi Party. There they picked up documents initialled by Hess which gave instructions for the staging of a revolt in the spring of 1938. According to this plan the German Wehrmacht would enter Austria as soon as Austrian troops tried to put down the revolt, to prevent German blood being spilt by Germans.[14] There was no need to put this or any similar plan into operation, as the Austrian Government capitulated.

On 12 March 1938, the morning that German troops marched into Austria, Hess and Himmler were the first Nazi leaders to appear in Vienna. On the next day, 13 March, Hitler, Goering, Hess, Ribbentrop and Frick signed the Anschluss Law for a 'free and secret plebiscite',[15] to determine the question of reunion with Germany, the results of which were predetermined, with Himmler's S.S. organising the polls.

On 24 July 1938 Hess and Himmler made a point of being present at the celebrations held on the anniversary of the murder of Dolfuss. Four years before, Hess and Hitler had disowned the revolt which had caused Dolfuss's death. At that time no reference had been made by Hess to the fact that thirteen Nazis, including Planetta, had been executed for their share in Dolfuss's murder. Yet on 24 July 1938 Hess proudly commemorated the unsuccessful Putsch by laying a wreath at the grave of the murderers and by eulogising them. 'Wherever in all the world National Socialists march, these dead comrades march with us.'[16] As a final touch, on 20 May 1938 Hess signed a decree extending the anti-Semitic Nuremberg Laws to Austria.[17]

In spite of Albrecht Haushofer's part-Jewish ancestry Hess had made an exception in his case, because his old friend Karl Haushofer had sheltered him after the Beerhall Putsch, and Hess was glad to repay his debt of gratitude by protecting the Haushofer family. Karl Haushofer spoke highly of the intellectual ability of his son Albrecht, and Hess was willing to consider Albrecht's technical reports on Volksdeutsch matters and Foreign Policy as well as on other topics including science and education. Albrecht however had no share in the formulation of Nazi policy. He could influence Hess only on matters of detail. Any line of policy emanating from Hitler was accepted absolutely by Hess and rational argument was impossible.

Nonetheless Hess was gradually declining in importance, and this became noticeable in 1937. His loss of influence was mainly due to the rise of Himmler and of Bormann in the Nazi Party. In 1937 the Volksdeutsche Mittelstelle was created and, with S.S. General Lorenz at its head, was effectively controlled by Himmler. Although Hess was still senior to Himmler his position was static, while Himmler's domain was rapidly growing. At the same time Hess's influence in the Nazi Party was declining, because Hitler was coming to realise that his Deputy was not an efficient or competent administrator. More and more work was undertaken by Bormann, who wheedled his way into Hitler's confidence by managing the Adolf Hitler Industrial Fund for Hitler's private uses. Putzi Hanfstaengl wrote: 'Hess gradually became a nobody, a flag without a pole. Even Hitler once said to me of his Deputy: "I only hope he never has to take over from me. I would not know who to be more sorry for, Hess or the Party." '[18]

On top of this Hess, according to Hanfstaengl, 'was already becoming highly peculiar and went in for vegetarianism, nature cures and other weird beliefs. It got to the point where he would not go to bed without testing with a divining rod whether there were any subterranean water-courses which conflicted with the direction of his couch.'[19]

It was no wonder that he was beginning to lose his place in the Nazi hierarchy to Himmler and Bormann. Even Ribbentrop had become a more powerful figure than Hess. The Dienststelle Ribbentrop had rapidly grown in numbers from about fifteen in 1934 to more than three hundred in 1937. It had become the boiler-room of Nazi diplomacy, and after Ribbentrop became Foreign Minister Hitler listened only to him when considering whether the British would tolerate the German enslavement of one country after another. Ribbentrop's advice to Hitler in 1938 and 1939 had been that the British would either not fight at all when Poland was attacked, or would not fight seriously when confronted with a *fait accompli*.

Hess did not question Ribbentrop's policy, because it was the policy of Hitler, whom Hess always supported. On 27 August 1939 Hess spoke of the exceptional restraint exhibited by Hitler towards Poland, and on 30 August he became a member of the Council of Ministers for Defence of the Reich.[20] His intimacy with Hitler remained unaltered and on 1 September he was reappointed Hitler's successor after Goering, whilst the German army was invading Poland.[21] On the same day Hess rang Karl Haushofer and told him that there would be a short thunderstorm, and the General Professor replied that one could not know how big a flood might follow, and that he who rode a tiger could not jump off.[22]

Two days later, on 3 September, Hess was beside Hitler when Hitler's interpreter Schmidt read out the British ultimatum, demanding withdrawal of German armed forces from Poland. Hitler turned to Hess and said 'My book has been written in vain.'[23] Sixteen years before, Hitler had dictated to Hess, whilst writing *Mein Kampf*, 'No sacrifice should have been too great in winning England's friendship'.[24]

After the fall of Poland, Hess was involved in the administration of the occupied territories. In September and October 1939 he signed decrees incorporating Danzig and German-occupied Poland into the Reich and on 12 October he signed another decree creating the administration of German-occupied Poland.[25] He aided Himmler in the recruiting of the S.S., which was already providing numerous extermination squads, and whose Waffen S.S. units were in his opinion more suitable than other units for policing the occupied eastern territories.[26]

Hess had no feelings of humanity towards the Poles. He had been involved in the formulation of penal laws for the Poles in the occupied eastern territories, based on the premise that the Pole was less susceptible to the infliction of ordinary punishment than other human beings. Hess therefore wanted them to do the heaviest forms of labour in concentration camps.[27]

Yet Hess never put the British into the same category as the Russians or any other people in Eastern Europe. He approved when Hitler offered a peace conference to the British Empire from the Reichstag on 6 October 1939, saying that if the opinions of Mr Churchill and his followers were to prevail, this statement would have been his last.[28] As a matter of fact it was only his first and it was promptly rejected by Neville Chamberlain, as the Germans showed no signs of withdrawing from the occupied territories. As Ciano caustically wrote, the only voices in Britain in favour of the conference suggested by Hitler were Lloyd George and Bernard Shaw, proving that the British considered Hitler's proposals to be quite unacceptable.[29]

As the Western Democracies had rejected his peace overture, Hitler turned his attention to the destruction of France in the spring of the next year. After demolishing the French armed forces, however, Hitler stopped his Panzer divisions from attacking the British Expeditionary Force at Dunkirk on 24 May 1940. General Guenther Blumentritt described Hitler's words:

> He then astonished us by speaking with admiration of the British Empire, of the necessity for its existence and of the civilisation that Britain had brought into the world. . . . He said that all he wanted from Britain was that she should acknowledge Germany's position on the Continent. . . . He concluded by saying that his aim was to make peace with Britain. . . .[30]

The next weeks characterised Hitler's love-hate attitude towards the British. On 18–19 June 1940 Ciano recorded that Hitler 'makes many reservations on the desirability of demolishing the British Empire, which he considers, even today, to be an important factor in world equilibrium'.[31] On 7 July again Ciano wrote that Hitler was 'rather inclined to continue the struggle and to unleash a storm of wrath upon the English. But the fatal decision has not yet been reached and it is for this reason that he is delaying his speech, of which, as he puts it, he wants to weigh every word.'[32] Hitler had for some time been thinking of invading Britain, but he was only toying with the idea, partly because he did not want to run the risk

of failure and partly because he intensely disliked the sea. He had
even told Field Marshal Rundstedt 'On the land I am a hero; on
the sea I am a coward.' [33]

Hence Hitler made his famous peace offer to the British Empire
on 19 July 1940 from the Reichstag. Before and after he spoke he
sat beside Rudolf Hess, to whom he paid a standard tribute. He
started by saying that he had warned Britain and France in his
former peace offer of 6 October 1939, and that a small clique of
British warmongers were keeping the war alive.

> For this peace proposal I was abused and personally insulted.
> Mr Chamberlain, in fact, spat upon me before the eyes of the
> world, and following the instructions of the instigators and
> warmongers in the background – men such as Churchill, Duff
> Cooper, Eden, Hore-Belisha and others – declined even to
> mention peace, let alone to work for it. . . .

With words flowing with sarcasm he poured scorn on the
British resolve to fight whatever the consequences.

> In the opinion of British politicians their last hopes, apart
> from allied peoples consisting of a number of kings without
> a throne, statesmen without a nation and generals with-
> out an army, seem to be based on fresh complications which
> they hope to bring about, thanks to their proven skill in such
> matters.
> A veritable 'wandering Jew' among these hopes is the belief
> in the possibility of a fresh estrangement between Germany and
> Russia. . . .

He said that any such hope was based on a false premise and he
then reverted to his constant theme that it was only this small war
clique in Britain which was causing the war, and that the British
people were longing for peace:

> Mr Churchill ought perhaps, for once, to believe me when I
> prophesy that a great Empire will be destroyed – an Empire
> which it was never my intention to destroy or even to harm. I
> do, however, realise that this struggle, if it continues, can end
> only with the complete annihilation of one or other of the two
> adversaries. Mr Churchill may believe that this will be Germany.
> I know that it will be different.

In this hour, I feel it to be my duty before my own conscience to appeal once more to reason and commonsense in Great Britain as much as elsewhere. I consider myself in a position to make this appeal since I am not the vanquished, begging favours, but the victor speaking in the name of reason.

I can see no reason why this war must go on. . . .

Possibly, Mr Churchill will again brush aside this statement of mine by saying that it is merely born of fear and of doubt in our final victory. In that case, I shall have relieved my conscience in regard to the things to come. . . .[34]

Winston Churchill regarded Hitler's peace offer as a gross affront, and did not condescend to reply. On 22 July the peace offer was casually rejected out of hand by Lord Halifax in a routine broadcast.

Even so Hitler had no heart for invading Britain, especially as he had clearly made up his mind to attack and annexe large parts of Russia. The date alone for the Russian venture had to be fixed, and Hitler was persuaded that an attack in the autumn of 1940 was not practicable. His commanders were having to restrain him, because Hitler's mind was adopting a new mould. He thought that Britain was refusing to make peace because she was hoping for help, above all from Russia, and that if Russia were smashed Britain could no longer have this hope and would therefore have to make peace. As Halder noted on 31 July 1940 after further talks with Hitler:

Britain's hope lies in Russia and the United States. . . .
Russia is the factor on which Britain is relying most. . . .
With Russia smashed, Britain's last hope will be shattered. . . .
Decision: Russia's destruction must therefore be made a part of this struggle. Spring 1941.
The sooner Russia is crushed the better.[35]

It has been suggested that Hess may not have known that Hitler was going to attack Russia. However there is a certain amount of evidence on this point from high-ranking Nazi sources which appears to point solely in one direction. Otto Dietrich, Hitler's Press Officer, wrote that Hess was one of the few who knew about the plan to attack Russia, and that Hitler was very much afraid in the latter half of May 1941 that Hess would give away the outline

E

of this plan to the British.[36] Fritz Hesse, Ribbentrop's Press Officer, recorded that Himmler too was very anxious lest Hess after his flight might betray to the British the Fuehrer's intentions towards Russia.[37] Walter Schellenberg, one of Himmler's most senior Intelligence Officers, was also aware of the concern of Hitler and Himmler, and wrote in his memoirs that Hess certainly knew about Hitler's decision to attack Russia.[38]

Albrecht Haushofer was in the secret as well,[39] and while the preparations for the Russian campaign were made from August onwards under the heavily camouflaged order entitled Aufbau Ost or 'Reconstruction East', Hess was becoming more and more impatient.[40] He had been kept in constant touch by Walter Warlimont of Hitler's Operations Staff in the OKW (Armed Forces High Command). Warlimont related that as Chief of the Section it was his responsibility to keep Hess in the picture as to the most recent military developments.[41] As Deputy Fuehrer of the Third Reich and as a member of the Council of Ministers for the Defence of the Reich, Hess obviously had to be kept informed. He probably knew about the decision to attack Russia months before Hitler issued his order for Operation Barbarossa on 18 December 1940.

Indeed Hess may well have known about Hitler's decision to invade Russia before anyone else. In June 1940, during the French Campaign, Hitler and Hess had a lengthy conversation, and Hess later admitted to Lord Simon that the plans for his Secret Mission stemmed from this date.[42] Presumably this was the conversation referred to by Dr Kersten, Himmler's doctor, in his diary entry for 24 June 1940. Hess was in an excitable condition, suffering from stomach pains, and in the course of his treatment from Kersten spoke about an era of Franco-German co-operation. When Kersten brought up the British question, pointing out that they were a stubborn people, Hess replied:

We'll make peace with England in the same way as with France. Only a few weeks back the Fuehrer again spoke of the great value of the British Empire in the world order. Germany and France must stand together with England against the enemy of Europe, Bolshevism. That was the reason why the Fuehrer allowed the English Army to escape at Dunkirk. He did not want to upset the possibility of an understanding. The English must see that and seize their chance. I can't imagine that cool, calculating England will run her neck into the Soviet noose instead of saving it by coming to an understanding with us.[43]

Hess had already made up his mind to restore himself in Hitler's personal esteem. He would help to make peace with Britain so that together Germany and Britain might oppose Russia, which Hess had described as 'the enemy of Europe'. His political aim was an open secret. He had laid it down as Hitler's secretary in *Mein Kampf* in 1923.

> If European soil was wanted by and large it could be had only at the expense of Russia. . . . For such a policy as this there was but one ally in Europe – England. Only with England covering our rear could we have begun a new Germanic migration.[44]

The only conclusion to be drawn is that Hess's immediate objective was to get Britain out of the war, so that Hitler's long-term aims for the establishment of a German Empire in the east could be realised. And so it was that the idea of a secret mission to the British came to germinate in the mind of Rudolf Hess.

2 A Tutorial for Hess: 8 September 1940

On 31 July 1940 Hitler told his commanders that an attempt must be made to finish preparations for the invasion of England by 15 September. There were several major complications however. The German Navy was inferior to the British Navy and had been severely mauled in the Norwegian campaign. Moreover the Luftwaffe, while numerically superior to the Royal Air Force, was quite unable to gain control over the air, and both the British Navy and R.A.F. wasted no time in harrying the German Invasion Fleet. On 17 September Hitler acknowledged that the R.A.F. had not been defeated and decided to postpone Operation Sea Lion indefinitely.[1]

During this time Rudolf Hess was attempting to discover whether the British might be susceptible to a peace feeler. For this purpose he sought the advice of Karl Haushofer, and had an eight-hour meeting with him on 31 August. The conversation took place when the Professor General went down to his Alpine Cabin, and was described by him in a letter to Albrecht on 3 September:

> I was rewarded, for it brought me a meeting with Tomo [Rudolf Hess] from 5 o'clock in the afternoon until 2 o'clock in the morning, which included a three-hour walk in the Grunwalder Forest, during which we conversed a good deal about serious matters. I have really got to tell you about a part of it now.

According to Karl Haushofer, Hitler was making preparations for launching an invasion against Britain, but was hoping for a peaceful way out and Hess was wondering whether a peace feeler could be made through a British intermediary in a neutral country.

> As you know, everything is so prepared for a very hard and

severe attack on the island in question that the highest ranking person only has to press a button to set it off. But before this decision, which is perhaps inevitable, the thought once more occurs as to whether there is really no way of stopping something which would have such infinitely momentous consequences. There is a line of reasoning in connection with this which I absolutely must pass on to you because it was obviously communicated to me with this intention. Do you, too, see no way in which such possibilities could be discussed at a third place with a middle man, possibly the old Ian Hamilton or the other Hamilton?

The last two persons mentioned were both known to Karl Haushofer. General Sir Ian Hamilton, the veteran of the Gallipoli Campaign in the 1914–18 War, had once had lunch with Hitler and Hess,[2] and Karl Haushofer had met the Duke of Hamilton (then Marquis of Clydesdale) once, before Munich.

Karl Haushofer told Hess that there was a good opportunity to send 'well disguised political persons' to Portugal for a meeting with a British contact, while the Portuguese were holding their centennial celebrations. The Professor General added in his letter to Albrecht that an old friend, Mrs Roberts, had just sent a message of greetings to the Haushofer family. Her address was c/o Post Box 506, Lisbon, and he felt that a channel to the British might be opened up through her, and 'that no good possibility should be overlooked'.[3]

Albrecht had been prepared by his father, and was in due course summoned by Hess to Bad Godesberg for a lengthy talk on 8 September. Hess had his reaons for calling Albrecht. He disliked Ribbentrop and knew that the Reich Foreign Minister had rejected the advice of Albrecht Haushofer, whom Hess had appointed to the Dienststelle Ribbentrop in order to keep Ribbentrop in check. He knew too that Ribbentrop had advised Hitler that it would be safe to tear Poland apart on the basis that the British would not fight seriously and that Hitler had acted on this information in disregard of the views expressed in Albrecht Haushofer's reports. He now turned to Albrecht in the belief that Albrecht knew a great deal more about the British than Ribbentrop. After the meeting Albrecht drew up the following memorandum.

TOP SECRET   Berlin, 15 September 1940.

ARE THERE STILL POSSIBILITIES OF A
GERMAN–ENGLISH PEACE?

On 8 September, I was summoned to Bad G. [Godesberg] to report to the Deputy of the Fuehrer on the subject discussed in this memorandum. The conversation which the two of us had alone lasted two hours. I had the opportunity to speak in all frankness.

I was immediately asked about the possibilities of making known to persons of importance in England Hitler's serious desire for peace. It was quite clear that the continuance of the war was suicidal for the white race. Even with complete peace in Europe Germany was not in a position to take over the inheritance of the Empire. The Fuehrer had not wanted to see the Empire destroyed and did not want it even today. Was there not somebody in England who was ready for peace?

First I asked for permission to discuss fundamental things. It was necessary to realise that not only Jews and Freemasons, but practically all Englishmen who mattered, regarded a treaty signed by the Fuehrer as a worthless scrap of paper. To the question as to why this was so, I referred to the ten-year term of our Polish Treaty, to the Non-Aggression Pact with Denmark signed only a year ago, to the 'final' frontier demarcation of Munich. What guarantee did England have that a new treaty would not be broken again at once if it suited us? It must be realised that, even in the Anglo-Saxon world, the Fuehrer was regarded as Satan's representative on earth and had to be fought.

If the worst came to the worst, the English would rather transfer their whole Empire bit by bit to the Americans than sign a peace that left to National Socialist Germany the mastery of Europe. The present war, I was convinced, shows that Europe has become too small for its previous anarchic form of existence; it is only through close German–English co-operation that it can achieve a true federative order (based by no means merely on the police rule of a single power), while maintaining a part of its world position and having security against Soviet Russian Eurasia. France was smashed, probably for a long time to come, and we had opportunity currently to observe what Italy is capable of accomplishing. As long, however, as German–English rivalry existed, and in so far as both sides thought in terms of security, the lesson of this war was this: every German had to tell himself: we have no security as long as provision is not made that the Atlantic gateways of Europe from Gibraltar to Narvik are free of any possible blockade. That is: there must be no English fleet. Every Englishman, must, however, under the same conditions, argue: we have no security as long as anywhere within a radius of 2,000 kilometres from London there is a plane that we do not control. That is: there must be no German Air Force.

There is only one way out of this dilemma: friendship intensified to fusion, with a joint fleet, a joint air force, and joint defence of possessions in the world – just what the English are now about to conclude with the United States.

Here I was interrupted and asked why, indeed, the English were prepared to seek such a relationship with America and not with us. My reply was: because Roosevelt is a man who represents a Weltanschauung and a way of life that the Englishman thinks he understands, to which he can become accustomed, even where it does not seem to be to his liking. Perhaps he fools himself – but, at any rate, that is what he believes.

A man like Churchill – himself half-American – is convinced of this. Hitler, however, seems to the Englishman the incarnation of what he hates that he has fought against for centuries – this feeling grips the workers no less than the plutocrats.

In fact, I am of the opinion that those Englishmen who have property to lose, that is, precisely the portions of the so-called plutocracy that count, are those who would be readiest to talk peace. But even they regard a peace only as an armistice.

I was compelled to express these things so strongly because I ought not – precisely because of my long experience in attempting to effect a settlement with England in the past and my numerous English friendships – make it appear that I seriously believed in the possibility of a settlement between Adolf Hitler and England in the present stage of development.

I was thereupon asked whether I was not of the opinion that feelers had perhaps not been successful because the right language had not been used. I replied that, to be sure – if certain persons, whom we both knew well, were meant by this statement – then certainly the wrong language had been used. But at the present stage this had little significance.

I was then asked directly why all Englishmen were so opposed to Herr von Ribbentrop. I suggested that in the eyes of the English, Herr von Ribbentrop, like some other personages, played the same role as did Duff Cooper, Eden and Churchill in the eyes of the Germans. In the case of Herr von Ribbentrop, there was also the conviction, precisely in the view of English-men who were formerly friendly to Germany that – from com-pletely biased motives – he had informed the Fuehrer wrongly about England and that he personally bore an unusually large share of the responsibility for the outbreak of the war.

But I again stressed the fact that the rejection of peace feelers by England was today due not so much to persons as to the fundamental outlook above.

Nevertheless, I was asked to name those whom I thought might be reached as possible contacts.

I mentioned among diplomats, Minister O'Malley* in Budapest, the former head of the South Eastern Department of the Foreign Office, a clever person in the higher echelons of officialdom, but perhaps without influence precisely because of his former friendliness towards Germany; Sir Samuel Hoare,† who is half-shelved and half on the watch in Madrid, whom I do not know well personally, but to whom I can at any time open a personal path; as the most promising, the Washington Ambassador Lothian,‡ with whom I have had close personal connections for years, who as a member of the highest aristo-cracy and at the same time as a person of very independent mind, is perhaps best in a position to undertake a bold step – provided that he could be convinced that even a bad and un-certain peace would be better than the continuance of the war – a conviction at which he will only arrive if he convinces himself in Washington that English hopes of America are not realisable. Whether or not this is so could only be judged in Washington itself; from Germany not at all.

As the final possibility I then mentioned that of a personal meeting on neutral soil with the closest of my English friends: the young Duke of Hamilton who has access at all times to all

* British Minister to Hungary.   † British Ambassador to Spain.
‡ British Ambassador to the U.S.A.

important persons in London, even to Churchill and the King. I stressed in this case the inevitable difficulty of making a contact and again repeated my conviction of the improbability of its succeeding – whatever approach we took.

The upshot of the conversation was H's [Hess's] statement that he would consider the whole matter thoroughly once more and send me word in case I was to take steps. For this extremely ticklish case, and in the event that I might possibly have to make a trip alone – I asked for very precise directions from the highest authority.

From the whole conversation I had the strong impression that it was not conducted without the prior knowledge of the Fuehrer, and that I probably would not hear any more about the matter unless a new understanding had been reached between him and his deputy.

On the personal side of the conversation I must say that – despite the fact that I felt bound to say unusually hard things – it ended in great friendliness, even cordiality. . . .[4]

As has been seen Albrecht was working for the German Resistance to Hitler as well as for the German Foreign Office and Hess. He was walking a tightrope, and it appeared to him that Hess was the only Nazi leader who would and could be of assistance to him, and further that he was the only Nazi leader at that stage whom he could use. As a patriotic German Albrecht believed that any peace with Britain was better than no peace. He was trying to open up a channel to Britain on Hess's behalf with, as he believed, Hitler's knowledge, and he had put forward Hamilton's name as a desperate man clutches at a straw. Albrecht knew that the British were in no mood for Nazi peace feelers, but by a strange irony had given Hess the name of the person whom Hess would approach. He had told Hess that his friend the Duke of Hamilton* had access at all times to all important persons in London and once the idea had been put into the mind of Rudolf Hess nothing in the world would get it out.

* Hamilton as it happened had been called up before the outbreak of war, and at the beginning of the Battle of Britain had been posted to command an Air Sector in the East of Scotland, since when he had been serving full-time with the R.A.F.

3 The Peace Feeler: 23 September 1940

THERE has been some doubt amongst historians as to whether Hitler knew that Hess was trying to make contact with the British through asking Albrecht Haushofer to send a written communication of some kind. However it appears from several sources that Hitler did know that Hess was going to try and make some such form of contact. Hewel, Ribbentrop's liaison man with Hitler, told Fritz Hesse that Hitler was using Albrecht Haushofer for making contact with the British, and that Haushofer had connections with Britain through the Swiss Professor, Carl Burckhardt.[1] Frau Hess was more definite: she wrote that her husband tried to get in touch with prominent circles in Britain through Albrecht Haushofer via Spain or Switzerland, with Hitler's knowledge.[2] As for Albrecht Haushofer himself, he had written in his memorandum on the possibilities of a German–English peace that Hess had given him the impression that their conversation as to how to make contact with the British by letter had been conducted with Hitler's prior knowledge. He also wrote that the chances were that he would not be required to take any action unless agreement on the subject was reached between Hitler and Hess.[3]

According to Otto Dietrich, Hess did have a conversation with Hitler. He asked Hitler whether his policy towards Britain remained unchanged and Hitler told Hess that he still desired an Anglo–German understanding.[4] The most that can be assumed from these sources is that Hitler gave a measure of approval to Hess to make enquiries through Albrecht Haushofer. It may well be that Hitler did not wish anyone else to know that such enquiries were being made with his approval. Be that as it may, Hess in due course took action. He got in touch with the Haushofers. On 10 September 1940 he wrote to Karl Haushofer referring to the letter of 3 September,* which the General Professor had sent to

* See above, page 132.

Albrecht. Obviously Hess had been toying with the mechanics of opening peace feelers.

> The prerequisite naturally is that the inquiry in question and the reply would not go through official channels, for you would not in any case want to cause your friends over there any trouble.
>
> It would be best to have the letter to the old lady, with whom you are acquainted, delivered through a confidential agent of the A.O. [Ausland Organisation] to the address that is known to you. For this purpose Albrecht would have to speak either with Bohle or my brother.* At the same time the lady would have to be given the address of this agent in L. [Lisbon] or if the latter does not live there permanently, of another agent of the A.O. who does live there permanently, to which the reply can in turn be delivered.
>
> As for the neutral I have in mind, I would like to speak to you orally about it some time. There is no hurry about that since, in any case, there would first have to be a reply received here from over there.
>
> Meanwhile let's both keep our fingers crossed. Should success be the fate of the enterprise, the oracle given to you with regard to the month of August would yet be fulfilled, since the name of the young friend and the old lady friend of your family occurred to you during our quiet walk on the last day of that month.
>
> With best regards to you and to Martha,
> Yours, as ever
R[Rudolf] H[Hess][5]

From the tone of his letter Hess was evidently quite determined to make a peace overture and Albrecht after seeing it wrote to his parents from Berlin on 18 September 1940, pointing out that it was not as easy as Hess imagined to make contact with a person such as Hamilton in a country with which Germany was at war. Also he did not wish to endanger their friend Mrs Roberts who would have to see that a message was conveyed from Portugal.

In the midst of a rather intensive activity only these lines for

---

* Hess's brother Alfred had been earmarked to be future Gauleiter of Egypt, and he would have been if the Germans had won the battle of El Alamein.

today as acknowledgement of the letter in question, I shall consider the whole case again for another twenty-four hours and
will then write to T. [Hess] directly. It really can not be done in
the way he imagines. Still, I could formulate a letter to D.H.
[Douglas Hamilton] in such a way that the conveyance in no way
endangers our old lady friend. Above all, I have to make it clear
to T. once again that without the permission of his authorities
of the highest responsibility my ducal friend can just as little
write to me as I can do it the other way round. . . .[6]

On the next day, 19 September, Albrecht wrote to Hess mentioning that he had seen the latter's letter to his father.

TOP SECRET

My dear Herr Hess,
    Your letter of the tenth reached me yesterday after a delay
caused by the antiquated postal service of Partnach-Alm. I
again gave a thorough study to the possibilities discussed therein
and request – before taking the steps proposed – that you yourself examine once more the thoughts set forth below.
    I have in the meantime been thinking of the technical route
by which a message from me must travel before it can reach the
Duke of H [Hamilton]. With your help, delivery to Lisbon can
of course be assured without difficulty. About the rest of the
route we do not know. Foreign control must be taken into
account; the letter must therefore in no case be composed in
such a way that it will simply be seized and destroyed or that it
will directly endanger the woman transmitting it or the ultimate
recipient.
    In view of my close personal relations and intimate acquain-
tance with D.H. I can write a few lines to him (which should be
enclosed with the letter to Mrs R. without any indication of
place and without a full name – an A would suffice for signature)
in such a way that he alone will recognise that behind my wish
to see him in Lisbon there is something more serious than a
personal whim. All the rest, however, seems to be extremely
hazardous and detrimental to the success of the letter.
    Let us suppose that the case were reversed: an old lady in
Germany receives a letter from an unknown source abroad, with
a request to forward a message whose recipient is asked to dis-
close to an unknown foreigner where he will be staying for a

certain period – and this recipient were a high officer in the air force (of course I do not know exactly what position H. holds at the moment; judging from his past I can conceive of only three things: he is an active Air Force General, or he directs the air defence of an important part of Scotland, or he has a responsible position in the Air Ministry).

I do not think that you need much imagination to picture to yourself the faces that Canaris or Heydrich would make and the smirk with which they would consider any offer of 'security' or 'confidence' in such a letter if a subordinate should submit such a case to them. They would not merely make faces, you may be certain! The measures would come quite automatically – and neither the old lady nor the Air Force officer would have an easy time of it! In England it is no different.

Now another thing. Here too I would ask you to picture the situation in reverse. Let us assume that I received such a letter from one of my English friends. I would quite naturally report the matter to the highest German authorities I could contact, as soon as I had realised the import it might have, and would ask for instructions on what I should do myself (at that, I am a civilian and H. is an officer).

If it should be decided that I was to comply with the wish for a meeting with my friend, I would then be most anxious to get my instructions if not from the Fuehrer himself, at least from a person who receives them directly and at the same time has the gift of transmitting the finest and lightest nuances – an art which has been mastered by you yourself but not by all Reich Ministers. In addition I should very urgently request that my action be fully covered *vis-à-vis* other high authorities of my own country, uninformed or unfavourable.

It is no different with H. He cannot fly to Lisbon – any more than I can! – unless he is given leave, that is unless at least Air Minister Sinclair and Foreign Minister Halifax know about it. If, however, he receives permission to reply or to go, there is no need of indicating any place in England; if he does not receive it, then any attempt through a neutral mediator would also have little success.

In this case the technical problem of contacting H. is the least of the difficulties. A neutral who knows England and can move about in England – presumably there would be little sense in entrusting anyone else with such a mission – will be able to find the first peer of Scotland very quickly as long as conditions in the Isle are still halfway in order. (At the time of a successful invasion all the possibilities we are discussing here would be pointless anyway.)

My proposal is therefore as follows:

Through the old friend I will write a letter to H. – in a form that will incriminate no one but will be understandable to the recipient – with the proposal for a meeting in Lisbon. If nothing comes of that, it will be possible (if the military situation leaves enough time for it), assuming that a suitable intermediary is available, to make a second attempt through a neutral going to England, who might be given a personal message to take along. With respect to this possibility, I must add, however, that H. is extremely reserved – as many Englishmen are toward anyone they do not know personally. Since the entire Anglo–German problem after all springs from a most profound crisis in mutual confidence, this would not be immaterial.

Please excuse the length of this letter; I merely wished to explain the situation to you fully.

I already tried to explain to you not long ago that, for the reasons I gave, the possibilities of successful efforts at a settlement between the Fuehrer and the British upper class seem to me – to my extreme regret – infinitesimally small.

Nevertheless I should not want to close this letter without pointing out once more that I still think there would be a somewhat greater chance of success in going through Ambassador Lothian in Washington or Sir Samuel Hoare in Madrid rather than through my friend H. To be sure, they are – practically speaking – more inaccessible.

Would you send me a line or give me a telephone call with final instructions? If necessary, will you also inform your brother in advance? Presumably I will then have to discuss with him the forwarding of the letter to Lisbon and the arrangement for a cover address for the reply in Lisbon.

With cordial greetings and best wishes for your health.

Yours etc.

A.H.[7]

On the same day Albrecht drafted a letter to Hamilton and

wrote to his parents. With his letter to his parents he enclosed
Hess's letter to his father, his own reply to Hess, the draft of his
letter to Hamilton, and the memorandum on the possibilities of a
German–English peace:

> Enclosed I am sending you some responsible documents:
> Firstly the letter of T. to father.
> Secondly my reply to T., which has already been despatched
> and which I hope has your belated approval.
> Thirdly the draft of a letter to D. [Hamilton], which I keep
> for myself and shall also not show to anybody, with the request
> for you to examine whether it contains any danger for the
> potential lady conveyer. I think actually that it sounds harmless
> enough. I have purposely fitted in the reference to the "author-
> ities" over there as a safeguard for the lady conveyer and for the
> recipient. Therefore, your honest opinion, please, and correc-
> tions, if necessary.
> Fourthly a record in writing of what I said in G. [Godesberg]
> on the eighth – as vindication before history (to be kept in your
> custody).
> The whole thing is a fool's errand – but we cannot help it.
> According to our latest news the Union agreements between the
> Empire and the United States are about to be signed. . . .[8]

On 23 September 1940 Albrecht wrote to Hess that the letter
to Hamilton had been despatched via Alfred Hess.

> My dear Herr Hess:
> In accordance with your last telephone call I got in touch with
> your brother immediately. Everything went off well, and I can
> now report that the mission has been accomplished to the extent
> that the letter you desired was written and despatched this
> morning. It is to be hoped that it will be more efficacious than
> sober judgement would indicate.[9]

He also wrote to his father on the same day enclosing a copy of
the letter to Hamilton which by this time had probably been
revised, and he admitted that the responsibility for sending it lay
with Hess.

> Enclosed a copy of a short significant letter, which is perhaps
> better kept in your custody than in mine. I have now stated

clearly enough that this is an action the initiative of which has not rested with me.

Now to English matters. I am convinced, as before, that there is not the slightest prospect of peace; and so I don't have the least faith in the possibility about which you know. However, I also believe that I could not have refused my services any longer. You know that for myself I do not see any possibility of any satisfying activity in the future.

If the 'total victory' from Glasgow to Capetown were to be achieved for our savages, then the drunk sergeants and the corrupt exploiters will call the tune anyhow; experts with quiet manners will not be needed then. If it is not achieved, if the English succeed in delivering the first blow with American help and in creating a long protracted war equilibrium with the aid of the Bolshevist insecurity factor, then, however, there will sooner or later be a demand for the likes of us – but in conditions in which little enough will be left to salvage any more. . . .

He wrote that his only hope of being able to influence affairs in Germany was that there would be a far reaching change. The head of the Foreign Office, Ernst von Weizsaecker, was in a similar position to himself. If there was no such change, then such men as Himmler's minion, Lorenz, would have the supremacy, and Albrecht would be in for a thin time.

I can only have a political future if in the end I am proved right with my Cassandra voice. . . . I recently talked with old Weizsaecker about the same topic. We occupy similar positions. He too tells himself that he would come into his own, only if external circumstances arose, which would deprive him of all pleasure in this activity: i.e. if he is proved right with his similar Cassandra reputation. Otherwise he could just as well go as myself: in that case the Lorenz types would have the greater historical justification on their side. . . .[10]

Albrecht had admitted in this letter that there was no chance of peace with Britain. He must have read Churchill's broadcast of 11 September 1940, in which Churchill had summarised the opinion of the British on Hitler:

This wicked man, the repository and embodiment of many forms of soul-destroying hatred, this monstrous product of

former wrongs and shame, has now resolved to try to break our
famous island race by a process of indiscriminate slaughter and
destruction. What he has done is to kindle a fire in British hearts,
here and all over the world, which will glow long after all traces
of the conflagration he has caused in London have been removed.
He has lighted a fire which will burn with a steady and con-
suming flame until the last vestiges of Nazi tyranny have been
burnt out of Europe. . . .[11]

Albrecht was looking for compromises, where there were none
to be made, and on 2 October 1940 he wrote to his parents:

> I now wait – without much confidence – for a chance of still
> being able to influence in some way or other the suicidal course
> of the struggle of the white master races with the modest powers
> of reason.
> But we have, at least on our part, done what was possible.[12]

A little later he wrote to his mother on 25 November:

> You know I do not easily forget and I am heavily weighed
> down by my share in the great collective guilt. . . .[13]

He seems to have felt that the sending out of a peace feeler to
Britain on Hess's behalf was never more than a completely forlorn
hope.

4 The British Secret Service

LATE in September 1940 the British Censor intercepted a letter. It was dated 23 September 1940 and had been sent from a person who signed himself 'A' via a Mrs V. Roberts in Lisbon, Portugal. The sender obviously intended that it should be forwarded to the Duke of Hamilton, and it is not clear how or when the letter was intercepted. It was a strange letter, and Hamilton did not learn about its existence until five months after it had been sent. During the interval the British Secret Service were probably making enquiries as to who 'A' was, and after a great deal of time, and possibly effort, they must have discovered that it was one Albrecht Haushofer who had close connections with the German Foreign Office. At some stage they advised the R.A.F. Intelligence that this matter should be followed up.

Accordingly Hamilton received a letter dated 26 February 1941 from Group Captain F. G. Stammers O.B.E. The latter asked whether Hamilton might be in London in the near future, as he was anxious to have a chat with him on a certain matter, in his office in the Air Ministry at Houghton House, the late London School of Economics.[1] Halfway through March 1941 Hamilton visited Stammers and was asked what he had done with the letter which Albrecht Haushofer had written to him. Hamilton thought that he was referring to the letter sent by Albrecht Haushofer in July 1939, which had been deposited in the vaults of a bank. It soon became clear that they were talking about different letters whereupon Stammers pushed across the desk a photographed copy of the intercepted handwritten letter which Hamilton had not seen before. It ran:

B. Sept. 23rd.

My dear Douglo,
    Even if there is only a slight chance that this letter should

reach you in good time, there is a chance, and I am determined to make use of it.

First of all, to give you a personal greeting. I am sure you know that my attachment to you remains unaltered and unalterable, whatever the circumstances may be. I have heard of your father's death. I do hope he did not suffer too much – after so long a life of permanent pain. I heard that your brother-in-law Northumberland lost his life near Dunkirk – even modern times must allow us to share grief across all boundaries.

But it is not only the story of death that should find its place in this letter. If you remember some of my last communications in July 1939, you – and your friends in high places – may find some significance in the fact that I am able to ask you whether you could find time to have a talk with me somewhere on the outskirts of Europe, perhaps in Portugal. I could reach Lisbon any time (and without any kind of difficulties) within a few days after receiving news from you. Of course I do not know whether you can make your authorities understand so much, that they give you leave.

But at least you may be able to answer my question. Letters will reach me (fairly quickly; they would take some four or five days from Lisbon on the utmost) in the following way: double closed envelope: inside address: 'Dr A. H.' Nothing more! Outside address:

> 'Minero Silricola Ltd.,
> Rua do Cais de Santarem 32/1
> Lisbon, Portugal'.

My father and mother add their wishes for your personal welfare to my own. . . .

Yours ever,
'A'.[2]

Hamilton was surprised to read this letter, as it had never occurred to him that Albrecht Haushofer would attempt to make contact with him during the war. Stammers explained that the Intelligence authorities were of the opinion that Haushofer was a significant person, who had close connections with the German Foreign Office. They also thought that it might be of considerable value to make contact with him. Hamilton told Stammers that, as far as he knew, Haushofer had been sent over to Britain by the

German Foreign Office in order to control Ribbentrop, that he had found this a hopeless task and that in any case he was not a man of war.

After this meeting with Stammers, very little happened for more than a month and then Hamilton received an order from the Headquarters of No. 13 Group that he was to report to Group Captain D. L. Blackford at the Air Ministry, on 25 April at 11.30 a.m. Hamilton duly appeared, and had a conference with Group Captain Blackford and Major Robertson. They were eager that Hamilton should volunteer to go to Portugal in order to acquire all information possible from Albrecht Haushofer. Hamilton said reluctantly that he would of course go if he was ordered, and he was told that for this type of job people volunteered and were not ordered. He would be given time to consider the proposition and the technical arrangements of getting him there and back could easily be laid on.

On 26 April Hamilton saw Lord Eustace Percy, the Rector of the University of Newcastle, as he wished to ask the advice of some-one for whose integrity and discretion he had the utmost respect. Percy had worked for the Foreign Office, had later served as a Cabinet Minister under Baldwin and had resigned in 1936 when Hitler remilitarised the Rhineland. He had been appalled that the British Government considered that the British Armed Forces were militarily too weak to repel the German invading forces.[3] He now advised Hamilton to proceed with caution on certain condi-tions. Two days later, on 28 April, Hamilton wrote to Blackford:

> I am prepared to go, if you wish it, but I think I must make two conditions: I should not, of course, like to hold any com-munication with X without the knowledge of and consultation with H.M. Ambassador at my destination. I presume that there will be no difficulty about this, and, to avoid any possible mis-understanding or delay at my destination, I would suggest that I should be authorised to explain the position to Sir Alexander Cadogan, at the Foreign Office, before I leave.
>
> I must be able to explain to X why I am answering his letter after a delay of seven months. It would be dangerous to allow him to believe that the authorities had withheld his letter from me last autumn and had now released it and had asked me to answer it. That would give the impression that the authorities

here had 'got the wind up' now, and want to talk peace. May I
therefore have an explanation of the circumstances in which the
letter was withheld from me last autumn?[4]

For a number of reasons this letter was not appreciated. First it
looked as though Albrecht Haushofer was making some sort of
peace overture, and the Intelligence authorities were only interested
in extracting technical information as to the plans and intentions
of the enemy. Indeed, when a section of the German Resistance
to Hitler was making a peace feeler to Britain via Josef Mueller
through the Vatican, Churchill had sent a minute to Eden, in-
sisting that it must be made clear to the Papal Nuncio that the
British did not wish to make any enquiries as to terms of peace
with Hitler, and that British agents had been 'strictly forbidden
to entertain any such suggestions'.[5]

Secondly, Hamilton had demanded that he should see the Head
of the British Foreign Office and the British Ambassador in
Lisbon, which meant that if anything went wrong it would be
harder for the British to disown him, as is usually the case with
unsuccessful agents.

Thirdly, the British Intelligence Authorities had already burnt
their fingers badly over the Venlo Incident when two British
agents, Captain Payne Best and Major R. H. Stevens, were kid-
napped over the Dutch Border on 9 November 1939. They had
expected to meet members of the German Resistance to Hitler,
and were shaken to discover that these 'representatives' turned out
to be agents of Himmler, and included Schellenberg. This had
proved embarrassing to the British, as Goebbels' propaganda
machine used their capture to maximum effect. In the present case
it was not clear who Albrecht Haushofer represented, and in the
light of the Venlo Incident it was certainly possible that he might
be a double agent.[6]

Lastly, Hamilton's letter had raised the point that the British
Secret Service had apparently been inefficient in withholding a
letter for five months, and Secret Service organisations do not like
questions being asked about their inadequacies, nor about their
methods. Blackford replied:

SECRET   3rd May 1941
Dear Hamilton,
    Thanks for your letter dated the 28th April. I am sorry not to

have been here when you came to London, but I had a casualty in the family and was compelled to go away for a bit.

2. I have discussed your letter with Air Commodore Boyle and he agrees with you that this may not be the right time to open up a discussion, the nature of which might well be misinterpreted.

3. You will realise, of course, that the Air Ministry are in no way concerned with the policy question involved and are only concerned with the problem whether or not it is practicable to open a channel with your assistance. I have, however, put your views to the Department concerned and I know they will receive careful consideration.

4. In my own view the delay which has occurred makes it extremely difficult to find a watertight excuse for action at the present time, and although quite a good one has been suggested on the lines of an enquiry from you as to why your previous letters have not been answered, it might not carry conviction and so have undesirable political consequences.

5. Incidentally, the delay was in no way due to any fault of Air Intelligence, another department having mislaid the papers.

6. It is Air Commodore Boyle's view that in the present circumstances a move of the kind suggested could not be made without Cabinet authority, and with this I agree. In the circumstances, will you, therefore, regard the matter as in abeyance. I will let you know at once should it come forward again.

7. Air Commodore Boyle has asked me to thank you for the trouble you have taken in this connection.

8. Should you be passing through town any time I hope you will find it possible to come in and see me and have lunch with me if you can spare the time.

9. I am sending copies of this letter to Air Commodore Boyle and Captain Robertson.

Yours sincerely,
D. L. Blackford.[7]

Hamilton replied to Blackford on 10 May.

I fully appreciate the position and will regard the matter as in abeyance until I hear from you that it has come forward again. I also realise that the Air Ministry is in no way concerned with the policy question involved, and that it was not the fault of the

Air Intelligence but another department for the papers having
been mislaid.

As regards the opening up of the channel, I am of the opinion
that a very good opportunity may have been missed owing to the
delay. I must admit I do not like the suggestion already made,
which you mention, on the lines of an enquiry from me as to
why my previous letters have not been answered. Quite apart
from the undesirable political consequences which might be
caused by failing to carry conviction, on the other hand X might
think that either the British authorities or the German authorities
had withheld a letter to him, either of which might also have an
undesirable effect.

If the proposition materialises and I am asked to go, I think
that probably the best way of overcoming the difficulty would
be if I adopted the following procedure. I would write to X –
'I did not reply to your letter last autumn because I saw no
opportunity of leaving this country at that time. It appears now
that I may have a chance of arranging a meeting with you
abroad some time during the next month or two. If you would
still like to see me, will you let me know.' I would then wait for
a reply before starting, so that I would only have to leave my
service duties for the minimum time and avoid the appearance
of waiting anxiously on his doorstep.

Many thanks for your kind invitation to come and see you
and have lunch. I should very much like to accept, if I am able
to come to London in the near future.[8]

Hamilton never received a reply to this letter for later on the
same day, 10 May 1941, R.A.F. Fighter Command Radar Stations
picked up a single enemy aircraft flying across the North Sea
towards Lindisfarne, and at 22.00 hours the Royal Observer Corps
identified it as a Messerschmitt 110. Shortly afterwards it had
crossed the Northumbrian coast. While the British Secret Service
and R.A.F. Intelligence were proceeding with slow and heavy
tread something had happened which rendered their actions
irrelevant.

5 The Leap into the Dark: 10 May 1941

BACK in Germany Hess's influence with Hitler had declined to an all time low. The American Under Secretary of State, Sumner Welles, wrote after an interview with Hess on 3 March 1940:

> Notwithstanding the impression so often given me previously that Hess possessed a powerful and determining influence in German affairs, the effect he made upon me at the time was that of a man who had only the lowest order of intelligence. . . .
> It was so obvious that Hess was merely repeating what he had been told to say to me . . . and that he had neither explored the issues at stake nor thought anything out for himself, that I made no attempt to enter into any discussion with him.[1]

Nobody was more aware of the situation than Hess himself. There was no question of his being disloyal in any circumstances; and, as Albrecht Haushofer explained to Rainer Hildebrandt:

> Hess leads a conventional bourgeois life but as soon as Hitler in some form enters his subconscious he automatically becomes liable to mental excesses. . . .
> During the first years I tried to warn Hess of the dangers which he could avoid and proved to him in black and white Hitler's mistakes. . . . Hess saw all this and was determined to intervene where necessary. At the end of our talk he said, 'I will ask the Fuehrer; I am sure he will understand and will turn everything to the best'. . . .
> It is Hess's dream to be able by some great mediating act to save the Reich for Germany, for his friends and first of all for Hitler, his idol. Hess is a Parsifal, and all injustice committed by Hess is in fact due to his bondage and under a kind of hypnosis.[2]

It was to be expected that Hess would feel that he could not play his part in saving the Third Reich by remaining tied to office work. In September 1939 he asked Hitler for permission to fly with the Luftwaffe at the Front. Hitler refused and demanded an assurance from Hess that he would not fly again, whereupon Hess promised not to fly for one year. By September 1940 Hess felt free from his promise.[3] During the same month he tried to put out his peace feeler to Britain through Albrecht Haushofer.[4] However, as this letter never received a reply, Hess thought that he would make another attempt, this time without the knowledge of his wife and the Haushofers, and above all without the knowledge of Hitler. He would embark on a personal unauthorised mission of a secret and dramatic kind.

He must have known about the suggestion which Goering had made to Hitler just after Britain's declaration of war against Germany. Goering then said, 'We must fly to Britain and I'll try to explain the position. . . .' When Hitler was informed he had said to Goering, 'It will be of no use, but if you can, try it.' For a long time the rumour had persisted that Goering might fly over to Britain, but Goering was not sufficiently enthusiastic about the possibility of success.[5]

Hess, however, took a different approach. He had always regarded Goering as a rival. Goering always managed to outshine him and was Hitler's first Deputy Fuehrer while Hess was only the second. After the fall of France, when Hitler made his peace offer to the British Empire, he had made Goering a Marshal of the Reich and merely complimented Hess as a loyal follower. Hess may well have felt that here was an opportunity to outshine Goering, by following the suggestion which Goering had not followed up himself.

It occurred to Hess that the making of a peace overture by original means would be welcomed by the British as a sporting gesture. He was influenced by the example of the American Colonel Charles Lindbergh who had been the first man to fly solo across the Atlantic from west to east. Hess had wanted to be the first man to fly the Atlantic solo from the east to the west, but in the end his plans fell through.[6] It was left to Hess to win, in 1934, the annual air-race round the Zugspitze, the highest peak in Germany, a feat of which he was very proud; and after it Lindbergh warmly congratulated him.[7] Hess had never met the Duke of Hamilton as he had met Lindbergh but he had read the *Pilots' Book of Everest* by Hamilton and Group Captain D. F. McIntyre and it had appealed to him.[8] If Hamilton had been the first pilot

to fly over Mount Everest and Lindbergh was the first aviator to fly
solo across the Atlantic, he, Hess, would be the first pilot to fly
from Germany to Britain with an offer of peace in the midst of a
great world war.

The Swedish author and explorer Sven Hedin had incorporated
a suggestion in his book *Ohne Auftrag in Berlin* that if Hitler had
flown over to Britain during the war, had offered to shake hands
and come to a 'reasonable' agreement, the British would have been
suitably impressed.[9] The British author Peter Fleming had written
very differently on the same theme in a comic vein in *The Flying
Visit* adding that if Hitler had parachuted into Britain nobody
would have been able to believe it.[10] Hess, however, was not to know
about Peter Fleming's book, and he made his preparations. He
went to Professor Messerschmitt at Augsburg airport, and with
his permission made frequent practice flights in a Messerschmitt
110. On Hess's orders extra fuel tanks were fitted to the aircraft as
well as radio equipment and Hess's secretary, Hildegard Fath,
obtained secret weather reports about conditions over Britain and
the North Sea.[11]

The mission was kept a closely guarded secret but one person
learnt about it, almost by mistake. In January 1941 Hess and his
Adjutant, Karl Heinz Pintsch, went to Augsburg airport, and
Hess told him that if he had not returned from his flight within
four hours Pintsch was to open the letter addressed to him and to
deliver the other letter personally to Hitler. Some four hours later
Pintsch opened the letter and read to his horror that his superior
had flown to Britain. He was not much relieved when Hess's
aircraft suddenly reappeared. On this occasion Hess had had to
turn back on account of bad weather.

Pintsch has given an account of the consequent conversation
between him and Hess, which should be treated with caution as it
was told many years later, but its broad outline is clear. Hess took
Pintsch into his confidence, because he was afraid that his plans
would be given away. He explained that Hitler had no designs on
the British Empire, which was the reason for not invading Britain
after Dunkirk. The enemy of the Third Reich was Russia and
Hitler wanted to expand in the east. Therefore it was essential to
get Britain out of the war, or else Germany might soon be fighting
the dreaded war on two fronts against most of the world, including
the U.S.A. as well as Russia and Britain. The Anglo–German

situation, so Hess thought, needed a personal approach. Naturally
there was an element of risk, but nothing in comparison with what
he might achieve if success were to smile upon him. He would save
millions of lives and the future of the Third Reich. He would fly
to the Duke of Hamilton's home, show him Albrecht Haushofer's
visiting card, and ask to see the King.[12]

Pintsch decided to keep this information to himself, and it may
be that others in Germany guessed that Hess had something in
mind. Shortly before he made his final flight Hess told Count
Schwerin von Krosigk, Hitler's Finance Minister, that the
Russians alone were benefiting whilst the British and Germans
were at each other's throats. He could not understand why the
British had not responded to Hitler's offer of peace, and could not
see why they had not understood that Bolshevism was the menace
threatening Europe and that Hitler had no demands to make of
Britain. He felt certain that if the matter were properly expounded
to the British, it would be possible to conclude an agreement.[13]

Winston Churchill gave an accurate analysis of Hess's motives in
his *History of the Second World War.*

> He knew and was capable of understanding Hitler's inner
> mind, his hatred of Soviet Russia, his lust to destroy Bolshevism,
> his admiration for Britain and earnest wish to be friends with
> the British Empire, his contempt for most other countries. No
> one knew Hitler better or saw him more often in his unguarded
> moments. With the coming of actual war there was a change.
> Hitler's meal-time company grew perforce. Generals, admirals,
> diplomats, high functionaries, were admitted from time to time
> to this select circle of arbitrary power. The Deputy Fuehrer
> found himself in eclipse. What were party demonstrations now?
> This was a time for deeds, not for antics. . . .
>
> Here, he felt, are all these generals and others who must be
> admitted to the Fuehrer's intimacy, and crowd his table. They
> have their parts to play. But I, Rudolf, by a deed of superb
> devotion will surpass them all and bring to my Fuehrer a greater
> treasure and easement than all of them put together. I will go
> and make peace with Britain. My life is nothing. How glad I am
> to have a life to cast away for such a hope! . . .
>
> Hess's idea of the European scene was that England had been
> wrested from her true interests and policy of friendship with

Germany, and above all from alliance against Bolshevism, by the warmongers, of whom Churchill was the superficial manifestation. If only he, Rudolf, could get at the heart of Britain and make its King believe how Hitler felt towards it, the malign forces that now ruled in this ill-starred island and had brought so many needless miseries upon it would be swept away. . . .

But to whom should he turn? There was the Duke of Hamilton, who was known to the son of his political adviser, Haushofer. He knew also that the Duke of Hamilton was Lord Steward. A personage like that would probably be dining every night with the King and have his private ear. Here was a channel of direct access.[14]

Just as some in Britain hoped that the German people might be separated from Hitler, so it was, Hess thought, that the British people, if encouraged, might be separated from Churchill. Hess knew that he was taking a considerable risk, but he well appreciated that nothing could have been more in Hitler's interests than to get Britain out of the war before the attack on Russia was launched. If he was successful he would be acclaimed as a popular hero in Germany.

On the whole he hoped to be back from his secret mission before too long. On 9 May 1941, one day before he made his flight, he wrote to Reichleiter Darré.

> I am contemplating an extensive journey and I do not know when I shall be back. I therefore cannot as yet tie myself down to a fixed date. I shall get in touch with you again after my return. . . .[11]

On the next day, Saturday 10 May 1941, he put on the uniform of an Oberleutnant in the Luftwaffe, went to Augsburg, obtained the Me 110 with the extra fuel tanks attached to it, left a letter for Hitler with his adjutant, and took off into the evening air, on a long and remarkable flight. By a strange paradox the most loyal and unimaginative of Nazi leaders was attempting a daring deed.

He flew north over Germany, straight for the North Sea towards the Farne Islands on a course for Dungavel House, the residence of the Duke of Hamilton in Lanarkshire. As he flew west over the British coast two Hurricanes came up to intercept him, but Hess nosed his aircraft downwards through the clouds and in the failing light gave them the slip. He flew on and eventually over Lanarkshire identified what he took to be Dungavel house. In order to check his bearings, he flew onwards over the Ayrshire coast, circled round and flew back. An R.A.F. Defiant was sent up from Prestwick Airport, but being in one of the fastest aircraft in the world Hess left it far behind.[16]

He flew back along the route which he had just taken, and made preparations for parachuting. He found great difficulty in getting out of the Messerschmitt, and in fact only managed to extricate himself from the aeroplane after a half-roll when it was flying upside down. He hurt his ankle on landing near the farm of Eaglesham, and was found getting out of his parachute by David McLean. He was taken into McLean's house and was treated with firmness and kindness as is the custom in the west of Scotland. He was dealt with as a prisoner of war, was collected by the Home Guard, and handed over to the army who took him to Maryhill Barracks, Glasgow, where at times he was in the custody of Corporal William Ross, a future Secretary of State for Scotland.

Meanwhile Hess had repeatedly given his name as Oberleutnant Alfred Horn, and had asked to see the Duke of Hamilton. This information was passed on, and the R.A.F. Sector Controller at Turnhouse airport telephoned Hamilton in the early hours of the morning, asking him to come to the Operations Room. Hamilton was there confronted with the surprising information that the pilot of the Me 110 which had flown across Scotland and had recently crashed in flames, had asked personally for him and had given his name as Oberleutnant Alfred Horn.

Hamilton made arrangements with the Intelligence Office – whose duty it was to interrogate captured German pilots – to leave for Glasgow early on the next day. He returned to his house by the airfield and, remembering that he had noted the names of various Luftwaffe officers whom he had met during the Olympic Games in 1936, looked through this list. However, Horn's name did not appear, so Hamilton returned to bed, somewhat puzzled but in readiness for what the next day might hold in store.

6 Hess, Hamilton and Churchill: 11 May 1941

ON Sunday 11 May 1941 Hamilton, together with the R.A.F. Interrogating Officer, arrived at Maryhill Barracks at 10 a.m. Hamilton first examined the personal effects of the prisoner, which included a Leica camera, a map, a large number of medicines, photographs of the prisoner and a small boy, and the visiting cards of General Professor Karl Haushofer and his son, Dr Albrecht Haushofer. These cards at once made Hamilton think that Oberleutnant Alfred Horn had a knowledge of the letter from Albrecht Haushofer which had so greatly interested the Intelligence authorities.

Accompanied by the Interrogating Officer and the Military Officer on guard, Hamilton entered the prisoner's room. Hess was in bed still suffering from the leg injury caused by his parachute landing the night before. Hamilton had no recollection of having seen him before, and the prisoner immediately asked that Hamilton should speak to him alone. The other officers were requested by Hamilton to withdraw, which they did. The most accurate account of what followed is given in Hamilton's report to the Prime Minister:

> The German opened by saying that he had seen me in Berlin at the Olympic Games in 1936, and that I had lunched in his house.* He said, 'I do not know if you recognise me, but I am Rudolf Hess.' He went on to say that he was on a mission of humanity and that the Fuehrer did not want to defeat England and wished to stop fighting. His friend Albrecht Haushofer told him that I was an Englishman who he thought would under-

* This was probably a reference to the dinner given by Hitler in honour of Lord Vansittart in Berlin during the Olympic Games, where Hess may have seen Hamilton across the room, but this dinner was not given in Hess's house. Hess was probably confusing the dinner in honour of Lord Vansittart with the lunch he gave in his own house to the International Olympic Committee.

stand his (Hess's) point of view. He had consequently tried to arrange a meeting with me in Lisbon. (See Haushofer's letter to me dated September 23rd, 1940.) Hess went on to say that he had tried to fly to Dungavel and this was the fourth time he had set out, the first time being in December. On the three previous occasions he had turned back owing to bad weather. He had not attempted to make this journey during the time when Britain was gaining victories in Libya, as he thought his mission then might be interpreted as weakness, but now that Germany had gained successes in North Africa and Greece, he was glad to come.

The fact that Reich Minister Hess had come to this country in person would, he stated, show his sincerity and Germany's willingness for peace. He then went on to say that the Fuehrer was convinced that Germany would win the war, possibly soon but certainly in one, two or three years. He wanted to stop the unnecessary slaughter that would otherwise inevitably take place. He asked me if I could get together leading members of my party to talk over things with a view to making peace proposals. I replied that there was now only one party in this country. He then said he could tell me what Hitler's peace terms would be. First he would insist on an arrangement whereby our two countries would never go to war again. I questioned him as to how that arrangement could be brought about, and he replied that one of the conditions, of course, was that Britain would give up her traditional policy of always opposing the strongest power in Europe. I then told him that if we made peace now, we would be at war again certainly within two years. He asked why, to which I replied that if a peace agreement was possible, the arrangement could have been made before the war started, but since Germany chose war in preference to peace at a time when we were most anxious to preserve peace, I could put forward no hope of a peace agreement now.

He requested me to ask the King to give him 'parole', as he had come unarmed and of his own free will.

He further asked me if I could inform his family that he was safe by sending a telegram to Rothacker,* Hertzog Str. 17, Zürich, stating that Alfred Horn was in good health. He also asked that his identity should not be disclosed to the Press.

* Frau Rothacker was an aunt of Hess.

It was the German radio which made the first public announcement about Hess's departure. On the evening of Monday 12 May the Germans broadcast that Hess, 'apparently in a fit of madness', had taken possession of an aircraft contrary to Hitler's orders and had disappeared. It was only after this broadcast that the British Press realised that the mysterious parachutist who had landed in Scotland was Hess.

At the first meeting Hamilton gained the impression that Hess, far from being mad, was a man of self-confidence who had numerous proposals to make which would have been highly favourable to the Nazi leadership, although certainly not to anyone else. Hess at one point said that the buying of fifty second-rate destroyers from the U.S.A. was a pointless exercise, because if Britain made peace such contracts with the U.S.A. would be unnecessary.

He also told Hamilton that while he had arrived without Hitler's knowledge, he knew how Hitler's mind worked so well that he could say with complete certainty what Hitler's peace terms would be, and what conditions Hitler would be prepared to accept in order to finish the war. By this time Hamilton had heard quite enough – certainly at that stage. His report continued:

> Throughout the interview, Hess was able to express himself fairly clearly, but he did not properly understand what I was saying and I suggested that I should return with an interpreter and have further conversation with him.

Hess then asked 'Will you please have me moved out of Glasgow, as I am anxious not to be killed by a German bomb', and Hamilton left him. Hamilton's report ended:

> From Press photographs and Albrecht Haushofer's description of Hess, I believed that this prisoner was indeed Hess himself. Until this interview I had not the slightest idea that the invitation in Haushofer's letter to meet him (Haushofer) in Lisbon had any connection with Hess.[1]

Albrecht Haushofer had previously described Hess as a dark, swarthy man with eyes sunken into his head and a sallow complexion. The prisoner answered this description, and Hamilton had now to consider how the matter should be best reported. The situation was one without precedent, and King's Regulations provided no guide.

Hamilton collected some of the photographs of the prisoner and told the officer commanding that the prisoner was probably very important, and that a strong guard should be put over him. He drove back to Turnhouse airport in the afternoon, when he collected the letter which Albrecht Haushofer had written in July 1939. Having obtained leave from his Air Marshal, he rang up and asked to see Sir Alexander Cadogan, the head of the Foreign Office. The official at the other end of the phone acted with all the superciliousness of which the British Civil Servant is a master. As Sir Alexander was a very busy man, if it was a matter of the greatest importance an interview might be fitted into his programme in a couple of weeks time. In frustration Hamilton immediately telephoned 10 Downing Street and spoke to Jock Colville, the Prime Minister's Private Secretary, demanding to see the Prime Minister, without delay, as there might be something very important to report. He was comforted with the information that the Prime Minister was more accessible than the head of the British Foreign Office. Hamilton said he would be at Northolt within two hours and asked Colville to make the necessary arrangements.

Colville has given his own account of what followed. He had spent the night of 10–11 May, which was perhaps the heaviest night of the Blitz, at 10 Downing Street and in the early hours of the morning had a curiously vivid dream centring on Peter Fleming's *Flying Visit*, which he had read some months before, and also on reports that Goering had been flying over London with the Luftwaffe to witness the damage which German bombs were causing. So strong was the impression left by this dream that it was still very much in his mind when he spoke to Hamilton on the telephone later the next morning. Hamilton said that something extraordinary had taken place, but declined to reveal what this extraordinary event was. All he did say was that it was like something out of an E. Phillips Oppenheim novel, and Colville, with his strange dream still in his mind, asked: 'Has somebody arrived?' There was a pause and then Hamilton replied 'Yes'. Colville thereupon rang up the Prime Minister, and received instructions not to go to Northolt, but to have Hamilton diverted directly to Kidlington and Ditchley.[2]

Winston Churchill records in his *History of the Second World War*:

F

On Sunday May 11, I was spending the weekend at Ditchley – presently a secretary told me that somebody wanted to speak to me on the telephone on behalf of the Duke of Hamilton. The Duke was a personal friend of mine, and was commanding a fighter-sector in the East of Scotland, but I could not think of any business he might have with me which could not wait till morning. However the caller pressed to speak with me, saying the matter was one of urgent Cabinet importance. . . . I therefore sent for him.[3]

Hamilton took off for Northolt in a Hurricane, and assembled his thoughts as he flew. He knew that Albrecht Haushofer must have played a large part in what had happened, because he himself had never had any connection with Hess before. He simply could not believe that Albrecht Haushofer could or would have sent Hess to see him. He recalled that years before Albrecht had once said casually to him that he hoped one day Hamilton might meet Hess. Yet Hamilton had never imagined that a meeting would take place in such circumstances. Although Hamilton could not know about it, neither had Haushofer, and Hamilton's astonishment was as nothing in comparison with the shock experienced by Albrecht. Indeed at the same time as Hamilton was flying to see Churchill, Haushofer was being taken to Hitler.

When Hamilton landed at Northolt he was given a message to fly on to Kidlington, near Oxford. The Prime Minister's car was waiting to take him to Ditchley Park, the country home of Ronald Tree where Tree's son was acting as host to some thirty guests, including the Prime Minister, Brendan Bracken and Sir Archibald Sinclair, the Secretary of State for Air. They were finishing dinner and Churchill welcomed Hamilton with great enthusiasm and asked him for his news. During the day information had been coming in concerning the heavy air raid on London during the night before, when the House of Commons had been hit by incendiary bombs and had been severely damaged. Adversity stimulated the Prime Minister, and he could not have been in more exuberant spirits or in better form, especially as thirty-three German bombers had been shot down in the last twenty-four hours. As the room was full of guests Hamilton replied that he must communicate his news to the Prime Minister in private. Accordingly the guests automatically withdrew, leaving the Prime

Minister, Hamilton and Sir Archibald Sinclair. Hamilton then explained that a German pilot had arrived in Scotland, had given the name of Oberleutnant Alfred Horn to everyone else, and had then told him personally that he was Rudolf Hess.

Hamilton had the impression that Churchill was looking at him sympathetically, as though he were suffering from war strain and hallucinations. On 15 May Churchill made the frank admission to the House of Commons: 'In view of the surprising character of the occurrence I did not believe it, although I was very interested when told in the course of Sunday.' Churchill then asked Hamilton very slowly and with great emphasis: 'Do you mean to tell me that the Deputy Fuehrer of Germany is in our hands?' Hamilton replied that the man had certainly declared himself to be Hess. He then produced the photographs of the unidentified prisoner. Churchill looked at them and said, 'Well, Hess or no Hess I am going to see the Marx Brothers.' [1]

By the time that the film-show was finished the Prime Minister had decided that it was necessary to go into the matter thoroughly, the time being about midnight. For the next three hours Hamilton went through every detail and was asked every conceivable type of question.

Hamilton explained that it was his personal view that the German was Hess, as he answered Albrecht Haushofer's description. He again showed Churchill the letter which Albrecht Haushofer had sent in July 1939 as well as a copy of the letter sent by Haushofer in September 1940. In the light of these letters it was clear that Hess's flight involved a peace offer, and that Hess was stating terms which would be acceptable to Hitler, although the flight was made without Hitler's knowledge.

It was, futhermore, Hamilton's impression that the prisoner was an energetic fanatical and stupid man, and that he had come to certain definite conclusions, one being that the British were losing the war and another that the British had been cowed by the bombing of their civilian population. Hamilton also said that Hess, if he was Hess, had said that Mr Churchill would not be very sympathetic to his point of view. After a momentary pause Churchill replied 'By God I would not.'

Hamilton was sworn to secrecy, and felt that Churchill was not entirely clear as to how the matter should be explained, for Hess's peace overture could not have been made in a more unconventional and unexpected way. At any rate it was decided that Hamilton should come up to London with the Prime Minister on the following day.

On the morning of 12 May the news of Hess's arrival had not broken, although there was some speculation around Glasgow and also East Renfrew, which Hamilton had represented as an M.P. until early 1940. The three cars left Ditchley for London at about 9.15 a.m. At one point speeding at 70 m.p.h. through a built-up area, a police car gonged the Prime Minister's car – whereupon without slackening speed a much louder gong resounded from somewhere in the depths of Churchill's car, and the police car immediately withdrew.

On arrival at 10 Downing Street, Churchill told the Foreign Secretary, Anthony Eden, the bare essentials and said that the prisoner must be identified. He then passed Hamilton over to Eden, who took him to the Foreign Office. The story was repeated, and was accepted with astonishment, or not accepted, as the case may be. Eden called in his German expert, Ivone Kirkpatrick, later permanent Under Secretary for Foreign Affairs. Kirkpatrick accepted the news very much as a matter of course, and it was arranged that he and Hamilton should fly to Scotland, so that Kirkpatrick might identify the German.

That evening Hamilton and Kirkpatrick flew north in a D.H. Rapide and on landing heard that an announcement had just been made on the German wireless that Deputy Fuehrer Rudolf Hess was missing. This dispelled any doubt in their minds as to the identity of the German prisoner. At Turnhouse airport they received instructions from the Secretary of State for Air to proceed with all possible speed to Buchanan Castle in Drymen, where the prisoner had been moved under armed guard, in order that identification should be made as soon as possible.

They arrived at Drymen after midnight and went in to interview the prisoner. At one o'clock on the morning of 13 May 1941 Kirkpatrick was summoned to the telephone. The Foreign Secretary had been unable to bear the suspense any longer. Kirkpatrick explained that the German had been talking for more than an hour and had said nothing. He still had no idea why he had come to Scotland, but there was no doubt that it was indeed Rudolf Hess.[5] Ivone Kirkpatrick then returned to the interview, but like Sir Alexander Cadogan he was 'a very busy man', and he behaved as though this particular episode in the war was an infernal bore.

7 Hess's Peace Terms: 12-15 May 1941

ON the way to Drymen, Kirkpatrick described the Nazi leaders to Hamilton, and said that of all of them Hitler was by far and away the worst. Behind all the bombast, histrionics and hysteria Hitler remained the most treacherous, calculating and cold-blooded devil in the world. It was an extraordinary scene which ensued. Kirkpatrick and Hamilton were treated to a speech in German by Hess, delivered from copious notes, which for the first hour consisted of a long eulogy of Hitler. Kirkpatrick sat looking like a sphinx.

During this interview Hess probably made a more complete statement of his ideas, hopes and aims, than at any other time. His views are recorded in detail in Kirkpatrick's first report to the Prime Minister, which gave a truer picture of what actually took place than the lighthearted account in his memoirs, *The Inner Circle*,[1] written years later.

Hess started [Kirkpatrick reports] by saying that he must go a long way back in order to explain the chain of circumstances which had led to his present decision.

Its origin lay in an English book called *England's Foreign Policy under Edward VII*. The author of this book who was an impartial and reputable historian,* admitted that from 1904 on, England's policy had been to oppose Germany and back France in the certain knowledge that this would lead to a conflict with Germany. Thus England was responsible for the war in 1914.

After the war came the Treaty of Versailles and the failure of the British Government to accord to the democratic system in Germany those concessions which would have enabled it to live. Hence the rise of Hitler and National Socialism.

* In a later interview with Lord Simon, Hess said that the English historian Farrar laid the main guilt for the Great War on the policies of Edward VII, so it appears that in this passage he was referring to Farrar.

Having given the interpretation of history accepted by the Nazis, he turned to more recent events. He said that Hitler had tried to negotiate the Anschluss through peaceful means, and after failing was forced to occupy Austria, as it was the wish of the Austrian people.

The Czechoslovak conflict was caused by the French trying to make Czechoslovakia an air base against Germany, and Hitler had to smother this attempt. Hess declared that Chamberlain's intervention at Munich had greatly relieved Hitler, but as the British and French had tried to arm the remainder of Czechoslovakia, Hitler had been compelled to act against this menace to Germany.

England had then caused the Polish crisis by opposing Germany, which was the strongest European power, for the Polish Government would have submitted to the German demands had it not been for the British. 'The conclusion was clear that England was responsible for the present war.'

The implication of this remark was that Hitler had never intended to go to war against Britain, that he had not expected the British to declare war, and that British intransigence in rejecting Hitler's peace offers had led to escalation.

When in May last year, Great Britain started bombing Germany, Herr Hitler had believed that this was momentary aberration; and with exemplary patience, he had waited, partly so as to spare the world the horrors of unrestricted air warfare, and partly out of a sentimental regard for English culture and English monuments. It was only with the greatest reluctance that after many weeks of waiting, he had given the order to bomb England.

The bombing of civilians in English cities was in his view a necessary expedient in order to make the British plead for peace. And as the British remained stubborn, Hitler had no alternative but to 'pursue the struggle to its logical conclusion'.

Hess then proceeded to explain why Germany was going to win the war. Germany was producing enormous numbers of aircraft and Britain could never reduce the lead which the Luftwaffe had over the R.A.F. As for naval warfare, a vastly increased number of submarines would be operating with the Luftwaffe against British convoys and shipping, and would have a deadly effect. Germany had obtained plenty of raw materials in German-occupied Europe and was self-sufficient. 'There is not the slightest hope of bringing about a revolution in Germany. Hitler possesses the blindest confidence of the German masses.'

Hess now turned to the most important part of his talk, dealing with peace proposals. He had been horrified at the idea of so much unnecessary killing, and had come without Hitler's permission in order to 'convince responsible persons that since England could not win the war, the wisest course was to make peace now'.

> From a long and intimate knowledge of the Fuehrer which had begun eighteen years ago in the fortress of Landsberg, he could give his word of honour that the Fuehrer had never entertained any designs against the British Empire. Nor had he ever aspired to world domination. He believed that Germany's sphere of interest was in Europe and that any dissipation of Germany's strength beyond Europe's frontiers would be a weakness and would carry with it the seeds of Germany's destruction. Only as recently as May 3, after his Reichstag speech, Hitler had declared to him that he had no oppressive demands to make on England.

> The solution was that England should give Germany a free hand in Europe, and Germany give England a completely free hand in the Empire, with the sole reservation that we should return Germany's ex-colonies which she required as a source of raw materials.

Furthermore it might be a mistake to keep Hitler waiting, for he could be impatient, even if he was a 'tenderhearted man'. Kirkpatrick tried to draw Hess on Hitler's plans towards Russia, and asked Hess whether he regarded Russia as being in Europe or in Asia.

> He [Hess] replied 'In Asia'. I [Kirkpatrick] then retorted that under the terms of his proposal, since Germany would only have a free hand in Europe, she would not be at liberty to attack Russia. Herr Hess reacted quickly by remarking that Germany had certain demands to make of Russia which would have to be satisfied, either by negotiation or as the result of a war. He added however that there was no foundation for the rumours now being spread that Hitler was contemplating an early attack on Russia.

Kirkpatrick wrote in his memoirs, 'I got the impression that Hess was so much out of things that he really did not know'.[2]

Hamilton, on the other hand, thought that Hess looked as though he had over-reached himself when he mentioned the possibility of war against Russia, and that he tried to recover his balance by denying that Hitler was thinking of an early attack.

> Finally as we were leaving the room Herr Hess delivered a parting shot. He had forgotten, he declared, to emphasise that the proposal could only be considered on the understanding that it was negotiated by Germany with an English Government other than the present British Government. Mr Churchill who had planned the war since 1938, and his colleagues who had lent themselves to his war policy, were not persons with whom the Fuehrer could negotiate.

Kirkpatrick admitted that his patience was exhausted long before the end of the interview, which had lasted two and a quarter hours, and he ended his report with these words:

> But in general, I allowed even the most outrageous remarks to pass unanswered, since I realised that argument would be quite fruitless and would certainly have deprived us of our breakfast.[3]

On the next day, Wednesday 14 May, the Foreign Secretary instructed Kirkpatrick and Hamilton to pursue their conversations with Hess. On his return to the prisoner's room Kirkpatrick noticed that Hess was surprised that nothing had been done to meet his demand for negotiations. Kirkpatrick later recorded that Hess still seemed to have some faith in the ability of Dukes to deliver the goods'.[4]

The interview which followed was not as important as the one which had preceded it. Hess requested the loan of certain books, including *Three Men in a Boat*, the return of his medicines and a piece of his aeroplane as a souvenir. He next described his flight and the extreme difficulty in parachuting out of a plane which was flying upside down.[5]

He then said that Germany had one or two additional demands. For example Germany could not leave Rashid Ali and the Iraquis 'in the lurch'. Britain would have to evacuate Iraq. Also there would have to be reciprocal indemnification of those Britons and Germans whose property had been requisitioned on account of the war.[6] Taken as a whole (he added) his proposals were more than fair.' If by any chance Britain continued the war, there would be a completely effective blockade, and if Britain capitulated, but tried to wage war from the Empire, it was Hitler's intention to continue the blockade so that the population of Britain would be deliberately starved to death. Kirkpatrick was beginning to find such interviews very irritating, but on Thursday 15 May he was instructed to interview Hess yet again, this time by himself, as Hamilton had been told to return to London in case he might be needed.[7]

The chief interest of this conversation between Hess and Kirkpatrick lay in the fact that Hess tried to make Kirkpatrick's 'flesh creep' by suggesting that the Americans wanted to take over the British Empire. Hess also reverted to his old theme that if Hitler's terms were rejected Britain would be subjugated. As Kirkpatrick recorded:

> I then threw a fly over him about Ireland. He said that in all his talks with Hitler, the subject of Ireland had never been mentioned except incidentally. Ireland had done nothing for Germany in this war and it was therefore to be supposed that Hitler would not concern himself 'in Anglo–Irish relations'. We had some little conversation about the difficulty of reconciling the wishes of the south and north and from this we passed to American interest in Ireland, and so to America.
>
> On the subject of America, Hess took the following line. The Germans reckoned with American intervention and were not afraid of it. They knew all about American aircraft production and the quality of the aircraft. Germany could outbuild England and America combined.
>
> Germany had no designs on America. The so-called German peril was a ludicrous figment of the imagination. Hitler's interests were European.
>
> If we made peace now America would be furious. America really wanted to inherit the British Empire.
>
> Hess concluded by saying that Hitler really wanted a permanent understanding with us on a basis which preserved the Empire intact. His own flight was intended to give us a chance of opening conversations without loss of prestige. If we rejected this chance it would be clear proof that we desired no understanding with Germany, and Hitler would be entitled, in fact it would be his duty to destroy us utterly, and keep us after the war in a state of permanent subjection.[8]

After this interview Kirkpatrick was permitted to return to

London, where he reported to the Prime Minister. Hess's flight
had not impressed Churchill, who was in bad humour in case it
might appear that peace negotiations were taking place. He told
Kirkpatrick, 'If Hess had come a year ago and told us what the
Germans would do to us, we should have been very frightened,
and rightly, so why should we be frightened now?[9]

One of the most interesting questions arising out of Hess's
mission is how a person like Hess, whose loyalty to Hitler had
always been unquestioned, could have acted so indiscreetly. The
answer must be that Hess was loyal to Hitler's innermost thoughts
in a way which Hitler himself was not, for Hitler, contrary to all
that he had said and written for many years, was seriously con-
templating a war on two fronts.

There were two essential matters which Hess with his over-
simplified Nazi outlook on the world did not understand. First,
the British were not prepared to contemplate peace with Hitler
or the Nazis. Hitler and the leaders of the Third Reich had broken
too many treaties, lied too often, and killed too many people. In
any case, the British would not have considered a peace proposal
even from a non-Nazi German Government unless it had been
coupled with a German withdrawal from all occupied territories.
Hess did not understand this. He relied for his information
primarily on Hitler and on Albrecht Haushofer, and he was unwise
enough to believe that it was Hitler rather than Albrecht Haushofer
who understood Britain best.

Secondly, Hess did not fully comprehend that Hitler had come
to believe in his own infallibility, as sometimes happens with men
who succeed against great odds. As Alan Bullock wrote, 'No man
ever more surely destroyed himself by coming to believe in the
image which he had himself created than Adolf Hitler'.[10] The turning point in Hitler's case came on 22 June 1941, six weeks after
Hess's flight, with the attack upon Russia, while a bitter war
against Britain was still being waged in the west. Hitler based his
gamble on the premise that he could knock out Russia with a
lightning blow and then return to settle the old score with Britain
and seize such parts of the British Empire as he desired. Hess, on
the other hand, believed that Hitler should not break the cardinal
rule laid down in *Mein Kampf*, never to conduct a war on two
fronts, and could not understand that Hitler was no longer worried
about the British resolve to fight.

As Kirkpatrick wrote, 'The Hess episode was one of the oddest in history, and the oddest thing about it was that it was not in character.'[11] It was not in character for one reason and one reason alone. Hitler was a master of deceit and a liar *par excellence*, while Hess was an arrogant fool who was only too anxious to reveal all the cards in his hand. It was not until he had been in Britain for some time that he realised that he had never held any cards, and that the British were not interested in a Nazi peace offer. Then in despair he tried to take his own life, but even in that was frustrated.[12]

Hess's secret mission, involving unconventional means, is easily understood in the light of what he himself said. Might he not make peace with Britain and return to Germany to be acclaimed a popular hero, second to none but the Fuehrer? Was there not a chance that before long the whole might and fury of the Third Reich would be turned on Russia alone?

8 The Silence of the British Government : 1941

IN spite of the fact that it was always the policy of Churchill to tell the British public the truth, however unpalatable, the British Government did not at any stage make a statement as to why Hess had come to Britain, nor was any information given as to what had been extracted from him. This led to wild guessing in the Press, and A. P. Herbert on 18 May 1941 gave a summary of the speculations which followed in the wake of Hess's flight, in a rhyme which he entitled *Hess*:

> He is insane. He is the Dove of Peace.
> He is Messiah. He is Hitler's niece.
> He is the one clean honest man they've got.
> He is the worst assassin of the lot.
> He has a mission to preserve mankind.
> He's non-alcoholic. He was a 'blind'.
> He has been dotty since the age of ten,
> But all the time was top of Hitler's men.
> (Indeed from all the tales he had to tell,
> Joe Goebbels must be slightly touched as well.)
> He is to pave the way to Britain's end.
> He is – as dear old Lindbergh was – a 'friend'.
> He's fond of flying. He was racked with fear.
> He had an itch to meet a British Peer.
> He thought that Russia was a crashing bore.
> He simply can't stand Hitler any more.
>
> In such rich fancies I am not engrossed
> For this is what appears to matter most –
> He came unasked, an enemy, a Hun;
> And nobody was ready with a gun.[1]

Very few people understood why Hess had come, and the

incident remained as a question mark in the mind of the British public. Eden in his memoirs told part of the inside story, starting on Monday 12 May. During dinner that day he heard the German wireless communiqué that Hess had disappeared. Churchill telephoned 'immensely excited', and wanted the Government to make an announcement quickly. The B.B.C. were instructed to announce Hess's presence in Britain later that night. Eden then went round to see Churchill, and together they concocted a statement, although they found it a problem as to how much should be said about Hess's 'confused obsessions'.[2]

On Tuesday 13 May Kirkpatrick telephoned the Foreign Office at 8.30 a.m., in order to give a brief account of his interrogation of Hess. He was told 'that the British Government were embarrassed by the whole affair and did not know exactly how to handle it'.[3] Later in the day the Prime Minister told the House of Commons 'I have nothing to add at present to the statement issued last night by His Majesty's Government', which had been an official recognition of the fact that Hess had arrived in Britain. Churchill went on, 'but obviously a further statement will be made in the near future concerning the flight to this country of this very high and important Nazi leader'. In answer to the suggestion that the Minister of Information should handle the news with skill and imagination, the Prime Minister replied, 'I think this is one of these cases where imagination is somewhat baffled by the facts as they present themselves.'[4]

However, Churchill had made no final decision, and on Wednesday 14 May Harold Nicolson, Parliamentary Secretary to the Ministry of Information, was included in a lunch party given by the Prime Minister. Nicolson tried to get directives on Hess and was merely told by Churchill that 'we must not make a hero out of him'.[5] That night Churchill rang Eden with a text of the statement which he wanted to make in the House of Commons about Hess on Thursday 15 May, quoting the trend of Hess's statements. Eden objected on the grounds that the Germans must be left guessing as to what Hess had said. Churchill then demanded an alternative draft and Eden 'struggled out of bed', drew up a statement and telephoned it to Churchill. A few minutes later Churchill telephoned back saying that Eden's statement had been approved by Lord Beaverbrook, Minister of Air Production but had upset Duff Cooper, Minister of Information, and was not to his own liking. Churchill said that he was either going to make his own statement or no statement, and which was it to be? Eden replied, 'No statement', whereupon Churchill answered angrily, 'All right, no statement', and the 'telephone was crashed down'; the time being 1.30 a.m.[6]

Accordingly no statement was made, and for once Churchill acted rather indecisively. Nicolson records in his diary that Duff Cooper persuaded Churchill that a directive must be put out as to the British attitude towards Hess. Churchill replied 'We must think this over. Come back at midnight and we shall discuss it again.' When Duff Cooper arrived he found Lord Beaverbrook with the Prime Minister, seeking to persuade him that a statement must not be made.[7]

Churchill was wavering and he brought up the subject again. Eden wrote: 'The Prime Minister reverted to his projected statement about Hess, this time at the Cabinet, but nobody liked it so that nothing came of it. Lord Beaverbrook told me afterwards that we might have to "strangle the infant" a third time, but fortunately it was not reborn.' Eden and Beaverbrook had got their way.[8]

Eden was no doubt opposed to making a full statement on the grounds that it would be best to keep the Germans guessing, while the German propaganda machine was floundering, and Beaverbrook probably thought this as well. Churchill himself finally decided to play down the whole episode and to remain silent.

As could be expected when the government lapsed into a mysterious silence, there was speculation. Harold Nicolson related, 'This is bad, since the belief will get around that we are hiding something and we shall be blamed in this Ministry', namely the Ministry of Information.[9] As it happened Duff Cooper had already issued inaccurate information to the B.B.C. which later had to be withdrawn. He told the B.B.C. that the Duke of Hamilton had met Hess at the Olympic Games at Berlin in 1936, and that Hess had written a letter which Hamilton had placed in the hands of the authorities.

Hamilton had never met Hess before May 1941. The British M.P. who had interviewed Hess had been Kenneth Lindsay, M.P., and after Hess's flight in May 1941 he suggested to several M.P.s that Hamilton might have seen Hess, as he did. Chips Channon, M.P., who had also been to the Olympic Games, was under a similar erroneous impression. Thus it was that a rumour of the vaguest description came to be accepted uncritically.

As to the belief that Hess had written a letter to Hamilton which had been handed over to the authorities, in fact it was Albrecht Haushofer who, with Hess's knowledge, had written the letter to Hamilton, which had been intercepted by the British censor. It was not until Hess's flight that the light dawned upon the British Secret Service, the Intelligence Branch of the Air Ministry and on Hamilton, that Albrecht Haushofer was the eminence grise behind Rudolf Hess.

Neither the British press nor the British public knew about the existence of Albrecht Haushofer and certainly nobody in Britain would have guessed that on 12 May 1941 Albrecht had been taken to Hitler's residence in Berchtesgaden, a summon which he most certainly did not enjoy. Instead, the British press, armed with Duff Cooper's inaccurate information, went speeding off along the wrong scent, imagining that all Rudolf Hess's ideas about the British emanated from conversations at the Olympic Games in 1936.

Hamilton had returned to London on Thursday 15 May, as the Prime Minister wished him to be available, and during the afternoon went to see Duff Cooper in order to emphasise that he had never met Hess before May 1941. Duff Cooper was very apologetic and offered to put out any statement which Hamilton wished to give him. Hamilton pointed out that the Prime Minister had sworn him to secrecy, and that no information of any consequence was to be divulged, so the matter was left in the air.

On Friday 16 May, Hess was transported late at night in great secrecy to the Tower of London. On the same day Hamilton had been asked to lunch with the King at Windsor. George VI was very curious to know what had happened, so Hamilton put him in the picture, and a few days later sent him the report on Hess which had been submitted to the Prime Minister, along with a covering latter:

> It is clear that Hess is still an unrepentant Nazi who repeats *ad nauseam* the usual Nazi 'claptrap'. While his action seems unlikely to affect the course of the war, his arrival here un-invited has been of considerable advantage to us, if only in the difficulties and discredit in which it has involved the German propaganda machine.
>
> I heard yesterday from Kirkpatrick that Hess had told him that he thought of flying to see Vansittart but gave up the idea

when he learned of the *Black Record*. It is indeed extraordinary
how little the Nazis understand us. . . .[10]

It is of interest to read what it was that Lord Vansittart had
written which had disturbed Hess. It was a book entitled *Black
Record: Germans Past and Present*, and if ever a book captured the
feelings of the British towards Nazi Germany early in 1941 it was
this book. What Vansittart wrote explained all too well that Hess
had made a fundamental miscalculation about the atmsophere in
Britain, and the determination of the British to fight on whatever
the consequences. Typical passages ran:

> But don't think Hitler was, or is, an exception. As early as the
> Franco–Prussian War of 1870 the King of Prussia was contin-
> ually thanking God in letters to his wife for the number of
> fellow-men whom he had killed. Even to our Victorian ancestors
> this seemed insufferable, and I think it was Punch that published
> a parody of the correspondence:

> > 'Thanks to the Lord, my dear Augusta,
> > We've hit the French an awful buster.
> > Ten thousand Frenchmen sent below!
> > Praise God from whom all blessings flow.'

> By the grace of God and for the salvation of man we shall
> rescue the earth from Germany and Germany from herself.[11]

When Hamilton returned to London, he found that he was not
required by the Prime Minister, who on Tuesday 20 May had
become preoccupied with the invasion of Crete. He was fitted in
for a ten-minute interview while Churchill travelled from 10
Downing Street to Buckingham Palace. Hamilton mentioned that
he was being pestered by the Press, and put it to him 'What do you
tell your wife if a prostitute throws her arms around your neck?'
Churchill roared with laughter, and said that whatever happened
the Press were not to be told a word. Nonetheless the point was
taken. On Thursday 22 May Sir Archibald Sinclair, Secretary of
State for Air, made a statement about the Duke of Hamilton's
position in relation to Hess's arrival, in answer to a question by
the M.P. Major Lloyd.

When Deputy Fuehrer Hess came down with his aeroplane
in Scotland on 10th May, he gave a false name and asked to see

the Duke of Hamilton. The Duke being apprised by the
authorities, visited the German prisoner in hospital. Hess then
revealed for the first time his true identity, saying that he had
seen the Duke when he was at the Olympic Games at Berlin in
1936. The Duke did not recognise the prisoner and had never
met the Deputy Fuehrer. He had, however, visited Germany
for the Olympic Games in 1936, and during that time had
attended more than one large public function, at which German
Ministers were present. It is, therefore, quite possible that the
Deputy Fuehrer may have seen him on one such occasion. As
soon as the interview was over, Wing Commander the Duke of
Hamilton flew to England and gave a full report of what had
passed to the Prime Minister, who sent for him. Contrary to
reports which have appeared in some newspapers, the Duke has
never been in correspondence with the Deputy Fuehrer. None
of the Duke's three brothers who are, like him, serving in the
Royal Air Force, has either met Hess or has had correspondence
with him. It will be seen that the conduct of the Duke of
Hamilton has been in every respect honourable and proper.[12]

Yet the question as to why Duff Cooper had given inaccurate
information to the B.B.C. still remained unanswered. Harold
Nicolson, on Tuesday 27 May, was asked by the M.P. Major
Adams how it was that the B.B.C. incorrectly broadcast that
Hamilton had received a communication from Hess. Nicolson
replied:

> The statement broadcast by the B.B.C. was based on informa-
> tion supplied by the Ministry of Information to the B.B.C. and
> the Press, which has since been found to be erroneous. The true
> facts are those stated in the reply given on 22nd May by my
> Right Honourable Friend the Secretary of State for Air to the
> Honourable and gallant Member for Renfrew [Major Lloyd]....[13]

Hamilton had returned to Scotland on 30 May to take up a
Group Captain's command and by this time had passed out of this
strange and eventful story. There had, however, been one last
attempt to make contact with him by the Nazis. On the early morning
of Monday 19 May, near Luton Hoo, while the Luftwaffe was
engaged in bombing, the searchlights picked out two parachutists
descending. They were S.S. men in plain clothes, who had a map

in their possession with circles drawn around certain places, one
of which was Hamilton's home in Lanarkshire. Clearly they
wished to make contact with certain persons in Britain in order to
find out where Hess was confined. It is not known whether they
were sent by Himmler, Schellenberg or Heydrich. All that is
known is that the British Secret Service picked them up, and drove
them to a secret establishment, where they were identified, interrogated and executed.[14] Such were the rules of war: Rudolf Hess
had at least arrived in uniform.

Even so his presence in Britain was never explained by the
British Government, and as no statement was made he could not
be exploited for propaganda purposes. Sefton Delmer, who was
working for the Directorate of Psychological Warfare, wrote that
he found it frustrating that the psychological warfare agencies and
the deception experts were not permitted to use the incident in
order to confuse and distress the Germans.[15] However, Churchill
was now adamant that no useful purpose could be served by telling
the British people that a Nazi leader had made a serious peace
initiative and that was the end of the matter. Churchill was quite
content to leave the Germans weltering in their own embarrassment.

Sefton Delmer remained dissatisfied; and he was not alone.
Dr Kurt Hahn believed that he, too, could see an opportunity in
Hess's flight. Hahn was a patriotic German of Jewish origin and
had been imprisoned by the Nazis in 1933 for his outspoken
opposition to Nazism. After the British Premier Ramsay Macdonald
interceded on his behalf Hahn was released; and he came to
Britain, where he founded Gordonstoun School. During the war
he worked for the British Foreign Office translating German news
cuttings, and on 20 May 1941 he submitted a report on Hess's
flight, suggesting that the Haushofers were behind it. His theme
was that Hess's action indicated that 'there was a great longing for
peace in Germany of which Hess had become the unconscious and
silent Ambassador. Now was the moment to encourage the German
Resistance and to make it clear to the German people that the
British would never make peace with Hitler, but that a cleansed
and liberated Germany had nothing to fear from Britain.'[16]

The blunt answer to Hahn's suggestions was that by May 1941
Churchill and the Cabinet believed that Nazism was too deeply
rooted in the German people and too firmly embedded in the

German mind for it to be removed by placing faith in a possible German Resistance to Hitler. Churchill and the Cabinet were thinking in terms of carrying the battle on to German soil at the first available opportunity, so that Nazism would be wiped off the map of Europe. There was a resolve that never again would Britain be tricked into an Armistice as in 1918, and that this time Germany would be crushed and occupied.

Thus secrecy was maintained and the Hess affair remained an enigma. Still Churchill did make use of the statement which he had prepared for the House of Commons. He asked Sir Alexander Cadogan to adapt it, so that it could be sent to President Roosevelt. His letter is worth quoting in full, because it shows in broad outline how Churchill would have described the episode to the British people, if his Cabinet had encouraged him to make a statement:

Former Naval Person to President Roosevelt. 17th May 1941.

Foreign Office Representative has had three interviews with Hess. At first interview on night of May 11–12,* Hess was extremely voluble, and made a long statement with the aid of notes. First part recapitulated Anglo–German relations during past thirty years or so, and was designed to show that Germany had always been in the right and England in the wrong. Second part emphasised certainty of German victory, due to development in combination of submarine and air weapons, steadiness of German morale, and complete unity of German people behind Hitler. Third part outlined proposals for settlement. Hess said that the Fuehrer had never entertained any designs against the British Empire, which would be left intact save for the return of former German colonies, in exchange for a free hand for him in Europe. But condition was attached that Hitler would not negotiate with present Government in England. This is the old invitation to us to desert all our friends in order to save temporarily the greater part of our skin.

Foreign Office Representative asked him whether when he spoke of Hitler having a free hand in Europe he included Russia in Europe or in Asia. He replied, 'In Asia.' He added however that Germany had certain demands to make of Russia which

---

* In fact this first interview with Kirkpatrick took place on the night of May 12–13.

would have to be satisfied, but denied that attack on Russia was being planned.

Impression created by Hess was that he had made up his mind that Germany must win the war, but saw that it would last a long time and involve much loss of life and destruction. He seemed to feel that if he could persuade people in this country that there was a basis for a settlement, that might bring the war to an end and avert unnecessary suffering.

At second interview, on May 14, Hess made two further points:

1. In any peace settlement Germany would have to support Rashid Ali and secure eviction of British from Iraq.
2. U-boat war with air-co-operation would be carried on till all supplies to these islands were cut off. Even if these islands capitulated and the Empire continued the fight, the blockade of Britain would continue, even if that meant that the last inhabitant of Britain died of starvation.

At third interview, on May 15, nothing much emerged save incidentally some rather disparaging remarks about your country and the degree of assistance that you will be able to furnish us. I am afraid in particular, he is not sufficiently impressed by what he thinks he knows of your aircraft types and production.

Hess seems in good health and not excited, and no ordinary signs of insanity can be detected. He declares that this escapade is his own idea and that Hitler was unaware of it beforehand. If he is to be believed, he expected to contact members of a 'peace movement' in England, which he would help to oust the present Government. If he is honest and if he is sane this is an encouraging sign of ineptitude of German Intelligence Service. He will not be ill-treated, but it is desirable that the Press should not romanticise him and his adventure. We must not forget that he shares responsibility for all Hitler's crimes and is a potential war criminal whose fate must ultimately depend upon the decision of the Allied Governments.

Mr President, all the above is for your own information. Here we think it best to let the Press have a good run for a bit and keep the Germans guessing. The German officer prisoners of war here were greatly perturbed by the news, and I cannot doubt that there will be deep misgivings in the German armed forces about what he may say.[17]

There is no doubt that Roosevelt did not accept this explanation as being the whole story. Robert Sherwood refers to a conversation which he had at dinner with Roosevelt, Harry Hopkins and Sumner Welles about ten days after Hess's flight. Knowing that Welles had met Hess in Berlin in 1940, Roosevelt asked him what he was like. Welles gave a picture of a stupid man possessed of a fanatical and mystical devotion to Hitler. After listening to this account Roosevelt was silent for a moment and then said, 'I wonder what is really behind this story.'[18]

Welles did not know and Sherwood learnt that Roosevelt was asking the same question as countless others in the U.S.A. Sherwood believed that Roosevelt and Hopkins imagined that there remained 'a small but potentially powerful minority' in Britain who were not averse to peace talks.[19] The British Ambassador in Washington, Lord Halifax, also telegraphed to Eden saying that the latter's speeches had received a good press in the U.S.A., which would be 'useful in counteracting rumours circulating that our silence about Hess connotes peace talks through him'. Eden's comment in his memoirs was to the point: 'So little was our temper understood even by our best friends'.[20]

9 A Prisoner of War: 1941-5

IN the summer of 1941 the Cabinet invited Lord Simon, who was a Minister, but not a member of the War Cabinet, to interview Hess. Lord Simon was sent because if Hess was an emissary from Hitler something of interest might be discovered, although the British had not the slighest intention of negotiating with him. Simon had already met Hess in Berlin when he and Eden were there in March 1935. Now, together with Kirkpatrick, he saw Hess again at Mytchett Place near Aldershot on 10 June 1941. It was considered vital that no one should know that a Minister had seen Hess so that there should be no rumours about peace negotiations. Simon and Kirkpatrick assumed the pseudonyms of Doctors Guthrie and Mackenzie respectively.[1]

The interview lasted for more than two hours and it can be split into three parts. First, Hess explained the reasons for his mission; secondly, he maintained that Germany had to reverse the Versailles Dictat and was in any case winning the war; and thirdly he declared that while he had come without Hitler's knowledge, he had been repeatedly told by Hitler the four indispensable conditions for the conclusion of an Anglo-German understanding. Many of his statements were a straight repetition of what he had said earlier to Kirkpatrick, but he did bring up additional points during this interview.

One such point was that the idea of making a peace overture had first occurred to Hess in 1940, during the German campaign against the French, while Hess was visiting Hitler. Convinced that Germany was in the process of conquering England, Hess had expressed the opinion to Hitler that Germany must demand from England the restitution of goods – such as the equivalent of the German merchant fleet, which had been confiscated from Germany under the Versailles Treaty. Hitler contradicted Hess.

Hitler thought that the war could possibly provide an occasion for coming to terms with England, something he had tried to accomplish ever since he had been politically active. Hitler told him that severe conditions should not be imposed on a country with which one hoped to come to an arrangement. This put the idea into Hess's mind that if the English knew Hitler's thoughts they might be ready to come to a suitable agreement. Hess believed that the refusal of Hitler's peace offer by the British after the French campaign stemmed from a reluctance to lose prestige by a peace agreement. He said:

> I had to realise my plan, because if I were over in England she would be able to cultivate negotiations with Germany without loss of prestige.
> I was of the opinion that, apart from the question of terms for an agreement, there would still be in England a certain general distrust to overcome. I must confess that I faced a very critical decision, the most critical in my life, of course, and I believed I was aided by continuously keeping before my inner vision the picture of an endless row of children's coffins with the mothers crying behind them on the German side as well as on the English side, and vice versa, the coffins of mothers with the children behind them. . . .

Whilst making these observations Hess never expressed concern at the thought of an endless row of children's coffins in relation to the Poles, the Jews or the Russians, peoples whom he had always regarded with the greatest disdain. He next turned to the Versailles Settlement, saying that this treaty was 'not only a frightful calamity for Germany but also for the whole world'. He explained that if the war, for which Britain was responsible, continued, the Fuehrer would have to act according to the rule of conduct of Admiral Lord Fisher. 'Moderation in war is folly. If you strike, strike hard and wherever you can.' Hitler had no alternative although 'It pained him deeply'. Hess listed all the terrible things which the Germans would do to Britain if the British remained stubborn. Britain would be doomed to total destruction at the hands of the Luftwaffe and would be starved into submission by U-boat warfare.

Hess admitted that he had come entirely without the knowledge of Hitler, but claimed that he knew the four conditions required by the Fuehrer prior to any peace agreement:

1. In order to prevent future wars between the Axis and England, the limits of the spheres of interest must be defined. The sphere of interest of the Axis is Europe, and England's sphere of interest is the Empire.
2. Return of German colonies.
3. Indemnification of German citizens who before or during the war had their residence within the British Empire, and who suffered damage to life and property through measures of a Government of the Empire or as a result of pillage, riot etc; indemnification of British subjects by Germany on the same basis.
4. Armistice and peace to be concluded with Italy at the same time.[2]

Hess went on to say that during their conversation, Hitler repeatedly put forward these points to him as the basis for an understanding with England. These remarks of Hess had their effect on Lord Simon. Instead of listening to Hess with the silent contempt which had been characteristic of Kirkpatrick, Simon forgot his Intelligence mission, and, as Sefton Delmer wrote, fell into 'the role of the heroic British statesman refusing to capitulate before a tyrannical enemy'.[3] Simon made the angry retort, 'There is a good deal of courage in this country and we are not very fond of threats.' In fairness to him, Hess's offer that the British must submit to an agreement or be destroyed could not have been couched in more offensive terms. Still, Simon felt a certain amount of contemptuous pity for Hess, and wrote in his memoirs, 'Nobody could see him as I did at Aldershot without feeling some sympathy for a man who had made such a frightful miscalculation. His ignorance of the British temper was colossal.'[4]

Hess must have known that his mission had totally failed; and the Nazi leaders hated failure. Five days later, at Mytchett Place, he dived over the banisters into the basement three floors below in a suicide bid, but merely broke his leg and pelvis.[5] It might have been a very serious matter since, if he had succeeded in taking his own life, Hitler might well have used his death as an excuse for the murder of thousands of British prisoners of war, as he had used the death of Vom Rath as an excuse to murder the Jews. Consequently, after 15 June Hess was watched more closely.

On 22 June 1941 Germany attacked Russia, and Churchill and

the Cabinet became a great deal less interested in Hess. Yet Hess did have one more interesting interview in Britain. It took place on 9 September 1941 when Lord Beaverbrook conversed with him for one hour. His talk with Hess centred around the topic of Germany's invasion of Russia which was dear to Hess's heart.

Hess completely changed the story he had given to Hamilton, Kirkpatrick and Simon. He now said that the purpose of his coming had been to make peace between Britain and Germany 'on any terms', provided that Britain would join Germany in an attack on Russia. Hess's line was that the British were mistaken if they believed that Operation Barbarossa would so weaken Germany and Russia that Britain's nineteenth-century position in Europe would be restored.

> A victory for England as the ally of the Russians will be a victory for the Bolsheviks. And a Bolshevik victory will sooner or later mean Russian occupation of Germany and the rest of Europe. England will be just as incapable of preventing this as any other nation. I am convinced that world domination awaits the Soviet Union in the future, if her power is not broken now.[6]

One naturally wonders why it was that Hess told a completely different story to Lord Beaverbrook. However, on close examination both stories fit into one pattern. It would appear that Hess wished to split his mission into two parts. First, he would have to make peace with the British through the use of an unselfish and sporting gesture. If all went well, as he hoped, he would go on to discuss the possibility of Anglo-German co-operation against Russia, in whatever form that might take. As Beaverbrook told Churchill, Hess was not insane.[7] In spite of his supposedly self-sacrificing act his proposals would have suited Hitler and the Nazis perfectly. It was one of the most cynical peace tenders of all time, and as far as the Russians were concerned it could with justice have been described as a mission of war.

It was not surprising that the news of Hess's arrival in Britain gave rise to the gravest anxiety in Russia, and there were fears that the British and Germans might be negotiating behind the scenes at Russia's expense. On 12–13 November 1940 Molotov, Russia's Foreign Minister, had visited Berlin for talks with Hess and the other Nazi leaders. At that time Molotov had not noticed any signs of insanity in Hess, and when Hess made his appearance in Scotland five months later Stalin was not prepared to accept the explanation from the German Ambassador in Moscow that Hess was crazy.[8]

Three years later Stalin asked Churchill about the Hess mission, and Churchill wrote:

> I had the feeling that he believed there had been some deep negotiation or plot for Germany and Britain to act together in the invasion of Russia, which had miscarried. Remembering what a wise man he is, I was surprised to find him silly on this point. When the interpreter made it plain that he did not believe what I said, I replied through my interpreter, 'When I make a statement of facts within my knowledge I expect it to be accepted'. Stalin received this somewhat abrupt response with a genial grin, 'There are lots of things that happen even here in Russia, which our Secret Service do not necessarily tell me about'. I let it go at that.[9]

Churchill had warned Stalin in early June 1941 that Germany was about to invade Russia, and when the German armed forces attacked on 22 June Churchill made one of his greatest speeches in support of the Russians. This went a long way to allay Russian suspicion, and in a speech of 6 November 1941 Stalin said that the Germans, as was obvious from Hess's mission, had intended that Britain and the U.S.A. should join them in a war against Russia, or at least give Germany a free hand in the east. Hess had failed, he added, because Britain, the U.S.A. and the Soviet Union were in one camp.[10]

Stalin had given an accurate appraisal of the position, and he might have been amused if he had known of the treatment Hess was receiving in Britain. Hess, under armed guard, had been turned over for examination to the British medical authorities, and had become the guinea-pig of British psychiatrists under Brigadier Rees. In Rees's Book *The Case of Rudolf Hess* it emerged that far from regarding Hess as a war criminal and as a man who would willingly kill anyone who stood in Hitler's way, they thought of him as a patient, and as a poor lost wayward brother who had strayed into the company of strange men. Even so they agreed that Hess was not insane medically or legally, and that he was mentally alert.[11]

The psychiatrists tried to explain Hess in medical terms. They argued that he was suffering from hysterical amnesia, paranoid schizophrenia, psychogenic disturbances, hypochondria, delusions of persecution, and last but hardly least, an inferiority complex. It is of relevance that the psychiatrist Douglas Kelley described Hitler as a psychoneurotic of the obsessive and hysterical type with pathological deviations and an inferiority complex.[12] While these views may be sound in medicine, they are not of much assistance to the historian, because at virtually all times Hess and Hitler were physically and mentally able to form and carry out their intentions. If there was a difference between Hess and other Nazi leaders it was not that he was mentally sick, since all Nazi leaders were mentally sick in varying degrees. Hess differed from the other members of the Nazi High Command because he was more loyal and less intelligent.

His flight had been a product of his fanatical devotion and of his steady decline. Indeed his uncritical devotion to Hitler had contributed to his decline, because he had allowed his will to be completely subordinated to that of Hitler. Consequently he had not possessed the ingenuity necessary for fitting into the role of a triumphant Nazi war leader. Besides, he genuinely disliked the thought of two Nordic peoples, the Germans and the British, killing each other although he never allowed himself to be burdened with such ideas about Russians, Poles or Jews. He had supported Hitler in word, thought and deed, and he gave himself away even to the psychiatrists, as can be seen in his attitude towards Russia, towards the Jews and towards Hitler.

When he was told about the invasion of the Soviet Union by Germany on 22 June 1941, he said 'So they have started after all'. He made out that very soon Germany would be victorious, and that she would then turn her attentions to the conquest of Britain. He still believed, however, that there was a possibility that Britain might come to a settlement with Germany, once Russia had been overrun. He later 'expressed satisfaction over the war with Russia, because he now felt that England would be more sympathetic towards Germany in her war against Communism'.[13]

As time passed, even Hess realised that Britain was not interested in Nazi peace offers. He made it clear that he regarded the Jews as being responsible for Britain's intransigence and for his present treatment. Indeed it appears that his hatred of Jews was so great

that, if he had been given the opportunity, he would have supported Hitler and Himmler in their policy of genocide. In June
1942 he wrote: 'It had not been one of my duties to decide the
treatment of Jews. However if this had been the case I would have
done everything to protect my people from these criminals, and I
wouldn't have had a bad conscience about it.' [14]

Never at any time did he waver in his loyalty to his Fuehrer, and
prior to his second attempt at suicide, when he tried to stab
himself with a breadknife, he wrote a letter to Hitler: 'I die in the
conviction that my last mission, even if it ends in death, will
somehow bear fruit. Perhaps my flight will bring, despite my
death, or indeed partly because of my death, peace and recon-
ciliation with England.' [15]

Perhaps the most accurate expression of Hess's motives was
given by his secretary, Ingeborg Sperr, who wrote of Hess that 'in
his fanatic love for the Fatherland, he wanted to make the greatest
sacrifice of which he was capable to Adolf Hitler and the German
people, namely, to leave nothing undone to bring the German
people the dearly desired peace with England, and thereby to risk
his life, his family, his freedom and his honourable name'. [16]

The evidence indicates that what mattered about Hess's secret
mission was not the neuroses which afflicted him after his lack of
success. The fact of importance is that he knew what he was doing,
why he was doing it, and had only one regret: that he failed.

By the end of May 1941 the war was over for Rudolf Hess, but
for Albrecht Haushofer back in Germany the crisis of his life was
about to unfold. He had known nothing of Hess's plans to fly to
Scotland. On 12 March 1941 however Hassell wrote in his diary
that he had met Albrecht Haushofer at Popitz's home and Haushofer had spoken about 'a desire for peace in high quarters',
although he agreed with Popitz and Hassell that owing to the
'distrust and abomination in which the world holds Hitler', the
existence of the Nazi regime constituted an insuperable barrier to
any peace talks. [17]

Hassell asked Albrecht to make use of his connections in
Switzerland, so that a guarantee might be extracted from Britain
that there would be peace negotiations once the Nazi Government
had been removed. Hassell's wife Ilse made preparations for
Albrecht's journey to the Swiss neutral Carl Burckhardt, who lived
in Geneva and was Vice-President of the International Red Cross.

She told Burckhardt in advance that 'Haushofer was coming with two faces. (Ostensibly for Hess, but actually for the resistance movement.)'[18]

Hess's authority gave Albrecht the opportunity to travel abroad as his agent, and by doing this Albrecht was pursuing his own objectives for the Resistance. With Hess's approval he met Carl Burckhardt on 29 April 1941, and asked Burckhardt to get in touch with certain persons in Britain. Burckhardt told him that Britain wanted peace on a 'rational basis', but not with the Nazi regime and time was possibly running short.[19] Hassell knew that Albrecht was playing a tricky and delicate game, and he said of him:

> I have a profound regard for him; he is a highly talented man and not for nothing do we jokingly call him 'Cassandra'. It is a pity that among young German politicians we have so few of his talent. But perhaps he is already too clever by half.[20]

When the news of Hess's flight to Scotland came through Albrecht was beside himself with anxiety. Rainer Hildebrandt wrote after seeing him on Sunday 11 May 1941.

> I found Haushofer, whom I had always known as being completely collected, in utter despair and helplessness. He said 'This motorised Parsifal wants to bring peace to Hitler, and he imagines that he could get round the Churchill government and could sit down at the negotiating table with the King.'
>
> Haushofer had calculated all possibilities. The most improbable and unusual developments were included in his reckoning, but here something had happened which brought his whole edifice of thought crashing down. Haushofer walked about like a wounded animal not knowing what to do with himself.[21]

Ever since 1933 it was as though Albrecht had been standing with a noose around his neck on account of his Jewish ancestry, and the chair upon which he had been standing was Rudolf Hess. He was now in the unhappy position of learning that this chair had been swept from under his feet. His protector had literally flown away. A few hours later two Gestapo agents came for him. Hitler wanted an account of his recent activities at the Obersalzberg, Berchtesgaden. Albrecht was under arrest.[22]

III | The Fate of Albrecht Haushofer

'And if, my Fuehrer, this project . . . ends in failure. . . . Simply say I was crazy.'
Rudolf Hess's letter to Hitler: 10 May 1941

'I know exactly that at present I am a small beetle which has been turned on its back by an unexpected and unforeseeable gust of wind, and which realises that it cannot rise to its feet by its own strength. . . .'
Albrecht Haushofer's letter to his parents from the Prince Albrecht Strasse Gestapo Prison: 7 July 1941.

*'There are times when madness rules the land
It is then that the best are hanged.'*
Albrecht Haushofer, No. 21 Sonnets of Moabit.

Turmoil at the Dictator's Court: 11 May 1941

EARLY on the morning of Sunday 11 May 1941 Hess's adjutant Pintsch arrived at Berchtesgaden and was told that Hitler was interviewing Todt, the Minister for Armaments, and that he was preparing a reception for Admiral Darlan of Vichy France after lunch.[1] Pintsch pressed his attentions, and when he handed Hess's letter to Hitler, the latter was 'overcome by a tremendous agitation'. Speer, who was also present, heard an 'inarticulate almost animal shout'.[2] The letter which had given rise to Hitler's trepidation and fury began with these words:

> My Fuehrer, when you receive this letter I shall be in England. You can imagine that the decision to take this step was not easy for me, since a man of 40 has other ties with life than one of 20. . . .[3]

It went on to give a lengthy description of the technical requirements necessary for such a flight, which had been attempted more than once. Hess underlined that he was not motivated by 'cowardice or weakness', and that his flight should not be regarded as an escape since undertaking a hazardous mission of this kind required more courage than it would to remain in Germany.[4]

His aim was to make contact between England and Germany by getting in touch with certain distinguished men in England. He felt that the interests of both England and Germany dictated that a serious attempt should be made to effect a peace settlement through negotiation. He reminded Hitler that he had recently asked him 'a point blank question' on his policy towards England, and was convinced the answer that Hitler still wanted an Anglo–German accommodation. He had not revealed to Hitler his plans to fly to Britain, because he knew that he would not have been allowed to go.[5]

Nonetheless Hess wrote that he considered himself to be

G

especially well qualified for this mission since he had been brought
up in Alexandria, Egypt, which was an English environment.
Naturally he would tell the British that his mission must not be
construed as an indication of 'German weakness'. He would
emphasise on the contrary that Germany was militarily invincible
and 'did not have to ask for peace'.[6] Hess's letter ended significantly
with these words:

> And if, my Fuehrer, this project – which I admit has but very
> small chance of success – ends in failure and the fates decide
> against me, this can have no detrimental results either for you
> or for Germany: it will always be possible for you to deny all
> responsibility. Simply say I was crazy.[7]

Hitler at once asked Pintsch what time Hess had disappeared
from Germany, and Pintsch confirmed that at about 6.10 p.m. on
the previous evening Hess had flown from Augsburg to Scotland.
Hitler promptly called Martin Bormann, who was ordered to telephone Ribbentrop, Goering, Goebbels and Himmler, the first two
of whom were summoned. Hitler asked the Luftwaffe General
Ernst Udet, who happened to be at hand, what chance there was
of Hess reaching Britain and Udet expressed the belief that with
the limited range of an Me 110 Hess would come down in the sea.[8]
Yet Hitler remained uncertain and shaken; his anger accumulated as the hours passed. His interpreter Schmidt wrote that it
was 'as though a bomb had hit the Berghof'.[9] Meanwhile all
personnel on Hess's staff, including his adjutants, Pintsch and
Leitgen, who were thought to have withheld information from
Hitler, were locked up. SS Gruppenführer Muller, head of the
Gestapo, made many arrests amongst personnel at Augsburg Airport, and when the reports of Heydrich's SD revealed that Hess
had been associating with astrologers, nature therapists and
anthroposophists, a large number of these individuals were imprisoned. Organisations which Hess had supported, such as the
Rudolf Steiner schools, were closed down.[10]
Karl Haushofer was temporarily placed under guard while his
house was searched. Amongst the documents found were Hess's
letter to him, Albrecht Haushofer's memorandum on the possibilities of a German–English peace, and also Albrecht's letter
to Hamilton sent at Hess's instigation. The Gestapo took these
papers. It emerged from the confiscated manuscripts and from

other enquiries that Hess's action had been one of personal initiative, and that there had been no disloyalty of any kind to Hitler.

Everyone in the proximity of Hitler at this time, when asked about it later, confirmed that never in his wildest moments had Hitler imagined that his Deputy Fuehrer would deliberately fly into enemy hands. It was true that Hitler had given Hess permission to make cautious enquiries through Albrecht Haushofer, but Hess's action infinitely exceeded the authority which Hitler had given him. As General Halder noted, Hitler told his army commanders that Hess's flight had taken him completely by surprise, and General Keitel saw Hitler on Sunday 11 May pacing restlessly up and down in his study, trying to frame as plausible an explanation as was possible for the German people. He was extremely concerned about Hess's flight on three accounts. First, he believed that once the German people learnt that his Deputy had flown to Britain on a peace mission, the German soldiers at the front would fight less hard. Secondly, he feared that Hess's action might result in the complete disintegration of the Anti-Comintern Pact between Germany, Italy and Japan, and that Mussolini, not to be outdone, would hasten to make his own peace terms with Britain. And, lastly, Hitler was afraid that Hess would reveal the Nazi plans to attack Russia. He kept muttering that a fool could cause unimaginable harm, and that the British might drug Hess and drag him before a radio, forcing him to make a statement. In these circumstances, Hitler felt that he had to make an explanation to the German people, and to Mussolini, and to confirm the date for the attack on Russia.[11]

To make matters worse, he had no idea whether Hess had reached Britain and, if he had, what his reception had been. Whatever happened, Hitler could never bear being associated with failure. He was not getting much support from Goebbels, the Reichsminister for Propaganda, who had disappeared to his country residence and had refused to give any directive to his Ministry, saying, 'There are situations which even the best propagandist in the world cannot cope with.' Goebbels confided to his subordinate, Rudolf Semmler, that he regarded the Hess episode as being more serious than the desertion of an army corps.[12]

The responsibility for issuing the first communiqué was left to

Dr Otto Dietrich, the Reich press chief who, along with Hitler, Goering and Ribbentrop, prepared a deliberately vague statement. In order to cover themselves in the event of the expected failure of Hess's mission, they took Hess's advice and attempted to suggest that he had suddenly and inexplicably gone off his head. The communiqué was redrafted many times and the final product, which was broadcast on the evening of Monday 12 May, ran:

> The Party authorities state – Party Member Hess, who had been expressly forbidden by the Fuehrer to use an aeroplane because of a disease which has been becoming worse for years, was, in contradiction of this order, able to get hold of a plane recently.
>
> Hess started on Saturday 10 May, at about 18.00 hours from Augsburg on a flight from which he has not yet returned. A letter which he left behind unfortunately showed traces of a mental disturbance which justifies the fear that Hess was the victim of hallucinations.
>
> The Fuehrer at once ordered the arrest of Hess's adjutants, who alone knew of his flights, and who in contradiction to the Fuehrer's ban, of which they were aware, did not prevent the flight nor report it at once. The National Socialist Movement has unfortunately, in these circumstances, to assume that Party Comrade Hess has crashed or met with a similar accident.[13]

This communiqué caused consternation and bewilderment in Germany. It was regarded as a serious and tragic matter that Hess had fled, especially as no signs of mental disturbance had been previously noted. The news that Hitler's deputy had for a considerable time been to all intents and purposes insane made many Germans wonder whether others of their leaders might not be in a similar condition. Hitler's interpreter Schmidt was asked by an old gardener, 'Didn't you already know that we are governed by madmen?'[14] Messerschmitt too expressed discontent when he was taken to task by Goering for lending Hess an aeroplane. He asked how on earth he could have been expected to know that one so senior as Hitler's Deputy was crazy, and why, if that had really been the case, his resignation had not been secured.[15] Hitler's first communiqué was clearly inadequate.

Late on Monday 12 May, at about 11.20 p.m., a British announcement was put out from 10 Downing Street to the effect that Rudolf

Hess had arrived in Britain. This announcement was accompanied by a total silence on the reasons for his arrival. Fritz Hesse, who worked for Ribbentrop, was asked by Himmler whether there was any possibility of peace negotiations with Britain arising out of Hess's flight, as this was the only matter that interested the Fuehrer. Fritz Hesse told him there was none, and Ribbentrop gave his opinion that the entire business was as stupid a piece of tomfoolery as could be imagined. According to Ribbentrop, Hitler had thought that Hess might have been successful and now that he no longer thought so members of Hess's staff would be victimised.[16] It was imperative that another explanation should be given to the German public and the following communiqué was published on 13 May 1941.

On the basis of a preliminary examination of the papers which Hess left behind him, it would appear that Hess was living under the hallucination that by undertaking a personal step in connection with the Englishmen with whom he was formerly acquainted it might be possible to bring about an understanding between Germany and Britain. As has since been confirmed by a report from London, Hess parachuted from his plane and landed near the place in Scotland which he had selected as his destination; there he was found, apparently in an injured condition.

As is well known in Party circles, Hess has undergone severe physical suffering for some years. Recently he had sought relief to an increasing extent in various methods practised by mesmerists and astrologers, etc. An attempt is also being made to determine to what extent these persons are responsible for bringing about the condition of mental distraction which led him to take this step. It is also conceivable that Hess was deliberately lured into a trap by a British party. The whole manner of his action, however, confirms the fact, stated in the first announcement, that he was suffering under hallucinations.

Hess was better acquainted than anyone else with the peace proposals which the Fuehrer has made with such sincerity. Apparently he had deluded himself into thinking that, by some personal sacrifice, he could prevent developments which, in his eyes, could only end with the complete destruction of the British Empire.

Judging by his own papers, Hess, whose sphere of activities

was confined to the Party, as is generally known, had no idea how to carry out such a step or what result it would have.

The National Socialist Party regrets that this idealist fell a prey to tragic hallucinations. The continuation of the war, which Britain forced on the German people, will not be affected at all. As the Fuehrer declared in his last speech, it will be carried on until the men in power in Britain have been overthrown or are ready to make peace.[17]

This statement did not clarify the confused picture in the mind of the German populace. Hess was still mad, but it was the madness of an idealist rather than of a lunatic. Weizsaecker, Secretary of State at the Foreign Office, touched on the crux of the matter when he wrote:

> To hold office meant, in fact, to be above criticism. That is why the fall of Hitler's Deputy, Rudolf Hess, in May 1941 seemed so fantastic; yesterday he had been a demigod and today he was nothing but a pitiful idiot. . . . I was sorry when his old friends attributed to him defects other than defects of intelligence.[18]

On 18 May Ulrich von Hassell wrote in his diary what must have been thought by many:

> The effect of Hess's flight . . . was indescribable, but immeasurably increased by the stupidity of the official communiqué, which could clearly be traced to Hitler's personal explosions of wrath. The first one especially, which implied that for months, even for years, he had presented to the people a half or even entirely insane 'Deputy' as heir-apparent of the Fuehrer. . . .
>
> The background of Hess's flight is not yet clear. The official explanations are, to say the least, incomplete. Hess's sporting and technical performance alone showed that he could not be called crazy.[19]

Nonetheless, Hitler's explanation had been given and on Tuesday 13 May all Reichsleiters and Gauleiters were summoned to Berchtesgaden. They were instructed that the official interpretation to be laid on this tragic case was that Hess, that everlasting idealist and sick man, had suffered from Messianic delusions and had tried to save the British Empire from the terrible destruction that awaited it. Whilst there, Goebbels had an interview with Hitler, whom he later reported as looking ten years older and in tears.[20]

On the same day Ribbentrop met Mussolini and Ciano in Rome. The official German record of the conversations signed by Schmidt relates that Ribbentrop had been sent to give information about Hess's disappearance. Hitler had been 'completely taken aback by Hess's action', which 'had been the action of a lunatic', although Hess 'had acted only from idealistic motives. His being unfaithful to the Fuehrer was utterly out of the question.' He had written to the Fuehrer 'a long and confused letter', explaining that he had flown in order to persuade the British that further resistance was hopeless, and he had confronted everyone with a *fait accompli*. 'When this letter reached the Fuehrer, Hess was already in England. It was hoped in Germany that he would perhaps have an accident on the way, but he was now really in England and had tried to contact the former Marquis of Clydesdale, the present Duke of Hamilton. Hess quite wrongly considered him to be a great friend of Germany and had flown to the neighbourhood of his castle in Scotland.'[21] Ciano entered in his diary on 13 May that Mussolini and himself were not very impressed with Ribbentrop's visit.

> Von Ribbentrop arrives in Rome unexpectedly. He is discouraged and nervous. He wants to confer with the Duce and me for various reasons, but there is only one real reason: he wants to inform us about the Hess affair. . . .
>
> The official version is that Hess, sick in body and mind, was a victim of his pacifist hallucinations, and went to England in the hope of facilitating the beginning of peace negotiations. Hence, he is not a traitor; hence he will not talk; hence, whatever else is said or printed in his name, is false. Ribbentrop's conversation is a beautiful feat of patching things up. The Germans want to cover themselves before Hess speaks and reveals things that might make a great impression in Italy.
>
> Mussolini comforted von Ribbentrop, but afterwards told me that he considers the Hess affair a tremendous blow to the Nazi regime. He added that he was glad of it, because this will have the effect of bringing down German stock, even with the Italians.[22]

Hitler's last concern had been that Hess would reveal his plans to attack Russia, but this was a matter about which he could do nothing and Hess's flight in no way altered his plans. On 12 May Hitler reaffirmed the decision to attack Russia on 22 June.[23] As it happened, Hess did not give away Hitler's planned operation against Russia, and the British interrogator Kirkpatrick had such intellectual contempt for him that he jumped to the incorrect conclusion that Hess did not know. But this oversight made no difference. The British already knew about the impending onslaught in the east, for they had broken the Luftwaffe code, and Churchill had warned Stalin.[24]

The only apparent effect of Hess's flight was the obliteration of his name from all public places. His photograph was to be removed from salerooms, shop windows, streets and public buildings. New books on the N.S.D.A.P. were to be published without pictures or information about him and eventually his name was erased from the Reich's Card Index and from the list of members of the Reich's Leadership Section. Hitler gave orders that he was to be shot if he returned. On 29 May 1941 Hess's office of Deputy Fuehrer ceased to exist and its functions were absorbed by the Party Chancellery under the leadership of Martin Bormann.[25]

Only a few days before, Hess had been a powerful Nazi but now that he was in disgrace there was a flood of derogatory criticism. Bormann, far from regretting the absence of his former superior, wrote to Himmler that Hess's flight was due to the fact that he had an inferiority complex, that he had been treated for impotence even when his son was born, and that he wanted to prove his virility to himself and his wife, to his party and to his people.[26]

Goebbels too was not reluctant to pour scorn on Hess and with great glee and pettiness declared that Hess had become impotent for reasons that were psychological, that he had visited astrologers and mystics with Frau Hess and that they had drunk mixtures before the child was born. After the birth of his son, Hess danced in a manner similar to the birth celebrations of South American Indians. Every Gauleiter was required to send a receptacle enclosing Germanic earth from each Gau to Hess, and the soil was put under a cradle so that the Deputy Fuehrer's son would begin to live on Germanic soil in a symbolic sense. Goebbels himself being Gauleiter of Berlin nearly sent a Berlin paving stone, but in the end decided to send some of the manure from his garden in an official container.[27]

If most Nazi leaders were glad to see Hess go, Hitler was sorry. Goebbels had seen Hitler in tears shortly after Hess's departure, and a few weeks later Mussolini told Ciano that in a conversation he had had with Hitler the latter had spoken about Hess and wept.[28]

There was an atmosphere of black comedy about the whole episode. His secret mission had astonished the British, bewildered the Americans, horrified the Germans, and struck fear into the Russians. It was remarkable to see how a man quite as unintelligent as Hess could make so many clever people run around in circles.

But if Hess's flight appeared to many as a comedy, to Albrecht Haushofer it was a fearful tragedy. When the first news of Hess's escapade was reported, Hitler had said darkly that this venture was due to the subversive influence of Professor Haushofer.[29] On Hitler's orders Albrecht was placed under close arrest and brought to Berchtesgaden. Since 1933 he had been sheltering under the protecting hand of Rudolf Hess, and he was now left with nothing. He knew that when giving an account of his activities to Hitler his life would hang in the balance.

2 Hitler and Albrecht Haushofer: 12 May 1941

ON arrival at the Obersalzberg, Berchtesgaden, on 12 May 1941, Albrecht Haushofer was not even admitted into Hitler's presence. Instead, he was given a pen and paper, under armed guard, and was ordered to make a report for Hitler entitled *English Connections and the Possibility of Utilising Them.* He knew that Hitler had a fair idea as to why Hess had disappeared, and well appreciated that he was writing for his life.

Consequently Albrecht's report was a plausible and convincing mixture of truths, half-truths and camouflage, designed not to implicate any of his friends in the Resistance. In his writing he used phrases and expressions in harmony with Hitler's prejudices for the purpose of clearing himself in Hitler's eyes and of reducing any suspicion. What he wrote did not represent his real belief, which was that Britain would never consider peace talks of any description with Nazi Germany. Nonetheless Albrecht hoped to convince Hitler that in any possible further negotiations with Britain he would be indispensable on account of his numerous English connections.[1]

The circle of English individuals whom I have known very well for years, and whose utilisation on behalf of a German–English understanding in the years from 1934 to 1938 was the core of my activity in England, comprises the following groups and persons:

1. A leading group of younger Conservatives (many of them Scotsmen). Among them are: the Duke of Hamilton – up to the date of his father's death, Lord Clydesdale – Conservative Member of Parliament; the Parliamentary Private Secretary of Neville Chamberlain, Lord Dunglass; the present Under Secretary of State in the Air Ministry, Balfour; the present Under Secretary of State in the Ministry of Education, Lindsay

(National Labour); the present Under Secretary of State in the Ministry for Scotland, Wedderburn.

Close ties link this circle with the Court. The younger brother of the Duke of Hamilton is closely related to the present Queen through his wife; the mother-in-law of the Duke of Hamilton, the Duchess of Northumberland, is the Mistress of the Robes; her brother-in-law, Lord Eustace Percy, was several times a member of the Cabinet and is still today an influential member of the Conservative Party (especially close to former Prime Minister Baldwin). There are close connections between this circle and important groups of the older Conservatives, as for example the Stanley family (Lord Derby, Oliver Stanley) and Astor (the last is owner of *The Times*). The young Astor, likewise a Member of Parliament, was Parliamentary Private Secretary to the former Foreign and Interior Minister, Sir Samuel Hoare, at present English Ambassador in Madrid.

I have known almost all of the persons mentioned for years and from close personal contact. The present Under Secretary of State of the Foreign Office, Butler, also belongs here; in spite of many of his public utterances he is not a follower of Churchill or Eden. Numerous connections lead from most of those named to Lord Halifax, to whom I likewise had personal access.

2. The so-called 'Round Table' circle of younger imperialists (particularly colonial and Empire politicians), whose most important personage was Lord Lothian.

3. A group of the 'Ministerialdirektoren' in the Foreign Office. The most important of these were Strang, the chief of the Central European Department, and O'Malley, the chief of the South Eastern Department and afterwards Minister in Budapest.

There was hardly one of those named who was not at least occasionally in favour of a German–English understanding.

This last statement was a fair point for Albrecht Haushofer to make, in that the persons mentioned wanted to avoid a Second World War, but, contrary to what Albrecht was writing, after the invasion of Poland none of these men would have considered peace talks with the Nazi regime. The report elaborated:

Although most of them in 1939 finally considered that war was inevitable, it was nevertheless reasonable to think of these persons if one thought the moment had come for investigating

the possibility of an inclination to make peace. Therefore when
the Deputy of the Fuehrer, Reich Minister Hess, asked me in
the autumn of 1940 about possibilities of gaining access to
possibly reasonable Englishmen, I suggested two concrete possibilities for establishing contacts. It seemed to me that the
following could be considered for this:
A. Personal contact with Lothian, Hoare, or O'Malley, all three
of whom were accessible in neutral countries.
B. Contact by letter with one of my friends in England. For this
purpose the Duke of Hamilton was considered in the first place,
since my connection with him was so firm and personal that I
could suppose he would understand a letter addressed to him
even if it were formulated in very veiled language.

   Reich Minister Hess decided in favour of the second possibility; I wrote a letter to the Duke of Hamilton at the end of
September 1940 and its despatch to Lisbon was arranged by the
Deputy Fuehrer. I did not learn whether the letter reached the
addressee. The possibilities of its being lost *en route* from Lisbon
to England are not small, after all.

Albrecht now came to the second peace feeler which he had
attempted to put out through Professor Carl Burckhardt:

   Then in April 1941 I received greetings from Switzerland
   from Carl Burckhardt, the former League of Nations Com-
   missioner in Danzig and now Vice President of the International
   Red Cross, whom I had also known well for years. He sent the
   message that he had greetings to pass on to me from someone
   in my old circle of English friends. I should please visit him
   some time in Geneva. Since the possibility existed that these
   greetings were in connection with my letter of last autumn, I
   thought I should again submit the matter to the Deputy of the
   Fuehrer, though with the reservation (as already last autumn)
   that the chances of a serious peace feeler seemed to me to be
   extremely slight. Reich Minister Hess decided that I should go
   to Geneva.

Carl Burckhardt read this report after the war and said that he
did not know any of Albrecht Haushofer's friends. He explained
that he had seen Lord Halifax in London in October 1939 and that
he had often seen the British Consul General in Geneva, mostly in

relation to the treatment of prisoners of war. However Burckhardt
denied that he had summarised the opinions of any British group
in the manner stated by Albrecht Haushofer.[2] Albrecht's report
continued:

> In Geneva I had a long conversaton with Burckhardt on 28
> April. I found him in something of a quandary between his desire
> to support the possibilities of a European peace and the greatest
> concern lest his name might somehow be involved with publicity:
> he expressly asked that what went on be kept strictly secret. In
> consideration of the discretion enjoined upon him he could only
> tell me the following.
>
> A few weeks ago a person well known and respected in
> London, who was close to the leading Conservative and city
> circles, had called on him in Geneva. This person, whose name
> he could not give, though he could vouch for his earnestness,
> had in a rather long conversation expressed the wish of im-
> portant English circles for an examination of the possibilities for
> peace; in search for possible channels my name had been
> mentioned.
>
> I for my part informed Professor Burckhardt that I had to
> expect the same discretion with regard to my name. Should his
> informant in London be willing to come to Switzerland once
> more and should he further be willing to have his name com-
> municated to me in Berlin through confidential channels, so
> that the earnestness of both person and mission could be
> investigated in Germany, then I thought that I, too, could agree
> to taking another trip to Geneva. Professor Burckhardt stated
> that he was willing to act as go-between in this manner: it would
> simply be communicated to England through an entirely safe
> channel that there was a prospect for a trusted representative
> from London, after he himself had given his name, to meet in
> Geneva a German also well known in England, who was in a
> position to bring such communications as there might be to the
> attention of the competent German authorities.
>
> My own conversation with Professor Burckhardt furnished a
> number of important points regarding the substantive part of
> possible peace talks. (Burckhardt has not only been in England
> during the war – for example, he had a long and detailed
> conversation with Halifax – but he also has frequent contact

with the English observer in Geneva, Consul General Livingston, who likewise is one of those Englishmen whom the war does not please.) Burckhardt's general impression of the opinions of the more moderate groups in England can be summarised as follows:
1. The substantive English interest in the areas of eastern and south-eastern Europe (with the exception of Greece) is nominal.
2. No English government that is still capable of action will be able to renounce (the aim of) a restoration of the western European system of states.
3. The colonial question will not present any overwhelming difficulties if the German demand is limited to the old German possessions and if the Italian appetite can be curbed.

All of this, however – and this fact could not be stressed seriously enough – under the assumption, which overshadowed everything else, that a basis of personal confidence could be found between Berlin and London; and this would be as difficult to find as during the Crusades or in the Thirty Years War.

As matters stood, the contest with 'Hitlerism' was being considered by the masses of the English people, too, to be a religious war with all the fanatical psychological consequences of such an attitude. If anyone in London was inclined toward peace, then it was the indigenous portion of the plutocracy, which was able to calculate when it, along with the indigenous British tradition, would be destroyed, whereas the indigenous, mainly Jewish element, had already in large part completed the jump to America and the overseas dominions. It was Burckhardt's own and deepest concern that if the war continued for a considerable length of time every possibility that the reasonable forces in England would force Churchill to make peace would disappear, since by that time the whole power of decision regarding the overseas assets of the Empire would be taken over by the Americans. Once the remainder of the indigenous English upper class had been eliminated, however, it would be impossible to talk sense to Roosevelt and his circle.[3]

Burckhardt, writing to Albrecht Haushofer's assistant, Walter Stubbe, after the war, emphasised that this report misrepresented what he had said, but he omitted to mention what had passed between himself and Albrecht Haushofer. It may be that

Burckhardt did not wish to reveal the precise extent to which he was prepared to act as an intermediary between the Nazi regime and the British.[4]

Hitler read Albrecht's report when he was still uncertain as to how Hess was being received in Britain, and he had no means of checking its truthfulness or accuracy. He thus decided to take no hasty and irrevocable action. Instead he merely gave orders that Haushofer was to be sent to the Prince Albrecht Strasse Gestapo Prison in Berlin, so that he could be interrogated by SS Gruppen-führer Mueller.

In the Gestapo Prison Albrecht was relatively well treated. His father, who had been arrested and then released after a short time, was allowed to visit him. The most unpleasant aspect of his imprisonment was the interrogations by Mueller. Haushofer had nothing in common with the head of the Gestapo. The latter was a coarse, ruthless and brutal man who had an instinctive distrust for a man like Albrecht Haushofer with his finely tuned intellectual mind. Mueller continually accused him of sending Hess to Britain, but was not intelligent enough to unravel the web of Albrecht's subtle activities. In no way was he able to incriminate Albrecht, although he regarded him with loathing and suspicion.[5]

There were other Nazi leaders interested in Albrecht and on 15 May 1941 Heydrich sent the following telegram to Himmler, after discussions with Albrecht's old enemy Gauleiter Bohle, of the Nazi Ausland Organisation:

1. After today's conversation with Gauleiter Bohle, the result of which I am transmitting to you today by courier within the next few hours, I have the profound impression that Rudolf Hess was in a particular measure under the influence of both Haushofer senior and Haushofer junior. Gauleiter Bohle thinks that Haushofer junior in particular influenced Rudolf Hess in his evaluation of British neutrality. He [Bohle] is also convinced that Haushofer junior is well able to supply possibly valuable information. I share this view and I would ask your permission to have Haushofer junior thoroughly interrogated about his knowledge of the matter. In the meantime I shall have his flat and office watched, so that, according to the result of the interrogation, any material found there can be seized. I shall of course once again ask for your views.

The postal and telephone surveillance ordered a few days ago
will be carried out. . . .
As regards Item 1. I shall be glad of an early decision.[6]

This telegram reached Himmler at a time when he was displeased with Heydrich. For some time Heydrich had been coveting
Himmler's position at the head of the S.S. and on Monday 12
May he grilled Himmler's doctor, Kersten, about his treatment of
Hess and only released him when Himmler intervened. Heydrich
knew that Himmler was interested in astrology and particularly
enjoyed helping to imprison astrologers in accordance with Hitler's
orders, in order to spite his senior.[7] Nevertheless it appears that
Himmler gave Heydrich permission to interrogate Albrecht. One
day Heydrich appeared in Albrecht's cell without warning and
asked many questions, which resulted in Albrecht giving a long
talk on the incompetence, inability and stupidity of Ribbentrop.
He may well have convinced Heydrich that Ribbentrop was a
disastrous Foreign Minister. That would not have been too
difficult. However, Heydrich also believed that Albrecht was a
potential traitor.[8] Ribbentrop, who had been described in such
disparaging terms to Hess and Heydrich by Albrecht, was
smouldering with hostility. He sacked Albrecht from his position
in the Foreign Office on 28 May and tried to get him suspended
from his Professorship, but without success, as Himmler refused
to let him be removed.[9] And Himmler had his reasons.

Two months before, Himmler had told his higher S.S. leaders
that the Slav population of Europe would have to be reduced by
thirty million.[10] He was not lacking in enthusiasm for the war
against Russia, but he had a clear sense of self-preservation. He
wished to make peace with Britain, as he did not want to fight a
war on two fronts. He wanted to keep alive anyone who might help
him to make such a peace behind Hitler's back, as he knew that the
British would not contemplate peace talks with Hitler.[11] And he
knew about Albrecht Haushofer. He knew about him through
Volksdeutsch work, through reading his reports after his missions
to Czechoslovakia and Japan and his memorandum on the possibilities of a German–English peace, and through examining the
recent report which Albrecht had written about the utilisation of
his English acquaintances. So when Lorenz of the S.S. recommended to Himmler after Hess's flight that it was the right moment

to finish off all the Haushofers, Himmler replied that he did not think it would be necessary yet.[12] For the time being Himmler abstrained from having Albrecht shot, in case he might prove potentially useful.

Nobody understood the position better than Albrecht, who wrote to his parents from the Gestapo prison on 7 July 1941:

> ... I know exactly that at present I am a small beetle which has been turned on its back by an unexpected and unforeseeable gust of wind, and which realises that it cannot rise to its feet by its own strength – and now, with some knowledge of two-legged creatures, does not entertain great illusions regarding its future. . . .
>
> I suppose you are now going to the Alpine pasture. My regards to the mountains! Sometime I shall, no doubt, see them again – and, if I am lucky, I shall be able to conclude my existence as a hermit on the Partnachalm. . . .[13]

While in prison Albrecht had been writing, with a sense of impending doom, a play called *The Macedonians*, in which the dictator Alexander was cast as a person with the characteristics of Hitler. He put these words into the mouth of Alexander's old teacher Aristotle:

> When Alexander exceeded all norms I knew that he would destroy himself and not only himself. . . . They will all thirst; they will fight, go berserk; they will think they are doing it for the Empire, for glory and power. But all that has passed is only a chase for the souls lost in the intoxication of Alexander's dreams. . . .[14]

By the end of May 1941 Albrecht had no more dilemmas as to what he should do. There was only one problem, and that was how to survive. Heydrich and Mueller had sent reports on him to Hitler which proved nothing against him, but which recommended that he should be kept in prison. For a month Hitler hesitated and then decided that he should be released.[15] The war against Russia had been launched, and no doubt Hitler intended to keep Albrecht alive for possible future dealings with Britain, once Russia had been overrun.

At any rate, in July 1941 after eight weeks, imprisonment Albrecht was released; an individual under the suspicious watch

of the Gestapo. It had become clear to the entire Nazi High
Command, to Mueller and Heydrich in particular, that Albrecht
Haushofer was not a good Nazi. He had English friends; he hated
the war; he had written that the British regarded Ribbentrop as
being in large part responsible for it and that they thought of
Hitler as 'Satan's representative on earth'. Albrecht had written
these things with too much enthusiasm, as though he believed
what the British had been saying.

Heydrich and Mueller were determined to liquidate Albrecht
Haushofer sooner or later. If they could not get him for being a
traitor they would get him for being partly Jewish. Albrecht's life
was hanging by a thread.

3 The Peace Memorandum: November 1941

IT had been hoped by the members of the Resistance in the Wednesday Society that Albrecht could soon go back and see Burckhardt in Switzerland, but after Hess's flight Hassell wrote that all possibility of advancing their cause through Haushofer was now gone.[1] Albrecht had emerged from the Gestapo prison in Berlin as a man in too vulnerable a position; in Nazi circles he had become a subject of the utmost suspicion. Previously Hess's authority had enabled him to travel abroad, but with Hess's disappearance any possibility of being despatched on foreign missions, or of escaping from Germany had disappeared. All that Albrecht had left to him was his post as Professor at the University of Berlin.

His father was unable to help him because he himself was out of favour with the Nazi regime after Hess's flight. This fact was emphasised by Martin Bormann in a letter dated 17 June 1942 from the Fuehrer's Headquarters to Rosenberg.

> I have been informed that Professor Dr Karl Haushofer was very prominently featured in the last number of the National Socialist Monthly magazine. It was on the occasion of a book review of his work on war geopolitics, in which the reviewer came to the conclusion that this book must by no means be overlooked.
>
> I am of the opinion that Professor Karl Haushofer and his son, Professor Albrecht Haushofer, should no longer be given any publicity and I would be thankful if you, too, would join in this decision. I would request information as to your position and conclusion in this matter.[2]

After Hess's flight Albrecht knew that he owed his survival to the fact that Hitler and Himmler had no wish for the time being to destroy an expert who might be able to formulate peace plans with

Britain. Consequently Albrecht wrote *Thoughts on a Peace Plan*[3]
for Hitler's consumption in November 1941, which was submitted
to Weizsaecker, the Secretary of State of the Ministry for Foreign
Affairs, who was a friend of his. It can safely be assumed that
Weizsaecker ensured that the document reached Hitler without it
being seen or blocked by Foreign Minister Ribbentrop, who
had become Albrecht's dedicated enemy.

The document, as one would expect, was not a model of social
democratic thought. The writing can hardly be taken to represent
what Albrecht really believed, which was that Germany should
have predominance only in Central Europe, where there were large
enclaves of Germans or of German-speaking citizens. It was his
desire that all other regions then occupied by German armed
forces should have autonomy,[4] and that German armed forces
should withdraw. It was impossible, however, to change Hitler's
belief that all Nazi gains should be held, that the conquered
peoples should be exploited and those who were no longer useful
should perish. Albrecht knew that if he wrote expressing his
personal views he would soon face a firing squad. In September
1940 he had written documents highly critical of the official Nazi
line and had got away with it. After his imprisonment he had to
try to blend more closely with his surroundings.

Even so his peace memorandum had more in common with
Resistance peace plans than with the Nazi line. By late 1941, when
he was writing, German troops had penetrated deep into Russia,
had occupied Norway, the Baltic States, the Low Countries,
France, Greece, east and south-eastern Europe including all the
countries of the Danube Basin. Even the Eastern Mediterranean
and large parts of North Africa were under German control.
Albrecht, far from maintaining that Germany could hold on to
these gains, was making proposals which would have involved
withdrawal and the establishment of a German hegemony only in
Central and East Europe. His suggestions were only slightly more
ambitious than the Resistance peace plans of Ulrich von Hassell,
written in February 1940, and of Goerdeler, written in May 1941.
Like Hassell and Goerdeler, Albrecht was of the view that
Germany's 1914 frontiers should be accepted as the blueprint for
further frontier revisions.[5]

Albrecht's memorandum was based on the premise that a
future world peace would have to be negotiated and that the war

could not be totally won by either side. He therefore put forward his four basic ideas: first, that the British–American alliance was economically and militarily unassailable; second, that Japan could not successfully monopolise control over Greater East Asia; third, that Russia with its nucleus on the Volga or in the Urals could not be forcibly subjugated any more than China could be; and fourth, that Germany's forces were sufficient to prevent military defeat on European soil and perhaps on Near Asian and North African soil, so that the naval powers of Britain and the U.S.A. would have to recognise Germany's preferential continental position.

His proposals advocated that Austria and the Sudetenland should remain within the Reich, while Germany's western frontiers were to be settled by negotiation. In the east he desired the creation of buffer states and suggested that the western frontiers of Russia should be under German control. Lastly he recommended that there should be an all-European responsibility for African colonisation and that Germany should acquire colonies, so that she might obtain raw materials and assist in economic development.[6]

His very lengthy document had no effect on practical politics, because it contained suggestions which were as unacceptable to Hitler as they were to everybody else. Nonetheless, it did help to keep him alive for a considerable period, as Hitler took a decided interest.

It appears that Hitler had not only read Albrecht's peace memorandum, but was receiving information about him from S.S. Gruppenführer Mueller and Heydrich. One of Albrecht's students, Frau Irmegard Schnuhr, had married a high-ranking S.S. man and came into contact with Nazi circles before she separated from her husband. She had come to detest the Nazi regime and became Albrecht's assistant. One day Mueller saw her and asked her to report on Haushofer's acquaintances, as well as on what he had said about the Hess case and his English friends. She was asked to make monthly reports on him. Frau Schnuhr accepted and told Albrecht, who saw to it that she gave carefully worded answers to the Gestapo.[7] She said that she performed this job in the belief that, had she refused, someone else less sympathetic to Albrecht would have continued to keep watch on him. Being under surveillance, Albrecht acted very cautiously and was therefore of little practical use to the Resistance. As Frau Schnuhr said of him, 'Finding himself in opposition he acted too timidly to have any

real effect. At every point he would have preferred a compromise
if that had been possible.'[8]

In December 1941 she was summoned by Hitler not long after
the U.S.A. had declared war on Germany. Hitler wanted to know
who Albrecht's acquaintances were and said that he had a 'special
interest' in Albrecht and was interested to learn whether he thought
there was a possibility of making peace with Britain. In February
1942 she was again called before Hitler and was asked the same
questions. She told him that Albrecht's views were that to the best
of his knowledge neither Britain nor Germany had any intention
of putting out a peace feeler. However, even if Hitler did desire
to negotiate with Britain, the very fact that the German Foreign
Minister was Ribbentrop would make it impossible for any
negotiations to get off the ground. Hitler told her that Albrecht
Haushofer was not as clever as he thought he was, and that it
would be easy to sack Ribbentrop if the British first sacked their
Foreign Minister, Anthony Eden.[9]

Frau Schnuhr asked Hitler whether he wanted to see Albrecht
Haushofer and Hitler replied that he would not dream of it, the
outcome of the war was going to be settled on the battlefield, and
he indicated that Albrecht Haushofer was only a *mischling*, a half-
breed.[10] Frau Schnuhr had the impression that Hitler, whilst
being fundamentally suspicious of Albrecht, wished to keep him
available should peace negotiations with Britain ever become a
possibility. Such thoughts almost certainly evaporated as the
months passed, and by the time of the crushing German defeats
at Stalingrad and El Alamein Hitler may well have had no further
use for Albrecht Haushofer.

However Albrecht had learnt that Himmler, of all people, also
had a decided interest in keeping him alive. Professor Rolf
Italiaander wrote:

> Superficial knowledge of Albrecht Haushofer may lead to the
> assumption that he was a cold, even icy, calculating intellectual.
> However, each intensive discussion soon made it clear that he
> was endowed with a deep kindness of heart and warmhearted-
> ness. These qualities combined with much melancholy were so
> strong that, in order to avoid becoming a victim of senti-
> mentality, he had to clothe himself, in his political tasks, in ice-
> cold sarcasm. Had he not done so, he would have been eliminated

much sooner by his protagonist Himmler, whom he hated passionately.[11]

It was not only Hitler and Hess who wanted to make peace with Britain. Himmler, the Reichsführer S.S., had taken up the idea of making peace overtures precisely where Hess had left off, the difference being that Himmler, unlike Hess, had no affection for Hitler. Himmler realised that the British would not make peace with Hitler in any circumstances, and he was therefore ready to enter into treacherous negotiations behind Hitler's back. Himmler's vanity was such that he thought that the British might regard him as being preferable to Hitler.

One of Himmler's neighbours on the Tegernsee, Munich, was Carl Langbehn, a friendly acquaintance of Albrecht Haushofer, a man who had gained entry to Admiral Canaris's Abwehr which made it easy for him to travel abroad. Himmler thought that Langbehn might be useful to him in trying to open up a channel to the British. Following Hess's example of sending Albrecht Haushofer to Switzerland, Himmler also sent Langbehn to Professor Burckhardt.

Langbehn was a curious character and like Albrecht Haushofer had been playing a double game, working for the Resistance and also for Himmler. On Sunday 17 August 1941, Langbehn, representing Himmler or the Resistance and quite possibly both, saw Professor Burckhardt in Geneva. As Gerald Reitlinger expressed it, Langbehn explored the possibilities of Britain making peace with a Hitlerless but not Himmlerless Germany.[12] Himmler apparently hated having to fight a war on two fronts especially after the entry of the U.S.A. into the war. On 9 April 1942, Ciano recorded in his diary that Himmler wanted a compromise peace, and it seemed that Himmlers plans for expansion into Russia were based on his hope of coming to an understanding with the West.[13]

All this had its importance for Albrecht Haushofer, who knew that for the time being Himmler and the S.S. might leave him alone if he was really cautious. Although he was under surveillance he was still collaborating with three important circles of the Resistance. He often attended the Wednesday Society, and there continued to meet with such members of the Resistance as General Beck, Popitz, Hassell and Jessen. They had contact with the generals in the Resistance including Witzleben, Hoepner, Olbricht and Wagner. Yet these military plotters remained hesitant.[14]

Albrecht also had contact with the Kreisau Circle. In the autumn of 1941, he lectured to those who surrounded Count Helmuth von Moltke, Count Peter Yorck von Wartenburg, Adam von Trott zu Solz and Stauffenberg on Moltke's estate at Kreisau. The Kreisau Circle had feelers of Resistance in the churches, in the Abwehr, in the military, and it was assisted by planners such as Albrecht Haushofer and Count Fritz Schulenburg, the Deputy Police President of Berlin.[15]

Fritz Schulenburg also worked in the Reich Office for Space Research, with Albrecht as geographical expert, and occasionally with Popitz. The three of them co-operated in the preparation of drafts for the internal reorganisation of Germany, which was to be of use to a non-Nazi German government, once Hitler had been destroyed. In those drafts Albrecht envisaged Germany's 1914 frontiers as a basis for the Reich once Nazism had gone.[16]

Strangely enough, Albrecht, who has been described as the 'darkest horse' of the German Resistance to Hitler, also had loose connections with the Rote Kapelle or Red Orchestra, a Communist Resistance movement in Germany. This organisation, through the use of more than a hundred short-wave transmitters, was supplying secret information to Russia. Its leader was Harro Schulze-Boysen, a grandson of Admiral von Tirpitz, who had through family influence got himself installed in an important position in the Luftwaffe Intelligence Service under Goering. One of Schulze-Boysen's most loyal adherents was Horst Heilman who had been a promising student of Albrecht's at the University of Berlin. Albrecht had met Schulze-Boysen through Rainer Hildebrandt and Horst Heilman, and they struck up a friendly relationship. The two men were representatives of different Resistance movements. Schulze-Boysen was working for the military defeat and economic collapse of Germany, whilst Albrecht was hoping to stir the hesitating generals to action against Hitler. Schulze-Boysen's friends were mostly of Communist persuasion, Albrecht's patriotic Germans.

Both Albrecht and Schulze-Boysen agreed that Hitler had removed the inferiority complexes which had overcome the German nation after the First World War, by appealing to their most primitive traits, and they both expected that the Russians would have advanced into the heart of Europe by the end of the war. But while Schulze-Boysen hoped for German–Russian co-operation, Albrecht expected the Russians to be hostile to a European standard of life which was higher than their own.

Although Albrecht had talks with Schulze-Boysen he was in no way involved in the latter's actions. But he did wish to know about the activities of his militant students such as Horst Heilman, so that if their activities were discovered he would not be implicated. He felt he was in far too vulnerable a position to take risks, and as his brother Heinz said of him, Albrecht's attitude of self-defence was very necessary to him as he did not possess the brute courage of a soldier. Accordingly Albrecht warned Schulze-Boysen and Horst Heilman that security and discretion were vital as there were thousands of Gestapo agents about, whose activities were not to be disregarded. Notwithstanding this advice, in August 1942 more than a hundred persons connected with the Rote Kapelle were arrested on the instructions of Himmler, who found it convenient to humiliate Goering by arresting a nest of conspirators in the Air Ministry. Schulze-Boysen and Horst Heilman were hanged as well as an unknown number of others.[17]

It was a depressing time for Albrecht. Three of his favourite students, Wolfgang Hoffman, Moser and Kinzler had been killed at the front. Another student, Paul Meller, was poisoned in a concentration camp, and Albrecht's girl-friend, who had parted from him some years previously and with whom he had never lost touch, died at Engadin in Switzerland.[18] He was always under surveillance by the Gestapo.[19] Albrecht, with his part-Jewish ancestry and his fingers in a number of anti-Hitler pies, was an obvious candidate for one of Himmler's extermination lists. But his name was omitted, part-Jewish or not, since Himmler kept anybody alive who might be of possible use to him.

Heydrich and Mueller had no such feelings about him. Heydrich was just as brutal as Mueller but he was more shrewd. He correctly guessed that Albrecht's assistant, Frau Schnuhr, was being of more assistance to Albrecht than to Mueller and Hitler. On one occasion Heydrich summoned her, and told her, with menaces, that he saw through her game and that she was not performing her duties as Hitler would have wished. No doubt he passed on his suspicions to Mueller.[20]

Mueller summoned Albrecht in to the grim surroundings of the Gestapo Headquarters on one occasion. He merely wished to tell

Albrecht how often he might write and lecture for the public. After this interview Albrecht found that his map briefcase, left in the anteroom, had in the interval been filled with communist pamphlets by some malicious person. Knowing that it might cost him his life to be found with them, he rapidly discarded them to learn that the precaution had not been in vain. He was unsuccessfully searched on his way out of the Gestapo Headquarters. It had been Mueller's way of playing a little joke.[21]

Hildebrandt wrote that the activities of Heydrich and Mueller were constantly present in Albrecht's mind, like a recurring nightmare which a man would long to forget. Whenever the telephone rang, whenever he went out, whenever he saw a friend the thought of Heydrich and Mueller was never far away. He loathed being a shadowed man.[22]

In April 1942 Albrecht heard from Frau Schnuhr that an S.S. man called Wilke had told her that Heydrich's staff was making plans for taking over Himmler's command forcibly. Armed with this knowledge Albrecht decided to do Heydrich a bad turn. He told Langbehn to report the matter to Himmler, which was done, and Himmler thanked Langbehn.[23] Himmler had been instrumental in recommending to Hitler that Heydrich should be appointed as Deputy Protector of Bohemia and Moravia, and it may be taken for granted that he took every precaution to ensure that Heydrich's presence remained as far removed from his own as possible. On 29 May 1942 Jan Kubiš and Josef Gabčík of the Free Czechoslovak Forces saw to it that Heydrich was blown up in his car by a bomb. At the end of the first week in June Heydrich died from his wounds, and shortly afterwards the S.S. murdered virtually the entire population of the small Czech village of Lidice.

Heydrich was dead but even so this fresh example of Nazi brutality can hardly have done anything to quieten Albrecht's apprehensions about his own future.

4 Himmler's Treachery and the July Plot: 1943-4

In 1943, the military plotters in the Resistance had still made no headway with their plans to remove Hitler. Albrecht was certain that the formula of unconditional surrender propounded by the Allies in January 1943 had acted as a dampening influence on the activities of the wavering Resistance generals.[1] In the summer he wrote a note to a friend, 'It is now either too late or too early for a successful action. What I could achieve is being ignored by those who seem to be able to do everything much better. Thus I sit in my home mountains and wait. I wait, in contrast to most of my coevals and contemporaries, but with the same helplessness in the face of the stream of events.'[2] Yet one of his acquaintances, whose thoughts were developing along a dangerous track, did not want to wait. This man was Langbehn, and Langbehn argued that there could be no *coup d'état* carried out against Himmler and the S.S.[3]

Langbehn had told Popitz and Albrecht Haushofer that in November 1941, after the failure before Moscow, Himmler and some senior S.S. officers had sensed defeat, had thought that Himmler could manage matters better than Hitler and had entertained the idea of forcibly changing the system. After the German defeats at Stalingrad and El Alamein Langbehn encouraged S.S. General Karl Wolff (Himmler's A.D.C.) to believe that Hitler would have to be 'written off' so that Himmler could save the Third Reich. Wolff thought that Himmler and the Waffen S.S. might be amenable to the idea of making a putsch in co-operation with army units under Himmler's control.[4]

Langbehn saw in this planned putsch a possibility of dispensing with Hitler and Himmler one by one. First, with Himmler's co-operation, the Resistance would destroy Hitler, and then, as soon as the army had reorganised, the Resistance would doublecross Himmler, kill him, take over the S.S. and disband it. Thereafter

peace negotiations would be instituted with the Allies. Thus it
was that a desperate plan was concocted.[5]

In principle Albrecht Haushofer was not against this stratagem.
He told his assistant, Walter Stubbe, that Germany could only be
freed by an act of violence carried out by the army. The war was
being lost, and in order to prevent a repetition of the 'stab in the
back' legend, it was important that the blame for any putsch should
be laid on Himmler and the S.S.[6] Naturally he hoped that Hitler
and Himmler would be knocked down like ninepins, but he did
not expect matters to take such a course. Yet, according to Rainer
Hildebrandt and H. W. Stahmer, Albrecht actively encouraged
Popitz to negotiate with Himmler through the medium of Lange-
behn, Himmler's solicitor.[7]

Langbehn considered himself in a good tactical position to
engage in this risky game. With the approval of Himmler and the
S.D., Langbehn had in December 1942 met a British official in
Zürich and Professor Bruce Hopper of the O.S.S. (U.S. Secret
Service) in Stockholm, in order to explore the chances of peace
negotiations.[8] He was periodically in touch with Himmler, and in
May 1943 he informed the military leaders of the Resistance that
Himmler was psychologically ready to be approached by those in
the opposition who wanted to play off Himmler and the S.S. against
the Hitler–Bormann clique.[9]

There were a considerable number of people in the Resistance
who liked this plan, including General Beck, General Olbricht,
Field Marshal Witzleben and General von Tresckow, as well as
Langbehn, Popitz, Albrecht Haushofer, Jessen and Planck. The
head of the Berlin Police, Count Helldorf, and the head of the
Criminal Police, General Nebe, who were both in the S.S. and
had dubious Resistance records, were also in favour of the idea.
Hassell and Goerdeler were in the secret and apparently did not
oppose it, although they had misgivings.[10] In May 1943 Langbehn
tried to arrange a Himmler–Popitz meeting through S.S. General
Karl Wolff. Langbehn explained to Wolff that with Hitler the
war could not be won, that a tolerable peace could be obtained for
Germany however with a Reich government of reliable persons
such as Himmler and Popitz, and that Hitler would be given an
'honourable position in retirement'. Wolff said that a reply from
Himmler would be forthcoming.[11]

Shortly afterwards Popitz and Langbehn heard from Field

Marshal von Bock's army group in Russia, through General von Tresckow that Bock was prepared to participate in a revolt if the putsch had Himmler's support.[12] Tresckow encouraged Popitz and told Langbehn to 'swallow the bitter pill and go into the lion's den'.[13] On 21 August Langbehn was informed by Wolff that Himmler would see Popitz in his office on 26 August.[14]

Himmler knew exactly why Langbehn was trying to arrange such a meeting, as he revealed a year later at Posen on 3 August 1944, in his speech before Bormann, Goebbels and the Gauleiters on the antecedents of the July Plot.

> Now there was another clue. An unusual man, a State Minister, Popitz, tried for some months to get into touch with me. He let it be known through a middleman that he wanted an urgent interview with me. We let this middleman chatter, we let him talk, and this is more or less what he said. Yes, it was of course necessary that the war should end, we must make terms of peace with England – just as the opinion is today – and the first requisite was that the Fuehrer must be removed at once and relegated by the opposition to an honorary president's post. His group was quite certain that this plan could not be carried out against the S.S. They therefore hoped, since I was an understanding and responsible German, that I would not interfere – only for Germany, of course, and in God's name no self-seeking matter.
>
> As soon as I was informed of the plot I went to the Fuehrer and said, 'I will kill the rascal! Such an unblushing thing to put an idea of this kind into my head, of all people's!' But the Fuehrer laughed and said: 'Oh no, if this is what he really intends you will not kill him, you will listen to him. Let him come and see you. It might be interesting, and if he says the same thing as at the first interview then you can arrest him. . . .'[15]

However, Himmler had given an entirely different impression to Popitz on 26 August 1943 at the Reich Ministry of the Interior, where he and Popitz had a serious discussion while Langbehn and Wolff waited in the anteroom outside. Popitz declared that the war situation was critical and that the Fuehrer, for his own sake, should be relieved of the many heavy responsibilities which he carried. The western allies would never negotiate peace with

Hitler and there could be no more appropriate person to supersede him than Himmler who could take firm action to save the Reich. Himmler listened and was very interested. Popitz was given to understand that, far from showing disapproval, Himmler was not against the proposals and found them somewhat appealing.[16]

Afterwards Popitz was informed by Wolff that the discussions were to be continued and that Langbehn and Field Marshall Witzleben were also to take part. A few days later Popitz told a friend that he had said things to Himmler which might cost him his head – if Himmler wanted it.[17] But at present Himmler did not want to arrest Popitz, nor did he wish to be too closely involved with the plan of the Resistance generals to destroy Hitler. Himmler liked to encircle his victims and render them defenceless before he struck them down, and Hitler was not defenceless. Himmler was content to wait in the hope that the Resistance would do his dirty work for him. Once done, he could thrust Bormann and Goering to one side, become Fuehrer, and take the credit with the German people for killing off those in the Resistance who could not be used. He was willing to play a double game until he saw which turn events were going to take.[18]

Albrecht Haushofer must have watched these machinations with dread, because the Resistance was operating from a position of extreme weakness. If Himmler chose to, he could take action against them at any time, and he was not such an easy man to outwit as Hess. Albrecht may well have feared that Langbehn and Popitz had insufficiently appreciated that in the art of playing off one group against another, in the doublecross and double doublecross of power politics, Himmler was equalled only by Hitler.

Hitler had advised Himmler to see Popitz for a second time, but the second interview did not materialise because Himmler's double dealing was very nearly discovered by Hitler. Himmler had been dubious about his own acceptability to the western allies as a peace negotiator in the event of Hitler's liquidation; like Hess before him, however, he hoped that the British could be brought round to his way of thinking and to this end he sent Langbehn to Switzerland yet again to make enquiries. Langbehn made contact with British and American Intelligence officers in Berne, and a certain allied agency sent a telegram to London to the effect that Himmler's lawyer had arrived to make a peace initiative. This telegram was decoded by the Abwehr and the S.D., and it is thought that it was Mueller who forwarded the telegram to Bormann and Hitler.[19]

As soon as he learnt that Hitler knew about Langbehn's trip to Switzerland, Himmler had Langbehn arrested for the sake of his own skin. When he was summoned to Hitler and asked what the telegram meant, Himmler naturally lied and denied all knowledge of peace negotiations, saying that the telegram must have been sent behind his back. Hitler was so dependent on Himmler that he accepted this 'unblushing' explanation, but from then on Himmler was forced to sit tight and watch carefully so as to avoid falling under suspicion.[20]

Langbehn was sent to Sachsenhausen Concentration Camp, but no efforts were made to bring him to trial: that would not have been in Himmler's interests. Instead he was subjected to endless interrogations by Leo Lange of the Gestapo, who admitted in June 1944 that strictly speaking Popitz ought to have been interviewed as well, but it was much too difficult.[21] By this he meant that he was not going to risk being liquidated by Himmler, simply by asking too many questions. In time Himmler discovered that Langbehn had sought to doublecross him on behalf of the Resistance, and he first tortured and then executed him.

Himmler had been keeping his options open. He had a good reason for wanting to keep Albrecht Haushofer alive, although he was having him watched. If the Resistance were to eliminate Hitler and thereby destroy an obvious obstacle to peace negotiations, resisters like Albrecht Haushofer and Dohnanyi, the senior Abwehr official who were believed to have connections in Britain and the U.S.A. could be utilised as middlemen in a bid for peace with Britain.[22] The only times that Himmler acted against the Resistance, prior to the July Plot, were when he suspected that Hitler had learnt about its activities from other sources. He took good care to keep up his pretence of loyalty.

By late 1943 Haushofer had lost all hope of a successful *coup d'état*. The plan to play off Himmler against Hitler had not worked to any satisfactory extent, and he believed it was now too late to eliminate Hitler. He felt that Nazism must burn itself out, and that there was no sense in the Resistance destroying Hitler only to be held responsible for Hitler's war. By 1944 he was opposed to any attempt on Hitler's life, because with or without Hitler Germany no longer had a card to offer her enemies in peace negotiations, as she had had in 1942.[23] He probably appreciated that if the Resistance did kill Hitler it would not be the Stauffenbergs and Haushofers who would gain, but the Himmlers and Muellers. Himmler was chief of the S.S., of the S.D., of K.R.I.P.O. and S.C.H.U.P.O., of the Ministry of the Interior, and had more than 500,000 S.S. men under his personal command who were ready to obey him unconditionally at any time, while Mueller's Gestapo, being subordinate to Himmler, had spread its tentacles into every town. Even if the Resistance did kill Hitler it was inconceivable that it could have withstood the savage counter-attack from Himmler's S.S. and Mueller's Gestapo, which were poised to strike.

Most members of the Resistance, like Albrecht Haushofer, were spending much of their time in trying to stay alive, and on 20 July 1944 when the bomb planted by Stauffenberg exploded at Rastenburg, there was not a single member of the Resistance who was prepared to check on whether Hitler was dead. Later that day Popitz was in Albrecht Haushofers's study; together they heard Hitler's grating voice over the radio saying that an attempt had been made on his life, and that an accounting would be given such as National Socialists were wont to give.[24] Popitz was arrested the following day and Himmler, newly appointed by Hitler as Commander-in-Chief of the replacement army, took ruthless measures to arrest all those circles of the Resistance about which he had previously known so much. It is reasonable to assume that Himmler was most disappointed that Stauffenberg's bomb had failed to do its work.

Albrecht knew that he was in imminent danger of arrest, partly because he knew about Himmler's treacherous dealings with Popitz and Langbehn, and partly because Himmler wanted to have an expert who could write and speak perfect English and was adept at drafting peace plans. In any case Albrecht's connections with the Resistance were being rapidly discovered.

Kaltenbrunner, who had taken over Heydrich's command at the head of the S.D., investigated the Wednesday Society's resistance activities, and Albrecht's name was mentioned in his reports of 25 July and 1 August 1944.[25] The Resistance plan for the reorganisation of the Reich, which had been written by Albrecht Haushofer and Fritz Schulenburg also fell into Himmler's hands, and he is said to have been much impressed.[26]

Fearing the worst, Albrecht went into hiding, and on 25 July

1944 left Berlin, travelling to his father's alpine hut at Partnachalm in Bavaria. He suspected that Himmler had already sent the Gestapo after him, and arrived only to discover that the Gestapo had arrested his father a few hours earlier, and had taken him to Dachau Concentration Camp. He found to his relief that his mother was still free. After a brief stay with her he fled again, this time to the house of his brother Heinz on the Ammersee. Heinz met him for a hurried discussion and told him that the Gestapo had been searching everywhere. There was little time to waste, and Albrecht continued his flight.

He was sheltered by the sisters of a convent for a night and then was sent on to stay with a doctor. The Gestapo were following close on his heels. They arrested his brother Heinz on his return to his job as an agriculturist in Vienna, and also Albrecht's sister-in-law and nephew, and the Mother Superior of the convent. They reached the doctor's house and Albrecht escaped into the woods with only seconds to spare. The doctor, his father and his wife were arrested. Albrecht was free, but his world was rapidly collapsing around him.[27]

5 Hunted by the Gestapo: Moabit Prison 1944-5

ONE day early in September 1944 Frau Zahler, who lived in a mountain chalet near Partenkirchen in the Bavarian Alps, heard a knock at the door. She had been a friend of the Haushofer family, and was surprised to find a dusty, tired and bearded man, whom she recognised as Albrecht Haushofer. She agreed to hide him. Her guest had hardly eaten for two days, had narrowly escaped being captured by the Gestapo in the forest, and was greatly relieved to be given shelter. That night he and Frau Zahler listened to the English radio, and heard that thousands of Germans were being sought by the Gestapo as a result of the July Plot, and that within weeks they would be freed by the Western Allied advance. Albrecht found it hard to decide whether he should try to escape to Switzerland across the strictly guarded border or whether he should lie low until the arrival of the British or the Americans. He decided to stay.

However, the British and Americans did not come: the Gestapo came instead. On 7 December Frau Zahler answered the door, and three Gestapo agents who were searching for Albrecht entered. They could find no one and were about to depart, when one of them decided to make a final examination before leaving. He climbed the ladder into the hayloft and gazed around. It was a cold winter's day and suddenly he noticed a column of vapour rising from the hay. He called the other Gestapo agents, and they burrowed down and found Albrecht buried beneath. Frau Zahler saw them bring him down from the hayloft with an expression of despair written all over his face. They took him and Frau Zahler to Munich Prison; Albrecht was particularly unhappy that she had been arrested as well. He told her that nothing would happen to her, a statement which turned out to be correct.[1]

Late on the evening of 9 December the Gestapo drove their newly acquired prisoner all the way from Munich to Moabit

Prison in the Lehrterstrasse, Berlin. It was a star-shaped building with several wings, containing in all some 550 cells joined together by a control tower, and supervised by the S.S. Sonder Commando. After the July Plot the R.S.H.A. (the Reich Security Main Office) under the overall charge of Himmler, had established the Sonder-commission on 20 July under Mueller, so that detailed investigations into the conspiracy could be made. Himmler and Mueller were working hand in glove, and as the Prince Albrechtstrasse Prison was not large enough to hold all resistance suspects, the Lehrterstrasse Prison of Moabit situated one mile and a half away was used as an annexe.²

Immediately after his arrival at the Lehrterstrasse Prison on 10 December Haushofer was taken to the Gestapo Headquarters at the Prince Albrechtstrasse Prison. There he was seen, quite by chance, by another prisoner, Prince Ernst August, who had been arrested on the Russian front under suspicion of having collaborated with the Resistance. Ernst August was sitting in the office of the Gestapo interrogator, when another Gestapo officer burst into the room with the exclamation, 'We have got him'. He said that they had driven all night from Munich and that the prisoner was in the next room. Both Gestapo agents went to look through the door at their prisoner, and when their backs were turned Prince Ernst August had time to raise himself from his seat and take a quick look at the written report which had been laid on the desk. It was entitled *Albrecht Haushofer*.

After a while Ernst August was taken into the next room and left there in the presence of a secretary. On entering he saw a man in a most dejected state. Slumped on a bench was a bowed figure, dressed in an old green hunting coat, with hair down to his shoulders and flowing beard, his elbows resting on his knees and his hands, which were manacled, hanging towards the ground. Written on the name card hanging around his neck were the words 'Albrecht Haushofer'.

The Gestapo guard who led Ernst August away told him, 'You have seen nothing – remember that. If anybody asks you, you saw nobody at all.' Ernst August replied, 'But I think I know that man. I have heard that he is a great friend of Ribbentrop.' He had a faint hope that he might be able to say something to help the drawn and bedraggled prisoner whom he had just seen. The Gestapo guard answered, 'No, he is one of the most dangerous traitors and

criminals alive. Remember you did not see anyone.' Evidently the
Gestapo were treating Albrecht as a very important prisoner.[3]

During the following days and months Albrecht was interrogated
constantly. His connections with the Resistance were established
beyond doubt. Dr Goerdeler had broken down under torture and
had disclosed the nature of the close association between Albrecht,
Popitz and Langbehn,[4] and whatever Albrecht might say there was
no adequate excuse to be given for his flight from Berlin after the
July Plot.[5] When Albrecht saw his brother Heinz after an interrogation he gave him the thumbs down sign.[6]

It was amazing that the Gestapo did not bring him to trial before
the Nazi Judge Freisler, and have him executed without delay. As
always the Gestapo had their reasons, which gradually became
evident to Albrecht's fellow prisoners. Albrecht remarked to them
that he had been taken to the Prince Albrechtstrasse Prison to state
his views on the possibility of a quick armistice, and that he had
taken this opportunity of telling his interrogators about the
disastrous mistakes of Ribbentrop. One Gestapo agent had said to
him, 'What a pity they did not listen to you',[7] and Albrecht said
to his fellow prisoners in the air raid shelter of Moabit Prison, 'I
would like to risk one more stake – and I can'.[8] He was almost certainly trying to present himself as an indispensable peace negotiator
with the Western Allies on account of his connections with Britain.

Albrecht once bitterly told the other prisoners that he had two
fears, that of the Rollcommando or Extermination Squad, and that
of being compelled to become Hitler's last Foreign Minister.[9] It is
of interest that in Albrecht's play *Sulla* the dictator orders the
Greek sage Zosias to assume office, and even under threat of death
Zosias refuses.[10] Perhaps Albrecht pictured himself in a role
similar to that of Zosias. If so it appears that Albrecht was given a
misleading impression, for the one man amongst the Nazi leadership who was keeping him available for possible use was Himmler
rather than Hitler.

Himmler knew that he would have to tread warily before making
any peace overtures to the west through imprisoned members of
the Resistance, in case Hitler might find out.[11] He well knew that
it was Hitler's policy to execute everyone connected with the
Resistance. So Himmler ensured that when the Gestapo caught
Albrecht Haushofer they would be suitably discreet, and for this
reason Prince Ernst August had been ordered to keep quiet about

what he had or had not seen. It was convenient for Himmler to have Albrecht Haushofer within his clutches, because less was known about him than about Langbehn and Popitz (the last of whom was under sentence of death). Besides, Himmler felt that he could trust a man when he was surrounded by armed S.S. men and could be taken out and shot if there were the slightest signs of non-co-operation.

In despair Albrecht wrote a poem *On the Threshold* indicating that even suicide might be preferable to his present existence, though he did not allow himself to entertain such thoughts for long:

> The means for leaving this existence
> I have tested them by eye and hand
> A sudden blow and no prison wall
> Is strong enough to touch my soul
> Ere the guard watching this door
> Puts in the heavy iron bar
> A sudden blow and my soul
> Would shoot into the night
> The belief, desire and hope
> That keeps others
> Is dead in me.
> Life, like a play of shadows
> Looks senseless to me, aimless
> What keeps me; the door is open.
> But we are forbidden to steal away
> Be it God or Devil who torments us.[12]

Albrecht was not the only prisoner in the Lehrterstrasse prison who was being kept alive temporarily by Himmler. Gerhard Ritter wrote that in March 1945 Himmler seemed to have hopes of Haushofer and of Dohnanyi.[13] The theologian the Reverend Eberhard Bethge, also in Moabit Prison, noticed that Albrecht had certain privileges, such as books to read and cigarettes to smoke. This was because Albrecht had been ordered to write an account of his political views for Himmler and to advise Himmler how he should comport himself in order to get a reasonable peace with the Western Allies. As Bethge wrote:

I was a co-prisoner and as such for some time an attendant in the prison passages, where I helped in the distribution of food, and on such occasions was able to speak to one or other of the prisoners; thus I was able on several occasions to have short talks with Haushofer. In this way I had an opportunity to see that Haushofer had objects in his cell which he could not have had there in the beginning. He also mentioned some very friendly interrogations when he was requested to write down things for Himmler. . . .

At any rate, in those days we watched with interest the change in Haushofer's treatment, and derived some measure of hope from it for all of us. We believed that it was the intention to make use of Haushofer at a later date.[14]

What Albrecht wrote for his captors we do not know. As he himself understood, peace plans for Himmler would not have been worth the paper on which they were written. He was using his time and energies in writing his last work *The Sonnets of Moabit*. In the course of his life he had written a number of plays, in all of which there was a political slant directed against tyranny, but it was the *Sonnets of Moabit*, written in the Lehrterstrasse Prison, which later made him known throughout Germany. They were desperate poems set down by a man who keenly felt the destruction of his country, and knew that his days were almost certainly numbered.

By March 1945 Himmler's interest in Albrecht Haushofer was beginning to slacken because he had found a more suitable inter-mediary to take messages to the Western Allies. In February he met Count Folke Bernadotte of the Swedish Red Cross and in April he despatched the Swedish Count with an offer to capitulate to the Western Allies but not to the Russians. Churchill and Truman rejected this offer on 25 April.[15] While the Himmler–Bernadotte talks were in progress (they have been described in Bernadotte's book *The Fall of the Curtain*) Himmler was scarcely in Berlin at all – he was too busy trying vainly to stem the Russian advance across the Vistula. On 19 April his chief inquisitor Kaltenbrunner left the Lehrterstrasse Prison. By this time Himmler no longer cared whether the last remnants of the Resistance in Moabit Prison lived or died and he was content to leave Albrecht Haushofer and his companions to the care of the head of the Gestapo. This was not welcome news for Albrecht as it was not the first time that he had come under the auspices of S.S. Gruppen-führer Mueller.[16]

It was clear that if only he could hang on for a few more days, the Russians would liberate him and his fellow prisoners in Moabit prison; for by the middle of April the bombardment of Berlin had begun, and between 16–21 April the Russians came much closer. On 21 April the Lehrterstrasse prison, which had already suffered bomb damage, was hit by shellfire from Russian artillery. The prisoners were moved down into the cellars, and there Albrecht shared a cell with Herbert Kosney, a young Communist. They struck up a friendly relationship, both men being equally helpless.[17]

On 20 and 21 April many prisoners, with the exception of the political ones were released or made to serve with the army. When this came to the ears of Goebbels, the Gauleiter of Berlin, he sent a telegram threatening that anybody who attempted to free other prisoners would be executed.[18] The remaining captives in Moabit suspected that Mueller would send the S.S. Rollcommando. Some of the prisoners determined to attempt a rising; however, when they heard that other prisoners had definitely been freed they decided to postpone their revolt.[19] It was a fatal decision.

They were not to know that on 21 April 1945 Mueller had called a meeting at the Reich Security Main Office to discuss the future of the last prisoners in Moabit. It was attended by the leaders of the S.S. Sondercommando and by the Commandant of Moabit Prison, S.S. Untersturmfuehrer Albrecht. It was at that meeting that Mueller gave his orders.[20]

6 The End: 1.05 a.m. 23 April 1945

IN Moabit Prison a great change came over Albrecht Haushofer, a change reflected in *The Sonnets of Moabit*. Unlike his letters to his mother these poems were expressed with great simplicity. In 1930 he had written to his mother that poems were 'better when one is very desperate',[1] and during those last weeks he was deeply despondent. From his *Sonnets* emerges the picture of a tormented man watching through prison bars the glow of Berlin burning, as a result of the war which he had sought to prevent.

The Reverend Edmund Walsh of the U.S. armed forces wrote that in the shadow of anticipated death Albrecht recaptured a whole lifetime of memories – his travels in Tibet, his colleagues Yorck and Moltke, Schulenburg and Schwerin, his mother, the scenes of happiness at Partnachalm, the voice of dead years and the ruins that now disfigured his devastated Fatherland and haunted his soul.[2] The *Sonnets* became for him the means through which he could finally resolve his inner conflicts, and he chose poetry as the medium for expressing his feelings. He described his loneliness in a poem called *In Fetters*:

> For him who nightly sleeps in it
> The cell is bleak but its walls
> Are full of life. Guilt and Fate are
> Veiled in grey in its vaults
> Of all the grief filling its frame
> There is below masonry and bars
> A breath alive, a secret flutter
> Revealing the deep pains of other souls.
> I am not the first in this room
> Whose wrists are cut by fetters
> And in whose grief alien wills rejoice
> Sleep turns to awakening

> Awakening to dream
> I listen and feel through walls
> The tremble of many brotherly hands.[3]

His words sprang out of the knowledge that all that he and his friends in the Resistance had attempted would be swept away amidst the ruins of Berlin. 'For a short while among dead walls sorrowful humanity will endure: thereafter all will be covered with ivy. . . . We are the last. Our thoughts tomorrow will be empty chaff, blown by the wind and without value where young morning dawns.'[4]

> When today I was lost in dreams
> I saw the whole host passing,
> Yorck and Moltke, Schulenburg, Schwerin
> Hassell, Popitz, Helfferich and Planck
> Not one with thoughts of gain
> Not one of them forgetting
> In pomp and circumstance, in mortal danger,
> The nation's desperate needs.
> My long despairing glance for them
> Who all had mind and rank and name
> And shared these cells with me
> And for them all the rope is waiting
> There are times when madness rules the land
> It is then that the best are hanged.[5]

Albrecht's thoughts were dwelling on the past. He remembered his girl-friend as in a dream, and she stood over him and asked whether he had yet come to terms with himself. 'Now you test me in my dream that had neither pain nor sorrow. You nod and you ask me: "Are you recovered now?" I lie still, slowly beats my heart. What has remained is gratitude that travels to your grave in Engadin.'[6] He thought of his brother Heinz who had been arrested for helping him to escape from the Gestapo. He very much hoped that his brother would survive,[7] for he saw Heinz as the anchor which would hold the remnants of his family together.

Albrecht had been reproached for not escaping from Germany after his flight from Berlin, and he explained in the sonnet *Home* that it had not been his wish to run away from his country. If he had decided to leave he would have done so long before. It was a source of great comfort to him that the beauty of the mountains of

southern Bavaria would remain untouched by the war; mountains
which had become for him a symbol of indestructibility:

> They asked me about my escape
> Why did I miss the way to the Rhine
> To nearby Switzerland, swimming away
> Before the chase for me began in earnest.
> I would not leave my homeland
> That had given such good shelter
> Then she could hide me no more
> And I shall not see her again
> I am glad to know that its wall of mountains
> Hides our Alm and hut
> Though I must miss the mountain's beauty
> The walls of silver grey will endure
> Whether man climbs them or flees
> Until fresh ice encircles their peaks.[8]

He likened the war to the launching of a vast avalanche, started
by 'criminals and madmen', which had led to 'a push, a flurry,
then a deadly cold'.[9] He wrote in *The Rats* that German soldiers
in their hordes had followed a Pied Piper who had wilfully led
them to destruction:

> A host of grey rats eats the land
> Approaching the stream in wild array
> In front a piper who with crazy sound
> Binds them in maddened twitches
> They leave full granaries abandoned
> Waverers are grimly pushed along
> Objectors cruelly chewed to death
> Thus they speed towards the stream
> Leaving ransacked fields behind
> They smell blood and flesh in the turmoil
> Shriller and harsher grows the sound
> Now they storm into the abyss
> A shrill whistle, a yelling screech
> The crazy noise drowns into the stream
> All rats are dead swept into the sea.[10]

Albrecht now acknowledged that as early as the Olympic Games
in 1936 he had foreseen that the magic of international co-operation

and friendship had been illusory, and that Germany's rulers were abusing the Games for their own warlike purposes. In *Arena* he recaptured the memory of a conversation with Lord Vansittart, head of the British Foreign Office at the time of the Olympiad, and Albrecht wrote that Vansittart had said to him: ' "They now celebrate victory with flags. But soon they will shout for blood. Then they will be themselves." Vansittart was silent. So was I. His Lordship was right.'[11]

In their separate countries Vansittart and Haushofer occupied roles which were in certain respects similar. In Britain Vansittart continually gave warnings about the dangers inherent in Nazism, and implored the Government of Neville Chamberlain to rearm rapidly, but his warnings went unheeded. He had told Chamberlain facts which Chamberlain had not wanted to hear, and consequently Vansittart had been relegated to a minor role in the British Foreign Office. In Germany too Albrecht Haushofer had given his warnings:

> They called me Cassandra in the office
> Since, like the seer of Troy,
> I had through bitter years
> Foreseen the whole agony of death
> Of people and country.
> Though they praised my deep knowledge
> They ignored all my warnings.
> They were angry when I dared to interfere
> When I adjuringly pointed to the future.
> They drove the boat full-sail
> In tempest on to the rocks
> With shouts of early victory
> Now they are shipwrecked and so are we.
> An attempt in final distress to grasp the rudder has failed.
> We now wait for the sea to engulf us.[12]

In June 1938 Albrecht had told Ribbentrop and Hitler in the clearest possible terms, both verbally and in writing, that if Germany launched a military invasion into eastern Europe, Great Britain would fight in earnest together with France, and Britain would receive the full support of the U.S.A., the end result being an incalculable Russian expansion into the heart of Europe. He had done everything within his power by non-violent means to prevent the outbreak of war. The broad outline of what he had said and written had been correct, and he could have given no better advice, but his warnings were discarded. Hitler thought that the British would at most only put up a token gesture of opposition, and, as always, Hitler was sure that he knew best.

In April 1945 it was manifest to everyone that the war was lost. The Russians were fighting within the outskirts of Berlin, slowly and determinedly burning their way towards the Unter den Linden and Kurfürstendamm, shattering virtually every house in their path. But Hitler even at this hour was not a man to acknowledge that he had been mistaken. He believed that a dead man would tell no tales.

Mueller saw Hitler on most days and would almost certainly have drawn his attention to the fact that the last remnants of the Resistance were in Moabit Prison. The precise instructions which passed between them during those last days will probably never be known, because between 20 and 22 April the Gestapo and R.S.H.A. destroyed all their files, including the records of Albrecht Haushofer's interrogations.[13] Mueller was covering all his tracks before he disappeared from Berlin without trace.

Even if the details of Hitler's instructions are not available for scrutiny, his policy was quite clear. Hitler had said 'I'm beginning to doubt whether the German people is worthy of my great ideals,[14] and it was his aim to kill any German who might be considered as a candidate for an alternative government to Nazism. If he could not rule, then as far as he was concerned nobody else would rule, and he would destroy as much as he could. That was Hitler's policy, and Mueller took measures to put that policy into effect on 21 April 1945.

Back in Moabit Prison during the afternoon of the next day, 22 April, twenty-one men had been freed, raising the hopes of those who remained.[15] Late that night two groups of eight men were summoned from the cellars to receive their personal effects, so that the release of all prisoners should not be delayed.

In the first group were Professor Albrecht Haushofer; Max Jennewein, a mechanical engineer; Herbert Kosney, a Communist; Carlos Moll; Lieutenant-Colonel Ernst Munzinger of the O.K.H., Armed Forces High Command; Major Count Hans Victor Salviati, the Olympic athlete who had been Field Marshal von Rundstedt's adjutant from 1941 to 1943, and was the brother-in-law of Prince

Friedrich Wilhelm of Prussia; Sosimoff, the Russian prisoner of war, whom the Gestapo had considered to be very important, and through whom Himmler may have wished to open peace negotiations with the Russians, and Colonel Wilhelm Staehle, a German Argentinian who had been a member of the Abwehr and Commandant of the Invalidenhaus, Berlin.

In the second group were Klaus Bonhoeffer, a barrister and legal adviser to Lufthansa and brother of the theologian Dietrich Bonhoeffer; Hans John, a lawyer and assistant of Rudiger Schleicher; Richard Kuenzer, a Counsellor of Legation in the Foreign Office; Karl Marcks, a merchant; Wilhelm zür Nieden, an industrialist; Dr Friedrich Justus Perels, the legal adviser to the Confessional Church; Professor Dr Rudiger Schleicher, Chief of the Institute for Aviation Law at Berlin University and brother-in-law of Dietrich Bonhoeffer, and Hans Ludwig Sierks, a former Councillor of State.[16]

They were a distinguished and varied group of men. They returned to their cells to pack what little clothing they had with them. Herbert Kosney helped his cell companion Albrecht Haushofer with his packing. Among his belongings was a loaf of pumpernickel which he gave to Herbert.[17]

Later that night the sixteen men were marched up the cellar steps to the prison yard, where they received the rest of their valuables such as pencils, cigarette lighters, watches, rings and wallets. They signed receipts and were asked to complete forms stating that they had been released, which they did. They were told by the prison Commandant that they would be immediately released.[18] One S.S. man mentioned to Herbert Kosney that he would see his wife soon.[19]

Even Albrecht Haushofer may have been momentarily filled with hope. How can one describe all the pent-up emotions of a man at such a moment when he desperately wants to live? He walked with the other prisoners towards the prison's entrance, through a narrow hallway, when suddenly a flashlight was switched on, and they saw on both sides of the passage about thirty-five S.S. Sondercommando armed with machine pistols.[20] Many of the faces under the steel helmets of the S.S. were those of youths.[21] Albrecht had been promised his freedom; he had signed documents confirming that he had been freed, but when he saw the S.S. it must have been too much to hope for, too much to believe.[22]

They went out on to the street outside the prison, surrounded by the S.S. who outnumbered them by more than two to one, and they were told by the S.S. Obersturmbannfuehrer that they were going to be transferred to another prison and would be shot if they tried to escape. The sixteen prisoners were marched down the Lehrterstrasse towards the Invalidenstrasse where they were halted. They were asked to surrender any valuables which they might have, such as their watches which had just been given to them and for which they had signed receipts a few minutes before.[23] Herbert Kosney noticed that it was 1.0 a.m. and Jennewein re-marked that there were some marks in his pocket book; and the S.S. Sergeant told him that the matter would be examined on the train.[24]

The S.S. men turned towards the bombed-out Ulap Exhibition site. All the prisoners knew that this was not the way to the Potsdam station, even if the S.S. sergeant said that they were taking a short-cut. The prisoners marched through the rubble and debris pitted with bomb-holes and craters and entered the ruins of the once-massive building; there the S.S. stopped. Albrecht Haushofer's group was marched to the left and the rest were taken to the right. On the left Munzinger went first, followed by Herbert Kosney, Albrecht Haushofer and the others.[25]

The prisoners were made to face the wall of the building. Then everything happened very quickly. Herbert Kosney heard shots nearby, and found himself staring at Albrecht Haushofer, who was standing absolutely still. Then they were mown down by a volley of shots in the back of the neck.[26]

But one man was not dead: Herbert Kosney. He had turned his head, and felt himself struck by a terrible blow from behind. The bullet had entered the back of his neck and had come out under his eye. Herbert lay on the ground still conscious and saw the S.S. Obersturmbannfuehrer walk up to Colonel Munzinger's body, shine a torch at him, and fire his revolver into Munzinger's face. He saw him walk down the row of prostrate forms, putting a bullet through each man's head.[27]

When he came to Herbert's body, Herbert heard him say that this pig had had enough, and that they would have to hurry, as they had more work to do.[28] He put his boot into Herbert's face, and thereafter the still-conscious Herbert heard the sound of moaning and more shots, until all sounds ceased.[29] Then he heard footsteps fading away and felt an uncanny stillness.

At last slowly and painfully he dragged himself towards his home, as he himself described it, like a hunted and wounded animal. At about 3.15 a.m. he crept up to his house in the Hagenauer Strasse, and it was some time before his wife realised that the battered figure covered in blood, collapsing in front of her, was her husband.[30]

When he recovered consciousness several days later in a public hospital he found in his pockets a bloody piece of bread – the bread which had been given to him by Albrecht Haushofer, and the only tangible memory he had of the man who had been murdered at his side. Through Herbert the news leaked out and Heinz Haushofer, after being freed by the Russians, set out to search for his brother.

On 12 May Heinz found Albrecht where he had been shot. Clutched in the dead man's hand were scraps of paper with poems written out in longhand entitled *The Sonnets of Moabit*.[31] The thirty-eighth sonnet was called 'Guilt':

> I lightly carry what the judge calls my guilt
> Guilt in planning and caring
> I would feel guilty had I not from inner duty
> Planned for the people's future
> But I am guilty other than you think:
> I should have sooner seen my duty
> I should have sharper condemned evil
> I have too long delayed my judgement.
> I now accuse myself
> I have long betrayed my conscience
> I have lied to myself and to others.
> I soon foresaw the evil's frightful path;
> I have warned,
> But my warnings were too feeble.
> I know today wherein lies my guilt.[32]

EPILOGUE

AFTER the July Plot Karl Haushofer had been imprisoned in Dachau Concentration Camp for a short period, but even that experience had not shaken his loyalty to the German State. To the old general patriotism meant everything, and the maxim 'My country right or wrong' had been one of the first articles of his political creed. He had always considered obedience to authority to be a moral necessity. His son Albrecht, on the other hand, did not shrink from the recognition that as an individual he had full responsibility for his own actions. Opposition might become a duty, and the plea of 'obedience to a superior authority' was never a valid excuse in his eyes where a moral issue was involved.

The German language contains two words for treason, *Hochverrat* and *Landesverrat*, and in all his activities with the opposition Albrecht attempted to draw a clear line between the two. The first word covers activities subversive to a particular system or regime and Albrecht had been prepared to engage in such activities. The second term is used for actions which are directed against the interests of the country itself, and he deliberately did not participate in such actions, as he was anxious to avoid the stigma of being called a traitor. His aim had not been to deliver Germany to her enemies but to secure a change of government which would enable Germany to negotiate a peace settlement, in which her interests as he saw them might be safeguarded.

For Karl Haushofer there was no such distinction; treason was treason and any German who worked against the State was a traitor. After the July Plot he learnt that Albrecht was being sought by the Gestapo and that he had been engaged in writing plans for the Resistance. Towards the end of the war he heard that Albrecht had been captured and interned in Moabit prison. Frau Schnuhr approached him saying that something must be done to get legal aid for his son, and he replied, 'Why should I do that? He has betrayed his country and his people and deserves no help from me.' At length he consented, but only for the 'honour of the family'.[1]

After the unconditional surrender, Karl Haushofer was a broken man. He understood that all his teachings had been in vain, saw his country in ruins and was well aware that the Third Reich, which he had always supported, had murdered his own son. Throughout the years of Nazism he had supported Nazi propaganda, had written that Hitler was 'a God-given leader' and that the German people must direct their course with that of the Fuehrer.[2] He now said that his teachings had been misused by the Nazis, and that for the last seven years – especially since Hess had left for England – he had lived under the fear that his half-Jewish wife would be taken to Theresienstadt or Auschwitz.[3] He was a nineteenth-century imperialist similar in thinking to the British imperialist Cecil Rhodes. He had supported the Third Reich, only because he would have supported any German state, and he was glad when his favourite pupil Hess became Hitler's deputy. Karl Haushofer was not a vicious man, but the only injustices he was prepared to struggle against those which directly affected his own family.

He explained in his *Last Defence of German Geopolitics* that he had interceded with Hitler on 8 November 1938 because he had hoped that Hitler would be satisfied with the solution reached at Munich, and he called the period from 1938 onwards 'The Way of Sorrow for German Geopolitics'.[4] Yet it had always been his belief that 'war was the highest test for human virtues such as could not be experienced in times of peace',[5] and his teaching of geopolitics had amounted in practice to little more than the study of how Germany might annexe, colonise and dominate other nations by stealth, cunning and covert aggression. Considerations of abstract morality never played a large part in his thinking.[6]

He had hoped that Albrecht would be the heir to his intellectual work,[7] but Albrecht at the end of his life had wanted nothing to do with his father's teachings. He felt no bitterness, but he firmly believed that an obsession with geopolitics had made his father close his mind to the results of a desire for domination and a lust for war. He wrote in his poem *Acheron, the River of Sorrow*: 'My father was still blinded by dreams of power. I have in advance felt the whole horror; Hunger, death, wounds, destruction and fire, the

whole calamity of such a devil's night. I often took deliberate leave
of all of life's beauty, of home, work, love, wine and bread. Now
darkness has fallen over me. Acheron is near and life is far. A
weary eye is searching for a distant star.'[8]

No prosecution was made against Karl Haushofer at Nuremberg
because the American prosecuting team regarded his role as being
academic and advisory.[9] He was taken to Nuremberg merely to
see Hess who was alleged to be suffering from amnesia and who
refused to recognise him. He was also asked to prepare a last statement on German geopolitics, which he agreed to do. On his way
back to his lodgings, Karl Haushofer said that Hess was completely sincere in his fanatical support of Hitler, that his flight to
Britain was characteristic of him, and that at no other time had
Hess concealed his plans from him. Whilst being driven back he
could see the ruins of the bombed city and he was dismayed.[10]

He had always been in favour of setting aside the Versailles
Treaty; now he saw Germany occupied and with far less territory
than she had had under the Treaty of Versailles. He did not want
to live in a Germany which had been defeated for the second time
in a world war. In 1943 he had quarrelled with Albrecht and had
told him that if the war was lost as Albrecht thought, he would kill
himself,[11] and his mind kept reverting to this theme.

Only the presence of his family kept him from putting his threat
into action. At the end of 1945 after the return of his son Heinz,
although his health was deteriorating, he did not wish to escape a
confrontation regarding his life's work. Once he had completed
his last defence of German geopolitics in which he claimed that
his teachings had been misunderstood, and once he had discovered
that Hess's counsel did not require him as a defence witness at the
Nuremberg war trials he felt freed from all obligations. He told
Heinz 'You no longer need me' and again and again emphasised
the right of the stoic to put an end to his life, once he had fulfilled
all his duties.[12]

He had been bitterly disillusioned, and harder than anything for
him was the denunciation by his murdered son. It had only
been because of the general's friendship with Hess, and because
of his influence and encouragement that Albrecht had worked for
the regime. But at the end of his life Albrecht bitterly regretted
having succumbed and unlike his father he had made a final break
with Nazism. His poem *The Father*, telling an Eastern legend

similar to that of Pandora's Box, signified that there had been an irrevocable parting of the ways between father and son:

> A noble tale from the Orient
> Relates of evil spirits captive
> In the sea's dark night
> Sealed there by divine decree
> Until in a happy millennium
> A fisherman gains the key
> To unseal the captives
> Unless he throws his catch back into the sea.
> For my father the fates have spoken
> He once had it in his power
> To cast the demon back into the dark
> My father broke the seal
> But failed to see the evil
> He let the demon escape into the world.[13]

Karl Haushofer had deep feelings of guilt which he admitted in private to a Roman Catholic priest, as is evident from the comments of the Reverend Edmund Walsh.[14] Apparently Karl Haushofer understood that Albrecht had chosen to stay in Germany in 1933 and after Munich, to a large extent because his mother, to whom Albrecht was very close, had decided to remain. The most poignant of all of Albrecht's poems is *The Mother*; he might almost have foreseen what was to come.

> I see you in a candle's light
> Waiting in the dark portal
> You feel the cool mountain air;
> You shiver, Mother, and yet you stay
> You watch me pass into the night
> Wondering about my future;
> You smile, and yet you cry
> Filled with hopeless pain
> I see you in your shining love
> I see your white hair trembling
> In the vast dark cool
> And slowly you lower your face
> While the candle still shines through
> You shiver, Mother, go inside.[15]

Throughout his life Karl Haushofer had been an admirer of the ancient Greek stoics and on 11 March 1946 he carried his admiration to its logical conclusion. On that Monday Karl and Martha Haushofer set out for their last walk through the woods. They stopped about half a mile from their house in a hollow by the stream under a willow tree. There they took poison. Martha was also hanged from the tree; the General was not strong enough to follow suit as the poison took effect. There they were found on the next day by Heinz.[16] The Reverend Edmund Walsh visited the place shortly after and wrote:

The lantern, with the extinguished candle which had lighted them through the darkness, lay beside them. Traversing their route step by step a few days after the double suicide – it was on the Ides of March – and attempting to reconstruct the scene as it was played out on that windy night on one of the loneliest hillsides in Bavaria, I could only liken it to some final act of a Greek tragedy. As if to seal his name and lifework to oblivion he left instructions to his son that no marker, memorial or other form of identification should ever be placed on or near his grave.[17]

This was not quite the end of the story: there yet remained Rudolf Hess.

After the war Hess was brought to Nuremberg to be tried as a Nazi war criminal, and while he was there some of the doctors began to have serious doubts as to whether he was fit to plead. In the view of some of the Allied psychiatrists, Hess appeared to be suffering from amnesia.[18]

As Hess later admitted his amnesia was a pretence – he had hoped to be repatriated, by faking mental disorders, and had tried hard but without success. He had, however, succeeded in deceiving some of the British psychiatrists and was proud of this fact. His game included feigning mental blackouts and then being unable to recall who or where he was. When he grew fed up with having such an 'attack' he would choose to remember his own name and would gaze around in astonishment. He was well aware of the fact that he had the ability to fool psychiatrists, and he realised when he arrived at Nuremberg that it could be a useful defence to suggest that he was suffering from amnesia. With this in mind he refused to take the witness stand. Instead he indulged in play-acting and insisted on reading an average of two books a day while the trials were in progress.[19]

He even refused to recognise Goering, Ribbentrop, Papen, Bohle of the Ausland Organisations and Karl Haushofer.[20] The doctors at Nuremberg were puzzled and, while they all agreed that Hess was 'medico-legally' sane, many of them thought that his amnesia was genuine or partly genuine and might interfere with his ability to conduct his defence and to understand the details of the past.[21]

Only one man told Hess to his face that he was a fraud – the American commandant, Colonel Burton C. Andrus who was in charge of the prison. Colonel Andrus told Hess that he was feigning and that this was 'not a very manly thing to do'. 'Hess, you owe it to yourself, your family and to the German nation to tell the truth. I think you should go into court and make a clean breast of this and tell them you have been faking amnesia.'[22] Hess thanked him, obviously uncomfortable that an appeal had been made to his sense of honour.

On the next day, part of the second afternoon session was taken up with a discussion as to whether Hess was fit to plead, when suddenly Hess rose in court and surprised everyone, not least his own Counsel, by making a declaration:

> In order to forestall the possibility of my being pronounced incapable of pleading in spite of my willingness to take part in further proceedings, and in order to receive sentence alongside my comrades, I would like to make the following declaration before the Tribunal. . . .
>
> Henceforth my memory will again respond to the outside world. The reasons why I simulated loss of memory were tactical. The fact is that it is only my ability to concentrate that is somewhat reduced. However, my capacity to follow the trial, to defend myself, to put questions to witnesses or even to answer questions, is not affected thereby.
>
> I emphasise that I bear the full responsibility for everything that I have done or signed as signatory or co-signatory.[23]

The court then declared Hess fit to plead, and when the psychiatrists Douglas Kelley and G. M. Gilbert saw Hess in his cell afterwards he was 'quite like an actor after his first night'. His memory was perfect and with alacrity he answered questions about his youth, his role in the Party, his flight to Britain and his imprisonment.[24] Hess later said that if it had not been for his acting ability he would have been sentenced to death.[25] There was certainly no question of his regretting anything that the Nazis had done.

When he was asked whether he thought differently of Hitler, having heard the evidence about the millions of human beings murdered in the concentration camps, Hess said, 'I suppose every genius has a demon in him – you can't blame him – it is just in him'.[26] His view of Hitler had not changed and he still worshipped him as his leader. In his final statement from the dock, Hess gave the court the impression that if he was given the opportunity he would do everything all over again:

> I was permitted to work for many years of my life under the greatest son whom my country has brought forth in its thousand-year history. Even if I could, I would not want to erase this period from my existence. I am happy to know that I have done my duty to my people, my duty as a German, as a National Socialist, as a loyal follower of my Fuehrer. I do not regret anything.
>
> If I were to begin all over again, I would act just as I have acted, even if I knew that in the end I should meet a fiery death at the stake.[27]

The court found Hess guilty of making preparations for war and conspiring against the peace. The presiding judge found it proven that Hess had been a willing participant in German aggression against Austria, Czechoslovakia and Poland. He also found it significant that his flight to Britain took place some ten days after the date on which Hitler decided that 22 June 1941 would be the date for attacking the Soviet Union. There had been no suggestion that Hess was not completely sane when the acts charged against him were committed and his sentence was one of imprisonment for life.[28] With others Hess was transferred to Spandau Prison in Berlin.

The Russian judge was not satisfied with the disposal of Hess's case and he dissented on the grounds that Hess was guilty of crimes against humanity in the eastern occupied territories, and that the only justified sentence could be death,[29] a view to which the Russian Government has adhered to this day.

As the Russian Government saw it, Russia lost between twenty and twenty-five million of its countrymen at the hands of the Nazi aggressors, and if Hess had succeeded in getting Britain out of the war in 1941 a great many more Russians might have died and the final outcome of the war might have been in doubt. So when he was sentenced to imprisonment for life as a war criminal, the Russian Government determined that that sentence would mean precisely what it said. On Friday 30 September 1966 Hess became the last prisoner in Spandau. The Nazi Youth leader Baldur von Schirach and the Nazi Minister for Armaments and War Production, Albert Speer, were released, and in silence Hess watched them depart.

During the years of his imprisonment he had kept himself occupied by working in the garden, and by writing letters to his wife which were published in three volumes. His letters were articulate, literate and erudite, showing a knowledge of history, linguistics, engineering, painting, music, folklore, geography, astronomy and languages. They also revealed a great interest in his son.[30]

These letters, published in book form, have sold better in Germany than any of the works on the German resistance to Hitler,[31] partly because his letters portrayed a human interest story, and partly because many Germans had a sneaking regard for the Nazi leader who tried to save the Third Reich from entanglement in ever-expanding war on more than one front. Besides, there was a widespread feeling in Germany that Hess was being used by the Russians as a pawn in East–West relations, and that they would not release him without major concessions in other fields from the British, Americans and French stationed in West Berlin.

For the last years of Hess's life the governments of Britain, U.S.A. and France would have preferred to free Hess, but they were not willing to make an international issue over his release with the Russians. Their outlook probably had a certain amount in common with the opinion expressed by Winston Churchill:

Reflecting upon the whole of this story, I am glad not to be responsible for the way in which Hess has been and is being treated. Whatever may be the moral guilt of a German who stood near to Hitler, Hess had in my view, atoned for this by his completely devoted and fanatic deed of lunatic benevolence. He came to us of his own free will, and, though without authority, had something of the quality of an envoy. He was a medical and not a criminal case, and should be so regarded.[32]

On the previous page Churchill had written, 'But he was more than a medical case',[33] and it may be that, if he had known the extent of Hess's direct participation and involvement in all of Hitler's actions up to May 1941, he might have been less magnanimous. Nonetheless the point remains that Churchill undoubtedly would not have wished Hess to have been sent to prison for life.

Many in the West shared Churchill's view with regard to Hess, and by 1970 few could see any point in his continued detention in Spandau under the guard of some two hundred soldiers. After the cataclysm of Nazism and its fall Hess had become a relic of the past, which brings to mind Albrecht Haushofer's prescient sonnet *The Great Flood:*

> I travelled once the Mississippi
> When under its brown floods
> For thousand miles towards the bay
> The fields around were buried.
> An empty image of former yields
> Of green crop, of golden harvest
> Where busy hands each year
> Had worked, home by home.
> All escaped who could:
> The rest were doomed to die.
> The plain was empty,
> Then the flood moved to the sea
> Sunlight courted the damp slime
> Soon the land woke to new life.[34]

In a sense Albrecht was correct: the flood which had convulsed Germany and Europe has gone and Germany has revived. Albrecht had stood in its way and had been swept out to the ocean, where he was drowned. The flood also destroyed the world of his father and mother, who followed in its wake. Only Rudolf Hess remained, one of the pieces of debris which were cast up, and a grim reminder of an age forever gone.

Appendixes

1 Peace Plan, drawn up by Albrecht Haushofer in the summer of 1940 for the German Resistance to Hitler.

The following document is a reproduction in full of the peace proposal drawn up by Albrecht Haushofer on behalf of the group in the German Resistance to Hitler around Ulrich von Hassell and Johannes Popitz. A former pupil of Albrecht Haushofer, H. W. Stahmer, who was Secretary of the German Legation in Madrid, delivered or had delivered this Report to the British Embassy in Madrid, for the attention of the British Ambassador Sir Samuel Hoare (later Lord Templewood).

A copy of this document was sent after the war on 1 June 1946 by Stahmer to the Duke of Hamilton. The introduction to the proposal said that in the event of either side again attempting to reach an understanding the following considerations would be recommended as a basis for negotiations.

Proposal for a provisional solution of problems

FOR an understanding with Britain the evacuation of the western and northern territories under German occupation must be accepted as a basis. Thus the sovereignty of Norway, Denmark, Belgium and Holland within the old frontiers would have to be re-established. The German–French frontier, in the event of Alsace–Lorraine remaining within the German Reich's territory, should be moved further west than before 1914, since the then frontier, seen from a geographical point of view, was distinctly unfortunate. (Map of frontier proposal attached.) This does not, however, mean that Alsace–Lorraine was to be unconditionally demanded by Germany. This problem should form the topic of a joint German–French discussion.

Italian demands for an Italian–French frontier revision must under all circumstances be dropped since they would not in any event correspond with Italy's power-political position in Europe, nor could they incontestably be justified from a historical viewpoint. Italian demands for Tunis should be clarified in an Anglo–French–Italian discussion in which Italy's request for a referendum must be anticipated. This does not mean that the incorporation of Tunisia into the Italian colonial sphere is regarded as desirable or necessary. (A proposal for settling the

Italian east frontier is attached separately.) As regards Italy's northern frontier, see annex.

Having regard to the fact that for Britain the way to India must be unconditionally secured, Britain's special interests in the eastern Mediterranean and Near East would have to be recognised. (Here must be added other problems which, like the extra-European ones, are dealt with in a special exposé, outside the scope of the original draft.) Moreover, there should be an appropriate understanding on the basis of which all European naval units would be available for the safeguarding of British interests.

Germany would have to be guaranteed, on the other hand, her special interests in the south-east European sphere, since the close ties with this region are of overriding importance for the economic existence of Germany and of the countries concerned. This position should find expression in Germany's privileged stand in south-east Europe without, however, in any way endangering the sovereignty of the countries concerned. From this complex Greece should be excluded for the reasons stated above, or she should receive special consideration. For individual state frontier delimitations in south-east Europe with their host of problems, a special exposé is submitted.

The regulation of her eastern frontier is regarded by Germany as a special problem which should be settled by the directly concerned states alone, without the participation of the other nations.

The foregoing proposals form an attempt at solving the most burning present problems of Europe. There should, however, be no doubt that the occasion of a peace conference must be used for a basic reorganisation of Europe since these proposals would offer no guarantee for a permanent solution. An attempt has therefore been made to illuminate the bases for a radical solution in the subsequent second proposal.

Constructive Peace Plan for Europe

THIS peace plan should, as mentioned, show the way to a constructive reorganisation of the European peoples' coexistence, and the equality of all nations, large or small, must play the decisive role. The difficulties that up to now have faced a reorganisation of the coexistence of European nations were rooted in historical development. The technical and economic evolution of recent times has, however, presented demands which under the existing egotistic national conceptions in Europe are incapable of fulfilment. Hence the necessity of finding a common basis for a number of European problems.

It is proposed that Europe should be enlarged to one economic region in which her peoples are led to a joint economic co-operation. This co-operation to be under the control of an Economic Council to which all

European nations would send their representatives. Each nation to have an equal vote in this permanent council. (If the small states, fearing to be smothered by the big powers, show reluctance towards this plan, one could even concede to them a double voting right.) One of the foremost tasks of the council would be, of course, the abolition of European customs frontiers in order to make possible the creation of an extensive common economic policy.

When this economic question is solved it should be easier to turn to the problems of national frontiers because a thorough regulation would remove the desire to snatch certain economic regions from a neighbour. In the new frontier order regard must be had to effective ethnological, geographical and cultural facts. In ethnologically mixed regions where a delimitation would create difficulties, the possibility of resettlement at the affected population's free will could be considered.

The desire of some countries to adhere to certain frontier delimitations for reasons of security will also die if an agreement is reached under conditions mentioned below on disarmament and military co-operation.

As in the economic sector of Europe, here too a common basis must be found. Each state should declare its willingness to contribute towards the creation of a European police force which then could carry out, jointly, all military and security measures. The German navy, like all other European naval units, would be placed under British command for safeguarding Europe's military co-operation, and would be available for the protection of British interests in the Indian Ocean. Air forces, like the police force, would be under a joint command and their strength would have to be adapted to joint European security requirements. To safeguard military co-operation an agreement should be reached in order to achieve the decentralisation in the production of war material, in such a way that, e.g., one country produces machine-gun barrels, another country the locks and the third country the ammunition.

Since the common European economic sector is to a high degree dependent on supplies from the African colonies, a solution should be found here too which would form part of the new economic framework. In this respect the foundation of a joint European colonial association would appear to be necessary. It would be the task of this association to ensure a joint and equitable distribution of all African economic goods in an all-European market and of the corresponding counter-supplies (exports). In this connection it must be specially emphasised that the economic reorganisation of Europe is only meant to serve for the removal of inner-European conflicts and not as an attempt at autarchy or a block-forming directed against other economic regions. For the rest, the interweaving with world economy would at any rate already be achieved through the world-wide ties of the British Empire. The cultural individuality of separate European nations must not be affected by this joint approach to economic and political problems.

By the proposal for the settlement of the colonial question a part of the aforementioned Mediterranean problem could be neutralised, while in regard to African colonies a community for all European nations should be achieved. India would remain, as before, the exclusive sphere of interest of Britain. This would also entail a recognition of special British interests in the Aegean and in the Near and Middle East as necessary protection for her passage to India.

This then is in rough draft an indication towards the solution of the European complex of questions. Further individual questions as well as extra-European problems will be dealt with separately.

II Albrecht Haushofer's Peace Plan, submitted to the German Foreign Office and Hitler in November 1941.

Late in 1941 Albrecht Haushofer submitted the following peace plan to the German Foreign Office. Nothing came of it, as it was as unacceptable to the Nazi leaders as it was to everyone else.

95 Federal Archives HC 833

Thoughts on a Peace Plan

Memorandum

Submitted to the Secretary of State of the Ministry for Foreign Affairs with the request kindly to examine it at the proper time for its suitability for a report to the Fuehrer.

November 1941

I POSTULATES

The events of the last few years have proved that the anarchy of fully sovereign states induced by weak International Law, has ceased to offer bearable forms of life at least on the territorially small continents. It has become no less apparent that the technical means of the present do not in themselves suffice in changing unilateral power solutions of a centralised nature into permanent historic value.

The present memorandum therefore proceeds from a basic postulate – with all it contains in regard to political-psychological conditions – that a future world peace has to be negotiated.

It is thus assumed that the present world war cannot be totally won by any of the fighting world powers, i.e. it cannot be won by a lasting dictate on a supra-continental scale. The following is, therefore, postulated for all that follows:

1. That the British–American power alliance in its essential nucleus (Atlantic and Indo-Pacific naval supremacy; unassailability of the entire area of the American continent) cannot be shaken. Here the fact is important that even hard blows against the British Isles and the British position in the East do not break up the overall Anglo-

Saxon naval supremacy; they merely accelerate the transfer of its centre of gravity to America.

2. That a successful monopolistic formation of Greater East Asia by Japan is as unlikely as a complete elimination of Japanese power in important parts of East Asia.

3. That the 'Great Russianism' – in Stalinist or another form – will retain possession of its Asiatic power nucleus on the Volga or in the Urals up to Lake Baikal, i.e. that a total forcible subjugation of Russian Eurasia from outside is just as incapable of attainment as a subjugation of China.

4. That German forces are sufficient not only to prevent a military defeat on European and perhaps even on (Near Eastern) Anterior Asia and North African soil, but also capable of productively organising great parts of Europe (against the passive resistance of most European peoples) to such an extent that the calculation of the naval powers of causing the internal crumbling of German power foundation would have to be recognised by them as a miscalculation.

All future peace negotiations will ideally hinge on the basic question of international treaty loyalty (including its application to the armament and economic field); regionally they will hinge on the following great problems:

A. A federative peace arrangement for continental Europe; the extent of a German leading position in it; its frontiers against Asia.

B. The relationship of continental Europe to British–American naval power (destiny of the West European glacis countries and their colonial possessions; Africa as a collective European responsibility; delimitation of Oriental spheres of interest; participation in overseas – South American, South-east Asian – sources of supply).

C. The internal balancing of power between London and Washington (within which the future of the South American countries will largely be decided).

D. The satisfaction of certain vital necessities of Japan (question: at whose cost?) against the entry of Japan into the Indo-Pacific supremacy of the naval powers.

E. The possibility or impossibility of a world-political isolation of Stalin (and of 'Great Russianism') in Siberia.

These five problem complexes – beside which everything else is secondary – form the great background context of any possible negotiation. Which parts of these problems can be made the subject of discussion at all will be expressed through the respective power relationships at the beginning and in the course of the negotiations.

The naval powers with their world-wide power network are interested in excluding from any discussion most of their special fields of interest (and of crises), or in isolating their treatment. They will endeavour to exclude from any negotiations the whole transoceanic and South American question C. They will strive to settle the East Asian question D in an isolated manner, and to mask their Asiatic colonial interest in question E (isolation of Bolshevism; decrease of Russian influence in India and China).

Stalin (or his successors, whoever they may be in the representation of Communist world-revolutionary or Great Russian nationalistic ideas and interests), the Japanese and perhaps even Chiang Kai-shek – one of the strongest personalities on the world political stage – will conversely tactically endeavour to join in the widest possible negotiations.

In this situation, Germany will also have to try – notwithstanding the internal and external necessity of regional restriction of her ultimate aims – to keep the negotiations open on the general sphere of world politics. Restriction is possible only as an aim, not as a method of negotiations. The conditions for a comprehensive world political participation of Germany exist as long as Paris, Brussels and The Hague, the constitutional centres for great parts of Central Africa and of South-east Asia, remain under German pressure. A premature willingness of the Reich to release the West European glacis (even though such willingness will presumably be necessary for a conclusion!) will remove this possibility just as would in present circumstances a highly unlikely and only barely imaginable Anglo-Saxon resignation regarding Western Europe. (The latter would make it possible to reach radical solutions in Africa and in South-east Asia without regard to the destiny of France, Belgium and the Netherlands, and would thereby considerably narrow the world political room to manoeuvre.)

The aims of Germany must be: by basically renouncing certain foreign political methods and by foregoing future disturbances of Asiatic and South American spheres of interest of the maritime powers, to achieve an Anglo-Saxon renunciation of total or part interference in a German-led continental Europe, as well as a German (or continental European) share in the development of Africa.

It goes without saying that beyond this a restoration of international trade and with it of German and all-European supplies by sea must be endeavoured. The political aims of the Reich could be narrowed or extended in the European as well as in the African field. Between the maximum solution, beyond which – regardless of external hindrance of their removal – looms an overstraining of German national strength and thereby its premature paralysis and the minimum solution, the shortcomings of which, seen as an admission of weakness, would open the way to hostile dictates, lies a wide margin for negotiations. In the following are demarcated in broad outlines the extreme limits of negotiations from the just endurable to the reasonably desirable.

I

II AIMS

1. The minimum requirements for the existence of a Reich still regarded as a great power, comprise:

   a. The full unity of the Reich for the entire national soil of Germany as it existed in 1914, without those national parts whose separation was confirmed in 1648 and not only started in that year.

   b. The establishment of Reich-protected countries (without a defence, economic and foreign policy of their own connected with the Reich by a personal union vested in the head of state) for peoples, whose living space is geographically, historically and economically so closely associated with Germany that the regulation of relations between them and the Reich must be exempt from any outside intervention. Among these peoples belong in any circumstances the Poles, the Czechs and the Slovenes.

   c. The return of the West African colonies of the Cameroons and Togo (rounded off at the expense of France) which are necessary for the safeguarding of German peacetime supplies of important tropical products.

2. In addition, the following would be required for the Reich as leaders of the Continent:

   a. A group of Reich-orientated countries which are associated with the Reich in durable, but less strict forms than the Reich-protected countries (personal union possible, but not necessary; long-term economic and defence agreements; bases; arbitral jurisdiction by the Reich; safeguards by the Reich of national characteristics). The circle of these countries would have to comprise Estonia, Latvia, Lithuania, Slovakia, Croatia and even Serbia.

   b. A group of countries to be allied to the Reich, among which have to be counted Hungary, Romania and Bulgaria; if necessary Finland, Greece and the Ukraine; at the worst, even the Caucasian countries (influences of the Reich to become effective only through long-term defence and economic agreements, as well as bases; in the case of White Russia, Ukraine and the Caucasus, after a longer transitional period of direct rule).

   c. Organisation of a European Federation (from the nucleus of a planning conference, necessary in any circumstances and resulting from the mobilisation of the European economy, equipped with wide powers). Apart from the countries already mentioned this should comprise: Sweden, Norway, and Denmark, Switzerland and Italy.

   d. Securing a larger West and Central African colonial empire.

3. Into the sphere of insolent pride ('hubris') not even justifiable under the present favourable power position – belong these:

a. Any attempt to prevent the restoration or continued operation of West European sovereignties. (It is at present unthinkable that Spain and Portugal, France, Belgium and the Netherlands together with their colonies, could be included in even the loosest form of a European Federation within the scope of a negotiated peace.) Special economic and traffic agreements (Rhine estuary) should be attainable, colonial concessions under the Belgian and Dutch flags should be possible (particularly if the peace treaty in the form of a joint guarantee by the naval powers and the Reich, were to contain special safeguards, perhaps for the entire Netherlands).

b. Any attempt to support Italian great power dreams in the Mediterranean or in Africa, or to adopt them.

c. Any attempt politically to break the British Orient position (even in the case of a successful military invasion! Its restoration is vital for England as long as she rules over India.) It goes without saying that the independent mid-position of Turkey – wanted also in Ankara – is of high value for a German–English settlement.

d. Any attempt at political infiltration into South America.

e. Any attempt at a permanent domination of the Greater Russian area beyond the line White Sea–Lake Onega–Volkhov–Central Russian ridge of land–Don bend–Volga estuary.

It is again emphasised that the renunciation, especially of the possibilities mentioned under 3 a–c, will be of the greatest tactical importance in negotiations for gaining points 1 and 2. A lasting peace is only possible, if it is understood by both sides that in the relationship Berlin–Prague there must be as little interference from London as from Berlin in the relationship London–Dublin; that the recognition of the British dominance in Cairo, Baghdad or Kabul depends on the recognition of the German dominance in Reval, Kiev or Sofia – and vice versa.

Greece will certainly be the subject of special intensive British interests. How far the Caucasus needs to be discussed will depend on the further development of the military situation. Turkestan – which will come into the political game only in the case of a serious Soviet collapse – should in this case be left to Anglo–Indian intervention.

III PROBLEMS

From the present survey, presented in the most concise form, an abundance of individual problems results, the regulation of which is indicated in outlines.

1. Frontiers of the German Reich and of Reich-protected countries:

12

A. Basic

It is of decisive importance that international negotiations should concern only the western frontiers of the Reich. The frontiers with Denmark, Hungary and Italy must be the subject of direct settlement with these countries. The frontiers of the Reich with the Reich-protected countries, Poland (at present a General Government), Bohemia and Moravia (at present a Protectorate) and Slovenia, are the concern of internal settlements.

Problems resulting from the demarcation of the Reich with these areas (the frontier of the area to be Germanised in Upper Carniola and South Styria with the remnants of Slovenia; the frontier of 1914 or coal railway line in the east; the destiny of Zichenau and of Litzmannstadt; the adjustment of the Protectorate frontier in numerous places, such as Brno-Breclav Lundenburg; Moravska Ostrava; Pilsen-Taus will not be dealt with at present. Should the Reich be forced to negotiate these points in detail with England or America, it would mean giving up the war as lost. It is among the general conditions of any thinkable peace that the regulation of the German–Polish, German–Czech and German–Slovene relationships must be brought about by methods which are justifiable within the framework of a common European culture.)

B. Territorial Problems

a. Against the sovereign states of the European West:

  1. The Netherlands: unchanged.

  2. Belgium: Eupen-Malmedy belongs to the Reich. Minor frontier corrections according to the Pangnage frontier in the area of Arel and west of Aachen are desirable.

  3. Luxembourg: belongs to the Reich.

  4. France: Alsace-Lorraine belongs to the Reich. Her western frontier (considered unsatisfactory as early as 1871) presents a number of special questions:

    A surrender of the French-speaking parts of the former Reich-regions, meanwhile evacuated – especially of Lorraine – is not desired. Shifting to the west of the Lorraine frontier inside of the uniform Minette region (Briey–Longwy), of the Alsatian frontier from the (strategically disadvantageous) main ridge of the Vosges Mountains over the (formerly Alsatian) forest and pasture area of the High Vosges up to approximately the line of Rombach–St Didel (Remirement–St Die) is urgently desired. The question of Belfort–Mompelgard should at least be raised.

  5. Switzerland–Liechtenstein: unchanged. Liechenstein is to be dealt with politically only within the scope of economic agree-

ments with Switzerland. Perhaps agreement with the Prince, who has property in the Reich, possible.

b. Against the states affiliated to the Reich or those which may belong to a European Federation:

1. Denmark: frontier correction, which will transfer Hoyer and Tondern, Apenrade and the island of Alsen to the Reich. Renunciation of the Hadersleben district, return of which to Denmark was already considered by Bismarck.

2. Lithuania: unchanged. In case of close economic co-operation the direct expansion of the immediate hinterland of Memel may be dispensed with.

3. Slovakia: unchanged.

4. Hungary: minor frontier corrections (Altenburg–Wieselburg, Odenburg, Guns) necessary for national-political reasons; major corrections (Steinamanger–Körmend–St Gotthard upon Raab) for traffic-political reasons (domination of the important Alpen–Ostrand line urgently desired). (More comprehensive possibilities are raised under the subject General Resettlement in the Danube Region page. . . .)

5. Croatia: unchanged.

6. Italy: South Tyrol as far as Salurner Klause including the Tyrolese – feeling Ladin valley regions of Groden, Enneberg, Fassa, Buchenstein and Ampezzo, as well as the Carnithian canal-valley, belong to the Reich. Individual improvement also of the frontier demarcation of 1914, necessary at Schilfes Pass (perhaps as far as Spol), in the eastern Dolomites and at the Plöcken Pass (Timau–Tischlwang). Affiliation of the old Ladin, now, however, strongly Italianised zone of Sulzberg, Unternonsberg, Zimmer and Fleims Valley, should at least be mentioned.

c. External frontiers of the Reich-protected countries:

1. Moravia with Slovakia: no problems.

2. Poland: the eastern frontier of Poland to comprise no part of the White Russian or Ukranian enclaves Grodno, Bialystock, Brest–Litowsk, Cholm and Lvov to remain outside Polish territory. For basic considerations on this point, see below.

3. Slovenia: frontier adjustment on a small scale (Rijeka to Croatia) with Croatia.

   A radical solution is necessary in respect of Italy: South Carniola, Görz and Istria (including Trieste and Pola) belong to a Reich-protected Slovenia. For the general problem of Italy raised thereby see page. . . .

2. Aims of Order in a German-led Continental Europe:

A. Basic

Regardless of which countries may be individually encompassed as Reich-affiliated or allied countries, whether a European Federation will materialise, which states it will comprise, the political fact emerges that the individual peoples of Europe will never be prepared in a uniform manner to recognise a German general leadership. Peoples who hitherto have been endangered or oppressed by others, not only Germans, who without imperial past and without imperial ambition cling to their national soil, will most easily be won over as co-supporters of a German order. Conversely, resistance against German leadership – independent of momentary alliance or antagonism – will be very persistent where there exists a supra-national sense of mission, a tradition of ruling over foreign peoples. A third group will be formed where terrorist procedures, if even failing to exterminate whole peoples – an aim, which not even the Mongols of Genghis Khan and the Spaniards of the American Conquest could achieve to a lasting degree – provoke the ones concerned to white heat and thus create completely unsolvable problems (often for decades).

Consequently, the peoples of Europe (the west Europeans, including the Swiss, who live under quite special psychological-historical conditions, are for the present not taken into account) can be divided into several groups:

a. Peoples, who for the last-named reasons must for a long time remain inviolate against a German leadership. To these belong the Great Russians, Poles and Serbs and perhaps also the Czechs. (Of course also European Judaism, especially Eastern Judaism.)

b. Peoples, in whom their own supra-national demand for domination opposes the German leadership. To these belong, apart from the already mentioned Great Russians and Poles, the Italians and the Magyars.

c. Peoples, whose internal changeover in favour of German leadership appears very difficult, but not completely hopeless: to these belong the Swedes, the Norwegians and the Danes and perhaps also the Czechs.

d. Peoples, who could comparatively easily be reconciled or won over through wise politics. To these belong the Finns, Estonians, Latvians, Lithuanians, White Russians, Ukrainians, Slovaks, Croats, Bulgarians, Romanians, Albanians and Greeks, possibly also some of the Caucasian peoples.

A powerful Reich will be obliged to examine and decide, be it alone or with others, a series of disputes among the said countries. In doing so, it will be advisable to avoid the frequently committed political mistake of wishing to reconcile irreconcilable enemies at the expense of possible friends. Scandinavian interests must in any circumstances be treated with care. Polish domination urges over Ukrainians, White Russians, Lithuanians and Slovaks must in these circumstances be given just as little room as Magyar desires concerning St Stephen's Crown and Italian Mare Nostro dreams.

B. Regional

    a. The Mediterranean: Italy has proved that she is lacking the conditions for a great power existence. The more thoroughly this is taken into account the better for the European future. Italian domination over other European peoples would lead to recurring trouble. The question must, therefore, not be introduced. The whole eastern shore of the Adriatic from Trieste to the Greek Islands must be released by Italy. Greece would have to be indemnified for the loss of West Thrace (to the Struma or Mesta) – but not of Greek Macedonia! – to Bulgaria or through the Dodecanese? A personal union with Albania would also have to be considered (in which, however, safeguards of Albanian autonomy against Greek desires of exploitation have to be provided). Croatia must gain free possession of the entire shore from Rijeka to Cattaro including Zara and all offshore islands. Montenegro may be united with Serbia (likewise under guarantee of a certain autonomy). Istria, as part of Slovenia, falls under the direct protection of the Reich. Italian demands against France must not be supported by the Reich; in the question of Italian East Africa, British interests have to be given preference; a favourable situation will result for Greece from the concurrence of German and British desires. In the case of an excessive British engagement for Athens the question of a Greek Cyprus could be raised merely as a tactical manœuvre. Spanish desires may be accepted in the Tangiers question. Syria must be left to a British–French settlement. In the whole Mediterranean spheres German, British and French interests can be settled without great difficulties, if no regard is paid to Italy. Italy is internally too decayed to enforce consideration of her demands in any direction.

    b. The Balkans: among the Slav peoples Bulgaria and Croatia must be furthered. Bulgaria should remain – with the exception of smaller territories in West Thrace and in Macedonia to be returned to Greece – in the possession of her gains through war and agreement (South Dobruja, West Thrace with an Aegean Sea entry, Pirrot, Inner Macedonia). Free

port in Salonica. The allocation of West Macedonian territories with Albanian enclaves to Albania may stand. As regards
the strengthening of the Croats, see above – Old Serbia
(including the former Sanjak of Novi Pazar and Montenegro)
will even in the best case remain for a long time a centre of
unrest. The question of dynasty will create difficulties in
Belgrade and in Athens. If the negotiations take place under
the auspices of a strong German position of power, the
abdication of the Greek King in favour of his brother Paul
would have to be arranged in Athens and a return of the
Karageorgeovitsches to be prevented in Belgrade. Resettlements on a great scale will hardly come into consideration in
the Balkans south of the Danube–San line.

c. The Danube Region: the central problem is Hungary. If a
quiet Central Europe is desired, not only must new Hungarian
demands be resisted, but already accomplished 'revisions' be
partly rescinded. Here it is necessary – apart from revision of
the Reich-frontier already mentioned – to make frontier im-
provements in favour of the Slovaks (especially around
Košice) and of Croats (Mur area, South Baranya). Surrender
of the Carpathian Ukraine to the Ukraine (and including the
towns of Ungvár and Munkács) mainly and politically most
important – the return of North Transylvania to Rumania.
This would reconcile the neighbours of Hungary with the new
order. In Hungary itself explosive events of nationalistic as
well as of social nature must be expected. However, the central
point must not be lost sight of. As long as they are tolerably
strong, the Magyars will never acquiesce in an arrangement
which gives other peoples of the Danube region even modest
rights. They have always proved the most adroit and most
persistent opponents of German influence in South-east
Europe, and the most artful persecutors of German nationalism. There is no reason to spare them, when the conditions
of power permit a radical treatment.

The outlined changes do not, however, offer a radical solution
of the involved questions of 'Volkstum' characteristics in the
Danube region. With modest frontier adjustments (and small
resettlements) the Croatian–Magyar and the Slovak–Magyar
frontier problem (the latter, however, in a rather unsatisfactory manner in the sense of economics and geography) can,
indeed, be solved, but the great questions remain politically
unsolved. They present themselves:

1. as a problem regarding German ethnic groups in Hungary,

Romania, East Croatia and in the areas of Batschka and Banat hitherto under Serbian administration;

2. as a problem regarding the Hungarian–Romanian ethnic and state frontier, especially the ethnic island of the Magyar Szeklers in Transylvania.

The experiences up to now give reason for the presumption that even a strong German Reich would again and again be forced to intervene in the home politics of Hungary, of Romania, of Croatia and of Serbia – but especially of Hungary – for the protection of an autonomy safeguarding the 2 million South-east Germans in their existence. It is likewise to be expected that in the Hungarian–Romanian relationship there will be no peace as long as either 5 million Romanians remain under Magyar domination or the same number of Magyars and Szeklers under Romanian domination. Minority autonomies are always endangered. Other solutions are, however, not attainable in the present settlement situation.

Here the question presents itself regarding the expediency of a large interchange of population to be carried out slowly and organically, which would have to go hand in hand with very considerable frontier adjustments. In doing so, more than one possibility of solution would have to be examined (particularly since radical interim developments in the Protectorate and in Slovenia threaten to incorporate these areas too into the large resettlement avalanche). As most important aspects, however, the following have at the same time to be kept in mind:

1. The restoration of the Transylvanian unity inside the Romanian not the Hungarian state (with the evacuation of the Magyar-conscious part of the Szeklers and with Romanian area sacrifices in the Banat).

2. The resettlement of the Danube Swabians in the parts of West Hungary to be ceded to the Reich by Hungary (up to the Bakony forest and Lake Balaton). The Magyar people would have to be indemnified by uniform settlement of the Batschka and the Banat.

Part problems will remain unsolved even with this proposition, which can be implemented only in years; so, for example, the final destiny of the Transylvanian Saxons.

d. Baltic Provinces and Karelia: the establishment of Estonian, Latvian and Lithuanian statehood in the form of countries affiliated to the Reich with the existing frontiers (Lithuania including Vilna) should meet with no difficulties, if the general question of the European eastern frontier proves solvable.

The Karelian question also belongs within this scope: a safeguarding of Finland (and of all North Scandinavia) against
recurrent Great Russian danger is possible only on the basis
of the Onega–Swir frontier, which gives the whole of Karelia
and of Kola to Finland, thereby presenting Finland with a
difficult and major colonisation problem, secures for Europe
important mineral resources, which are partly unique in
Europe, but cuts off Russia from the ice-free part of the Arctic
Ocean. The destiny of Petersburg remains open even with this
solution. The best security line of Baltic North Europe would
follow the River Volkhov to the Ilmen Lake and would join
an independent White Russia (i.e. to be supported and
equipped for a long time by the Reich) in the Valday area
(historically at the most to be connected with the short-lived
principality of Polzk). The possibility or impossibility of such
solutions would largely depend on the extent to which mass
migration has already been enforced by the course of the war
itself and by the politics of Stalin in these areas.

e. The Ukraine, White Russia and the Caucasus: this last great
set of problems of central and eastern Europe leads even more
profoundly than the foregoing to the decisive basic question:
under what conditions can the pacification of eastern Europe
be achieved at all. Probably there is only one – troublesome
and costly chance; the establishment of a belt of states,
separated from Moscow, leading from White Russia over the
Ukraine to the Caucasus and to the Hindu Kush. In order to
be durable, such states must be desired and carried by their
peoples. That is out of the question for the time being – at
least for the more closely situated areas of the Ukraine and of
White Russia. Such willingness would first have to be created.
It could only be created under the two-fold condition; that
the national consciousness of the White Russians and of the
Ukrainians (if necessary, also that of the Georgians and of the
other Caucasus peoples) against 'Great Russianism', is partly
supported and partly roused and that at the same time land
policies are pursued, which are completely contrary to those of
the Bolsheviks. The first requires that a Ukranian and a White
Russian or leading and cultural class be furthered or newly
created; the second necessitates that any exploitation-policies
concerning large holdings in the style of the Sowchos and of
Kolchos economy be abandoned and the land be left to the
peasant. Even if this policy proves to be workable, a German
'military frontier' of long duration on the River Don or the
River Volga will even in the most favourable case be necessary

to safeguard a lasting order. The last postulate in this case is also that Stalin can be world-politically isolated in Siberia, that the naval powers be induced to cease assisting him; and that by wise agricultural policy even in occupied parts of Russia the pacification of Pan-Russianism on both sides of the front, with or without Stalin, can be achieved. If these prospects are rejected, it will become necessary to vacate great parts of eastern Europe, to shift the military frontier further to the west and to expose the next generation to a new Russian and Communist war under completely unpredictable conditions. It will therefore not be possible to do anything but at least to try the way outlined above. A postulate for this is that any surrender of Ukrainian or of White Russian national soil to other peoples be avoided, i.e. that Eastern Galicia must not be Polish, the Carpathian Ukraine must not be Magyar, Northern Bukovina, and especially Odessa, must not be Rumanian. Beyond this the Ukrainian northern and eastern frontiers would have to be generously arranged, the Ukrainian state area would have to be extended to the lower Volga and the central Caucasus (i.e. including the Kuban area). In conclusion, attention is drawn to the incalculable diversity of national problems in areas, which are still – and perhaps permanently – situated outside the scope of German armed power; to the Caucasian and Turkestan problems (with their religious complications: Islam, Panturanism).

f. Northern and Western Europe: the question presents itself more profoundly for the northern and western European countries than for those in eastern and south-east Europe (where, given a favourable point of departure, much may be regulated according to the unilateral wishes of the Reich): can the former be won for or incorporated into a European federative system? Is a supra-continental and a supra-national peace regulation based on an agreement between continental Europe and the Anglo-Saxon powers thinkable? Within such a peace regulation formulas would also have to be found for the West European countries and their colonial empires provided that the continental and the oceanic leading powers, too, accept the introduction of supra-national planning and control authorities in the military-political and in the economic-political fields. However little the prospects in this respect may be, even if they are regarded as pure Utopia, it is certain that programmes of world organising character are being prepared on the part of the Anglo-Saxons, which have at least great psychological significance. Northern and western

Europe, apart from questions about the immediate frontier extent of the Reich, is free from territorial problems. All the more a struggle will be fought here not only for European but also for world-political forms of organisation, which will take effect in the shape of many graded restrictions of sovereignty of the individual state. It would be premature to examine at present the series of these restrictions in their applicability or non-applicability to this or that country (beyond what has already been said under the heading Reich-protected countries, countries affiliated to the Reich and countries allied to the Reich). It is important to consider them in principle. The simple international forms of law and of relationship of the nineteenth century will not return. They will be replaced by direct governing forms of differently grouped confederations (such as have already been formed or at least appear in outlines in all great continental power spheres, especially in the British Commonwealth of Nations, as far as time and psychology are concerned). In northern and western Europe the result of the war will find external expression in the number of states ready to unite in independent confederations and those willing to follow predominantly Anglo-Saxon or predominantly German leadership. The political forms of such unions will have to be very numerous as far as law is concerned. Fully developed confederations are just as conceivable as are part solutions of a different nature: defence unions, total or partial (stronger standardisation of air or of sea power as against the national traditionally bound land power; bases); economic unions (part solutions possible here, too, in the currency and money, postal and traffic; customs and financial spheres); technical and social planning communities (which could assume supreme significance).

Such solutions suggest themselves on European soil in the event that once again attempts be made to by-pass the greatest political question: that of a world-economic planning of production and consumption, of labour and population – this time in continental instead of (as in 1919) individual state isolations. The tasks of such planning are obvious. They extend from the co-ordination of scientific research to the distribution of raw materials and consumer goods; from armament control to the basic questions of division of labour according to climates and races (the Jewish problem, too, as an eastern European as well as world problem is solvable only within such a scope). But especially at a time when the technical-economic and with that also the political-organisational concentration of peoples into large scale areas, of the large scale areas into world planning is deemed inevitable, it emerges with increased emphasis that Europe – and not only Europe! – is in need of a Magna Carta Libertatum in all religious and cultural spheres.

3. Africa

Africa is only a special field of application for many of the things which have been said in the foregoing paragraph. An all-European responsibility for the development of Africa proper (negroid and hamitic negroid) (from which the Atlantic–Mediterranean northern margin of Morocco up to Egypt is excluded: here the traditional status of possessions – including that of an Italian Libya–Cyrenaica – should be preserved) should be aimed at. The form of a modern colonial organisation for Negro Africa should be all-European, i.e. supra-national, so that the territorial structures of the development area (which are partly very bad regarding geography and economics) should be removed or become obsolescent. Within the scope of such general planning room should then be found for the activity of persons from those parts of Europe, which have hitherto been under excessive population pressure (among others Italy). A satisfaction of the specific German colonial demands in the form of isolated strips of land (even with geographical and economic sensible rounding off) would, though useful for the Reich and even necessary in the sense of a great power minimum of existence within the scope of all-European tasks, only be an expedient. If this has to be accepted, then the areas around the Guinea Gulf would regionally be eligible: i.e. a Greater Cameroons solution – to which British and French as well as Belgian and (perhaps in exchange for the northern half of German South West Africa) Portuguese areas could contribute. The southern half of South West Africa belongs into the settling context of a uniform white South Africa. German as well as Italian East Africa will never be surrendered by Britain as long as India and the Indian Ocean are dominated by Britain.

Real concessions in the colonial field will, however, only be made by the naval powers when one of two conditions exists: a breakthrough of the German Army to Central Africa (possible only if either the British Orient position is broken or French North Africa comes under German command) – or a genuine world-political willingness to reach an understanding, within which also the remaining responsibility for maritime communication lines between the Reich and her tropical possessions could be borne by the Atlantic fleets. Willingness to reach an understanding is, however, conditional on circumstances which are far beyond the possible scope of this memorandum.

Sources

PROLOGUE

1. Karl Heinz Harbeck, 'Die Zeitschrift fur Geopolitik 1924–44'.
2. Edmund Walsh, *Total Power*.
3. William Shirer, *Rise and Fall of the Third Reich*, 69–70.
4. Konrad Heiden, *Der Fuehrer*, 83.
5. *Ibid.*, 163–4.
6. Walsh, *op. cit.*, 26.
7. *Ibid.*, 14, 15; Heiden, *op. cit.*, 225, 254, 255.
8. Adolf Hitler, *Mein Kampf*, 141, 143.
9. Ernst Hanfstaengl, *Hitler – The Missing Years*, 115–31.
10. Heiden, *op. cit.*, 285–6. *The Earl Goebbels Diaries*, 77.
11. Hanfstaengl, *op. cit.*, 73.
12. Fritz Thyssen, *I Paid Hitler*, 129. Otto Dietrich, *The Hitler I Knew*, 172–3. Heiden, *op. cit.*, 127. *Ibid.*, 313–14. *Ibid.*, 398.
13. Donald Hawley Norton, '*Karl Haushofer and his Influence on Nazi Ideology and German Foreign Policy 1919–45*', 57–82. *Ibid.*, 95. Rudolf Hess, *Reden*, Address to Overseas Germans.
14. Norman H. Baynes, *Hitler's Speeches 1922–39*, vol. I, 309. Joachim C. Fest, *The Face of the Third Reich*, 189; Baynes, *op. cit.*, 288. Rudolf Hess, *Reden*.
15. Gerald Reitlinger, *The S.S. Alibi of a Nation*, 64, ff.
16. Fest, *op. cit.*, 191; *National Zeitung*, 27 April 1941.
17. Rudolf Hess, *Reden*.
18. Shirer, *op. cit.*, 279. Alan Bullock, *Hitler, A Study in Tyranny*, 306.
Trial of German Major War Criminals at Nuremberg, Proceedings: Part VI, 148.

I. The Work of Albrecht Haushofer
1. EARLY DAYS

1. Allen Dulles, *Germany's Underground*, 122.
2. Verger, *Revue des spectacles et des lettres en Allemagne occupée*; Heinz Haushofer, '*Souvenirs sur mon frère Albrecht*', 24.
3. Carl von Weizsaecker, *In Memoriam Albrecht Haushofer*, 19.
4. Rainer Hildebrandt, *Wir sind die Letzten*, 44.
5. Ursula Michel, *Albrecht Haushofer and National Socialism*, 15.
6. Hartschimmelhof Papers.
7. *Ibid.*
8. *Ibid.*

9. Michel, *op. cit.*, 94.   17. *Ibid.*
10. *Ibid.*, 96.   18. *Ibid.*
11. Hartschimmelhof Papers.   19. *Ibid.*
12. *Ibid.*   20. *Ibid.*
13. *Ibid.*   21. *Ibid.*
14. Michel, *op. cit.*, 69.   22. *Ibid.*
15. *Ibid.*, 73–74.   23. *Ibid.*
16. Hartschimmelhof Papers.   24. *Ibid.*

2. PROTECTION FROM HESS: 1933

1. Michel, *op. cit.*, 120.   9. *Ibid.*
2. Hartschimmelhof Papers.   10. Norton, *op. cit.*, 94.
3. *Ibid.*   11. Hartschimmelhof Papers.
4. *Ibid.*   12. *Ibid.*
5. *Ibid.*   13. Federal Archives in Koblenz,
6. *Ibid.*   HC 833.
7. *Ibid.*   14. *Ibid.*
8. *Ibid.*   15. Hartschimmelhof Papers.

3. PERSONAL ADVISER: 1934

1. Verger, *op. cit.*; Jacques Nobe-   16. *Ibid.*
   court, '*A la trace d'Albrecht*   17. Norton, *op. cit.*, 139.
   Haushofer', 8.   18. *Ibid.*, 140.
2. Federal Archives in Koblenz,   19. Hartschimmelhof Papers.
   HC 833.   20. *Ibid.*
3. *Ibid.*   21. Federal Archives in Koblenz,
4. Hartschimmelhof Papers.   HC 833.
5. Hans   Adolf   Jacobsen,   22. Eva Braun, *The Private Life of*
   Nationalsozialistische Aussen-   *Adolf Hitler*, 64.
   politik 1933–38, 587, 588, 593,   23. Hartschimmelhof Papers.
   790.   24. Jacobsen, *op. cit.*, 196.
6. *Ibid.*, 794.   25. Ballhorn,   Franz   von,   'In
7. *Ibid.*, 340.   Memoriam   Albrecht   Haus-
8. Hartschimmelhof Papers.   hofer and his friends', *Das*
9. *Ibid.*   *Freie Wort*, 20 April 1951.
10. Michel, *op. cit.*, 153.   26. Jacobsen, *op. cit.*, 196.
11. *Ibid.*, 153.   27. Ballhorn, Franz von, *op. cit.*
12. *Ibid.*, 154.   28. Verger, *op. cit.*, Heinz Haus-
13. *Ibid.*, 154.   hofer, 25.
14. Norton, *op. cit.*, 113–15.   29. Hartschimmelhof Papers.
15. Hartschimmelhof Papers.   30. *Ibid.*

4. MISSIONS FOR HITLER AND RIBBENTROP: 1936-7

1. Jacobsen, *op. cit.*, 196.   memorandum for Hess, 'The
2. Federal Archives in Koblenz,   Operation   of   Germany's
   HC 833. Albrecht Haushofer's   Foreign Policy'.

3. Weinberg, G. L. 'Secret Hitler–Beneš negotiations in 1936–7', *Journal of Central European Affairs*, January 1960, 367.

4. Michel, *op. cit.*, 166.

5. Weinberg, *op. cit.*, 368.

6. *Ibid.*, 369, 370.

7. *Ibid.*, 370, 371.

8. *Ibid.*, 371.

9. *Ibid.*, 372.

10. *Ibid.*, 372, 373.

11. Michel, *op. cit.*, 149; Hartschimmelhof Papers.

12. Dr Eduard Beneš, *Memoirs*, 20.

For a more detailed analysis of the Haushofer–Beneš negotiations see the original German document written by Albrecht Haushofer in the Manuscript Division of the Library of Congress, Washington, D.C.

13. Hartschimmelhof Papers.

14. Walsh, *Total Power*, 8, 9, 42.

15. Michel, *op. cit.*, 177.

16. *Ibid.*, 178.

17. Hildebrandt, *op. cit.*, 57.

18. Rolf Italiaander, *Besiegeltes Leben*, 21, 22.

5. THE OLYMPIC GAMES AND THE BRITISH: 1936-8

1. Michel, *op. cit.*, 162.

2. Walter Stubbe, 'In Memoriam Albrecht Haushofer', *Vierteljahreshefte für Zeitgeschichte*, July 1960, 239, 240.

3. Italiaander, *op. cit.*, 23, 24.

4. Fritz Hesse, *Das Spiel Um Deutschland*, 64, 65.

5. Ward Price, *I Know These Dictators*, 32.

6. Hamilton Papers.

7. *Ibid.*, the transcript of Albrecht Haushofer's lecture to

Chatham House was sent by the latter to the Duke of Hamilton after the war on request.

8. *Ibid.*

9. Stubbe, *op. cit.*, 240.

10. Harbeck, *op. cit.*, 252.

11. Hamilton Papers.

12. *Ibid.*

13. *Ibid.*

14. Stubbe, *op. cit.*, 241–242.

15. *Ibid.*, 242.

6. MUNICH AND DECLINE: 1938

1. Hartschimmelhof Papers.

2. Michel, *op. cit.*, 191.

3. *Ibid.*, 194.

4. Hildebrandt, *op. cit.*, 23.

5. Hartschimmelhof Papers.

6. Ibid.

7. Hildebrandt, *op. cit.*, 23.

8. Michel, *op. cit.*, 202.

9. Heinz Haushofer, statement made to Dr John Campsie after the war.

10. Michel, *op. cit.*, 206.

11. Federal Archives in Koblenz,

HC 833, draft in handwriting with amendments and deletions written by Albrecht Haushofer.

12. Harbeck, *op. cit.*, 70; Michel, *op. cit.*, 204.

13. Harbeck, *op. cit.*, 68, 69; Walsh, *op. cit.*, 350–1; Hildebrandt, *op. cit.*, 38; Heinz Haushofer, statement made to Dr John Campsie after the war.

14. Hartschimmelhof Papers.

15. Hesse, *op. cit.*, 155.

16. Harbeck, *op. cit.*, 255.

7. A MESSAGE OF DESPAIR: JULY 1939

1. Stubbe, *op. cit.*, 243.
2. Michel, *op. cit.*, 246–7.
3. Hartschimmelhof Papers.
4. *Ibid.*
5. *Ibid.*
6. Hansard 1938–9, vol. CCCXLIX, 1785–6.
7. Hamilton Papers.
8. Hartschimmelhof Papers.
9. Weizsaeker, *In Memoriam Albrecht Haushofer*, 22.
10. Stubbe, *op. cit.*, 244.
11. Hansard 1938–9, vol. XXXL, 377–8.
12. William Temple (Archbishop of York), letter to *Daily Telegraph*, 4.12.39; A. C. Lindsay, Master of Balliol, letter to *The Times*, 7.10.39; Arthur Salter, article in *Spectator*, 27.10.39.
13. BBC transcript of broadcast by Archbishop of York, 2.10.39.
14. Clydesdale, letter to *The Times*, 6.10.39.
15. Letter from Dr Kurt Hahn (9.10.67) to Duke of Hamilton, quoting from a letter of Frederick Ogilvie to Dr Hahn (11.10.39). NOTE: For a detailed analysis of Ribbentrop's intentions towards Poland see Douglas-Hamilton, J., 'Ribbentrop and War' in *Journal of Contemporary History*, Vol. V, No. 4, 1970.

8. A BITTER DILEMMA: DECEMBER: 1939

1. Michel, *op. cit.*, 206.
2. Hartschimmelhof Papers: Albrecht Haushofer's enclosure with his letter to his father, 5.10.39.
3. *Ibid.*
4. *Ibid.*

9. THE DOUBLE GAME: 1940

1. Hartschimmelhof Papers.
2. *Ibid.*
3. *Ibid.*
4. Hesse, *op. cit.*, 235–6.
5. Gerald Reitlinger, *The SS: Alibi of a Nation*, 163.
6. Hildebrandt, *op. cit.*, 79.
7. *Ibid.*, 16, 17.
8. *Ibid.*, 58, 99, 100.
9. *Ibid.*, chapter entitled 'No. 50 Brentano Strasse'.
10. *Ibid.*, 99.
11. Hans Bernd Gisevius, *To the Bitter End*, 293–4.
12. Sir John Wheeler-Bennett, *The Nemesis of Power*, 484–93. For a more detailed analysis read also the *Diaries* of Ulrich von Hassell.
13. See Appendix I.
14. Michel, *op. cit.*, 262.
15. Viscount Templewood (formerly Sir Samuel Hoare), *Ambassador on a Special Mission*, 275.
16. Hildebrandt, *op. cit.*, 112.

II. The Hess–Haushofer Peace Feelers

1. HESS'S DECLINE AND HITLER'S PEACE OFFERS

1. Hitler, *Mein Kampf*, 180–1.
2. Trial of German Major War Criminals at Nuremberg, *Proceedings*, Part 6, 148.
3. *Ibid.*, Part 14, 329: Part 6, 152.
4. *Ibid.*, Part 6, 148–9: Part 3 89–90.
5. Dietrich, *op. cit.*, 189.

6. Stephen H. Roberts, *The House that Hitler Built*, 79–81.
7. Trial of German Major War Criminals at Nuremberg, *Proceedings*, Part 6, 152.
8. *Ibid.*, 153.
9. Hans Kohn, *The Mind of Germany*, 337.
10. Rudolf Hess, *Reden*: 'Essence and Endeavour of the NSDAP' 16.1.1937.
11. Trial of German Major War Criminals at Nuremberg, *Proceedings*, Part 6, 152–3; Part 19, 375.
12. *Ibid.*, Part 22, 259; Mau and Krausnick, *German History 1933–45*, 123.
13. Hess, *op. cit.*, 'Essence and Endeavour of the NSDAP'.
14. Shirer, *op. cit.*, 397. Trial of German Major War Criminals at Nuremberg, *Proceedings*, Part 6, 151.
15. *Ibid.*, 151.
16. Sir Robert Vansittart, *Black Record: Germans Past and Present*, 12.
17. Trial of German Major War Criminals at Nuremberg, *Proceedings*, Part 6, 153.
18. Gerhard Boldt, *In the Shelter with Hitler*, 30–1; Hanfstaengl, *op. cit.*, 231.
19. *Ibid.*, 230.
20 Trial of German Major War Criminals at Nuremberg, *Proceedings*, Part 6, 148, 157.

21. *Ibid.*, 148.
22. Hildebrandt, *op. cit.*, 38.
23. Ansel, *Hitler Confronts England*, 10–11; Trumbull Higgins, *Hitler and Russia*, 33.
24. Hitler, *op. cit.*, 143.
25. Trial of German Major War Criminals at Nuremberg, *Proceedings*, Part 6, 158.
26. *Ibid.*
27. *Ibid.*, 158–9.
28. Hitler, *My New Order* Raoul de Roussy de Sales, 755.
29. Ciano's Diary, ed. Malcolm Muggeridge, 165.
30. Shirer, *op. cit.*, 881.
31. Ciano's *Diary*, 266.
32. *Ibid.*, 275.
33. William Shirer, *The Rise and Fall of the Third Reich*, 757.
34. Hitler, *My New Order*, 816, 834, 837, 838.
35. Gerhard Weinberg, *Germany and the Soviet Union*, 115.
36. Dietrich, *op. cit.*, 64.
37. Fritz Hesse, *Hitler and the English*, 125.
38. Schellenberg, *Memoirs*, ed. Louis Hagen, 201.
39. Hildebrandt, *op. cit.*, 78.
40. *Ibid.*, 111.
41. Walter Warlimont, *Inside Hitler's HQ*, 33–4.
42. Trial of German Major War Criminals at Nuremberg, *Proceedings*, Part II, 12, 13.
43. Kersten, *Memoirs*, 88.
44. Hitler, *Mein Kampf*, 143.

2. A TUTORIAL FOR HESS: 8 SEPTEMBER 1940

1. Alan Bullock, *Hitler, A Study in Tyranny*, 596.
2. Ian Hamilton, *General Sir Ian Hamilton*, 448–9.
3. Documents on German Foreign Policy 1918–45: Series D, vol. XI, 15, 16 ff.
4. *Ibid.*, 78–81.

3. THE PEACE FEELER: 23 SEPTEMBER 1940

1. Hesse, *Hitler and the English*, 93.
2. Ilse Hess, *Prisoner of Peace*, 15.
3. Documents on German

Foreign Policy 1918–45, Series D, vol. XI, 81.

4. Dietrich, *op. cit.*, 62–3.
5. Documents on German Foreign Policy 1918–45, Series D, vol. XI, 60–1.
6. Federal Archives in Koblenz HC 832 (C.002.195).
7. Documents on German Foreign Policy 1918–45, Series

D, vol. XI, 129–30.
8. Federal Archives in Koblenz HC 832 (C.002.197–202).
9. *Ibid.* (C. 002.203).
10. *Ibid.* (C.002.204–205).
11. Churchill, *War Speeches*, comp. Charles Eade, vol. I, 256.
12. Federal Archives in Koblenz HC 832.
13. Hartschimmelhof Papers.

4. THE BRITISH SECRET SERVICE

1. Hamilton Papers.
2. This is an exact reproduction of the original letter, written in English, which was intercepted by the British Censor. The letter reproduced in the Documents on German Foreign Policy 1918–45: Series D Vol. XI, 131–2, is a translation of the copy in German, which Albrecht Haushofer sent to his father, and its terms do not coincide exactly with the original letter.

3. Lord Percy of Newcastle, *Some Memories.*
4. Hamilton Papers.
5. Churchill, *The Second World War*, Vol. II, 152.
6. Captain S. Payne Best, *The Venlo Incident.*
7. Hamilton Papers.
8. *Ibid.*

5. THE LEAP INTO THE DARK: 10 MAY 1941

1. Sumner Welles, *The Time for Decision*, 90–1.
2. Hildebrandt, *op. cit.*, 36.
3. Ilse Hess, *Prisoner of Peace*, 16.
4. See Memorandum on the Possibilities of a German–English Peace, Part II, ch. 2; Ilse Hess, *op. cit.*, 15.
5. Paul Schmidt, broadcast reproduced in the *Listener*, 16.4.70.
6. James Leasor, *Rudolf Hess, the Uninvited Envoy*, 85.
7. Hess and Lindbergh met on a number of occasions.
8. Leasor, *op. cit.*, 84–5.
9. Ilse Hess, *op. cit.*, 28–9.

10. Colonel Peter Fleming, *The Flying Visit.*
11. Leasor, *op. cit.*, 208.
12. *Ibid.*, 73–80.
13. Eugene Davidson, *The Trial of the Germans: Nuremberg 1945–6*, 112.
14. Churchill, *Second World War*, Vol. III, 44–5.
15. National Archives of U.S.A., Washington, D.C., Record Group No. 242.
16. Hamilton Papers: Wing Commander Duke of Hamilton's Report to the Prime Minister on his Interview with Hess, Sunday 11 May 1941.

6. HESS, HAMILTON AND CHURCHILL: 11 MAY 1941

1. Hamilton Papers: Wing Commander Duke of Hamilton's Report to the Prime Minister on his interview with Hess, Sunday 11 May 1941.
2. This account was given in

writing by Mr Jock Colville, summer 1969.

3. Churchill, *The Second World War*, vol. III, 43.

4. Some garbled versions have been given of the words which

Churchill used from second-hand sources. The words which Churchill in fact used are as stated in the text.

5. Sir Ivone Kirkpatrick, *The Inner Circle*, 175.

7. HESS'S PEACE TERMS: 12-15 May 1941

1. Kirkpatrick, *op. cit.*, ch. 8.
2. *Ibid.*, 180.
3. Hamilton Papers: Kirkpatrick's report on an interview with Hess at midnight on Monday 12 May 1941.
4. Kirkpatrick, *op. cit.*, 179.
5. Hamilton Papers: Kirkpatrick's report on an interview with Hess on afternoon of Wednesday 14 May 1941.
6. *Ibid.*

7. Kirkpatrick, *op. cit.*, 180.
8. Kirkpatrick's report on an interview with Hess on 15 May 1941; Trial of German Major War Criminals, Proceedings, Part 6, 162.
9. Kirkpatrick, *op. cit.*, 181.
10. Bullock, *op. cit.*, 385.
11. Kirkpatrick, *op. cit.*, 184.
12. J. R. Rees, *The Case of Rudolf Hess*, 47–8, 71.

8. THE SILENCE OF THE BRITISH GOVERNMENT: 1941

1. A. P. Herbert, *Let Us Be Glum*.
2. Sir Anthony Eden, *The Reckoning*, 256.
3. Kirkpatrick, *op. cit.*, 178.
4. Hansard, 1940–1, vol. 371, 1085.
5. Harold Nicolson, *Diaries and Letters 1939–45*, 166.
6. Eden, *op. cit.*, 256.
7. Nicolson, *op. cit.*, 167.
8. Eden, *op. cit.*, 256.
9. Nicolson, *op. cit.*, 167.
10. Hamilton Papers.
11. Vansittart, *op. cit.*, 2.
12. Hansard, 1940–1, vol. 371, 1591.
13. *Ibid.*, 1701–2.
14 This incident was confirmed

by an Intelligence Officer who saw the map, and the episode is referred to indirectly in Leasor, *The Uninvited Envoy*, 149–50.

15. Sefton Delmer, *Black Boomerang*, 43, 44, 52–60.
16. Hamilton Papers: report of Dr Kurt Hahn for the British Foreign Office entitled 'The Flight of Hess: An Attempt at Reconstruction'.
17. Churchill, *The Second World War*, vol. III, 46–7.
18. Robert Sherwood, *Roosevelt and Hopkins*, 294.
19. *Ibid.*, 374.
20. Eden, *op. cit.*, 259.

9. A PRISONER OF WAR: 1941-5

1. Lord Simon, *Retrospect*, 261–3.
2. Trial of German Major War

Criminals at Nuremberg: Proceedings, Part 10, 13–15.

3. Delmer, *Black Boomerang*, 56, 57.
4. Simon, *op. cit.*, 263.
5. Rees, *op. cit.*, 47–8.
6. Delmer, *op. cit.*, 59–60.
7. Leasor, *op. cit.*, 161.
8. Alexander Werth, *Russia at War 1941–45*, 120.
9. Churchill, *Seccnd World War*, vol. III, ch. XX, 49.
10. Werth, *op. cit.*, 235–6.
11. Rees, *op. cit.*, 56, 76, 94, 217–24.
12. Douglas Kelley, *22 Cells in Nuremberg*, 235.
13. Rees, *op. cit.*, 52, 59.
14. *Ibid.*, 56, 70, 126.
15. *Ibid.*, 44.
16. *Ibid.*, 137–9.
17. Ulrich von Hassell, *Memoirs*, 159–60.
18. *Ibid.*, 176.
19. *Ibid.*, 177.
20. Rolf Italiaander, *Besiegeltes Leben*, 25.
21. Hildebrandt, *op. cit.*, 112–3.
22. *Ibid.* 112–3.

III. The Fate of Albrecht Haushofer

1. TURMOIL AT THE DICTATOR'S COURT: 11 MAY 1941

1. Otto Dietrich, *The Hitler I Knew*, 62.
2. Albert Speer, *Erinnerungen*, 189.
3. Article in *Weltbild*, 2nd, 3rd, 4th and 5th issues in 1951 under the title of 'And this Fool flies to England'.
4. Dietrich, *op. cit.*, 62–3.
5. *Ibid.*, 62–3.
6. *Ibid.*, 62–3.
7. Ilse Hess, *Prisoner of Peace*, 27.
8. Dietrich, *op. cit.*, 63; Speer, *op. cit.*, 189.
9. Dr Paul Schmidt, *Hitler's Interpreter*, 233.
10. Walter Schellenberg, *Memoirs*, 199, 200.
11. Shirer, *op. cit.*, 998; Speer, *op. cit.*, 189–91. Articles in *Weltbild*, see Footnote 3 above.
12. Curt Reiss, *Joseph Goebbels*, 205; Rudolf Semmler, *Goebbels, The Man next to Hitler*, 32.
13. Hamilton Papers: translation of the first communiqué by Dr Kurt Hahn for the British Foreign Office, May 1941.
14. Schmidt, *op. cit.*, 233.
15. Ilse Hess, *op. cit.*, 18.
16. Fritz Hesse, *Hitler and the English*, 126.
17. Hamilton Papers: translation of the second communiqué by Dr Kurt Hahn for the British Foreign Office, May 1941.
18. Ernst von Weizsaecker, *Memoirs*, 168.
19. Ulrich von Hassell, *Diaries 1938–44*, 176.
20. Semmler, *op. cit.*, 33.
21. Trial of Major German War Criminals at Nuremberg, *Proceedings*, Part 6, 163–4.
22. Ciano's *Diary* 1939–43, 341–2.
23. Bullock, *op. cit.*, 645.
24. Churchill, *The Second World War*, vol. III, 320–3.
25. Bullock, *op. cit.*, 645; Joseph Wulf, *Martin Bormann*, 131; National Archives of U.S.A., Washington, D.C., Record Group No. 242, T580-Roll 36.
26. James Mcgovern, *Martin Bormann*, 61.
27. Semmler, *op. cit.*, 34–6.
28. Ciano's *Diary* 1939–43, 352.
29. Speer, *op. cit.*, 190.

2. HITLER AND ALBRECHT HAUSHOFER:
12 MAY 1941

1. Walter Stubbe, 'In Memoriam Albrecht Haushofer', *Viertel-jahreshefte für Zeitgeschichte,* July 1960, 253–4.
2. *Ibid.,* 253.
3. Documents on German Foreign Policy, 1918–45 : Series D, vol. XII, 783–7.
4. Hesse, *Hitler and the English,* 95.
5. Hildebrandt, *op. cit.,* 114, 115.
6. National Archives of U.S.A.,

Washington, D.C., Record Group No. 242, T175, Roll 128.
7. Schellenberg, *op. cit.,* 200.
8. Hildebrandt, *op. cit.,* 114.
9. Michel, *op. cit.,* 270.
10. Reitlinger, *op. cit.,* 161.
11. *Ibid.,* 160–66.
12. Michel, *op. cit.,* 269.
13. Hartschimmelhof Papers.
14. Hildebrandt, *op. cit.,* 121.
15. *Ibid.,* 115, 122.

3. THE PEACE MEMORANDUM: NOVEMBER 1941

1. Hassell, *op. cit.,* 177.
2. Walsh, *op. cit.,* 40.
3. See Appendix II; Weizsaecker, *Memoirs,* 182.
4. Michel, *op. cit.,* 200.
5. *Ibid.,* 276.
6. Federal Archives in Koblenz, HC 833, see Appendix II.
7. Hildebrandt, *op. cit.,* 130.
8. Statement made by Frau Schnuhr to Dr J. Campsie after the war.
9. Hildebrandt, *op. cit.,* 131.
10. *Ibid.,* 132.
11. Italiaander, *op. cit.,* 19–20.
12. Hildebrandt, *op. cit.,* 99–102; Reitlinger, *op. cit.,* 160–66,

289–313.
13. Ciano's *Diary,* 455.
14. Allen Dulles, *Germany's Underground,* 33, 34.
15. Christopher Sykes, *Troubled Loyalty,* 375; Hildebrandt, *op. cit.,* 130; Michel, *op. cit.,* 287.
16. Gerhard Ritter, *The German Resistance,* 207–8; Michel, *op. cit.,* 287–8.
17. Hildebrandt, *op. cit.,* 158.
18. *Ibid.,* 176.
19. *Ibid.,* 79.
20. *Ibid.,* 131.
21. *Ibid.,* 133.
22. *Ibid.,* 131–2.
23. *Ibid.,* 135.

4. HIMMLER'S TREACHERY AND THE JULY PLOT:
1943-4

1. Hildebrandt, *op. cit.,* 176.
2. Michel, *op. cit.,* 293.
3. Hildebrandt, *op. cit.,* 135–7; Sir John Wheeler-Bennett, *The Nemesis of Power,* 576–7.
4. *Ibid.,* ch. 11; Hildebrandt, *op. cit.,* 135.
5. *Ibid.,* 136.
6. Michel, *op. cit.,* 293.
7. Hildebrandt, *op. cit.,* 135;

Statement made by Stahmer to Dr J. Campsie after the war.
8. Hassell, *Diaries,* 251; Wheeler-Bennett, *op. cit.,* 577.
9. *Ibid.,* 577,
10. Dulles, *op. cit.,* 153–62; Hassell, *op. cit.,* 275; Hildebrandt, *op. cit.,* 137; Gisevius, *To the Bitter End,* 516.
11. Dulles, *op. cit.,* 158.

12. *Ibid.*, 149.
13. *Ibid.*, 158.
14. *Ibid.*, 158.
15. Reitlinger, *op. cit.*, 300–1.
16. Hildebrandt, *op. cit.*, 137.
17. *Ibid.*, 137.
18. Wheeler-Bennett, *op. cit.*, 578;
    Reitlinger, *op. cit.*, 289–313.
19. Hassell, *op. cit.*, 287–8.
20. Wheeler-Bennett, *op. cit.*, 579;
    Reitlinger, *op. cit.*, 289–313.

21. Hassell, *op. cit.*, 312.
22. Reitlinger, *op. cit.*, 289–313.
23. Michel, *op. cit.*, 294.
24. Gisevius, *op. cit.*, 566–7;
    Stubbe, *op. cit.*, 256.
25. See the Kaltenbrunner Reports
    (Wiener Library, London).
26. Michel, *op. cit.*, 288; Ritter, *op.
    cit.*, 208.
27. Hildebrandt, *op. cit.*, 186.

5. HUNTED BY THE GESTAPO: MOABIT PRISON
1944–5

1. Hildebrandt, *op. cit.*, 188–90
2. Peter Paret, 'An Aftermath of
   the Plot against Hitler: the
   Lehrterstrasse Prison in
   Berlin 1944–45', *Bulletin* of the
   Institute of Historical Research, vol. 32, no. 85 (1959),
   88–93.
3. Statement of Prince Ernst
   August, Duke of Hanover, to
   Dr J. Campsie after the war.
4. Hildebrandt, *op. cit.*, 192;
   Gisevius, *op. cit.*, 580.
5. Hildebrandt, *op. cit.*, 192.
6. *Ibid.*, 196.
7. Michel, *op. cit.*, 298.
8. Hildebrandt, *op. cit.*, 199.

9. *Ibid.*, 133.
10. Dulles, *op. cit.*, 162–4.
11. Reitlinger, *op. cit.*, 289–313.
12. Albrecht Haushofer, *Sonnets of
    Moabit*, Sonnet No. 5.
13. Ritter, *op. cit.*, 302.
14. The Rev. Eberhard Bethge,
    Letter to the author dated
    4.1.69; see Bethge, *Dietrich
    Bonhoeffer: A Biography*, 807–8.
15. Count Folke Bernadotte, *The
    Fall of the Curtain*.
16. Hildebrandt, *op. cit.*, 203.
17. *Ibid.*, 204.
18. *Ibid.*, 203.
19. *Ibid.*, 203.
20. Paret, *op. cit.*, 98.

6. THE END: 1.05 a.m. 23 APRIL 1945

1. Hartschimmelhof Papers.
2. Walsh, *op. cit.*, 64.
3. Albrecht Haushofer, *op. cit.*,
   No. 1.
4. *Ibid.*, No. 47.
5. *Ibid.*, No. 21.
6. *Ibid.*, No. 73.
7. *Ibid.*, No. 36.
8. *Ibid.*, No. 22.
9. *Ibid.*, No. 12.
10. *Ibid.*, No. 40.
11. *Ibid.*, No. 26.
12. *Ibid.*, No. 59.

13. Paret, *op. cit.*, 98.
14. H. Trevor-Roper, *The Last
    Days of Hitler*, 35.
15. Paret, *op. cit.*, 99.
16. *Ibid.*, 100; *Frankfurter Allge-
    meine Zeitung*, 'Fifteen
    Murdered at the Last Moment,
    18.7.62; Wheeler-Bennett, *op.
    cit.*, 685, 744–52.
17. Cornelius Ryan, *The Last
    Battle*, 346–8.
18. Hildebrandt, *op. cit.*, 204;
    Ryan, *op. cit.*, 346–7.

19. *Ibid.*, 346–7.
20. Eric H. Boehm, *We Survived*, 47–8.
21. *Frankfurter Allgemeine Zeitung*, 'Fifteen Murdered at the Last Moment', 18.7.62.
22. Paret, *op. cit.*, 100.
23. Boehm, *op. cit.*, 48.
24. *Frankfurter Allgemeine Zeitung*, 'Fifteen Murdered at the Last Moment', 18.7.62.
25. Boehm, *op. cit.*, 48–9.
26. *Ibid.*, 49.
27. Ryan, *op. cit.*, 348.
28. Ryan, *op. cit.*, 348.
29. *Ibid.*, 348.
30. Boehm, *op. cit.*, 50.
31. Albrecht Haushofer, *op. cit.*
32. *Ibid.*, No. 38.

Epilogue

1. Statement made by Frau Schnuhr to Dr J. Campsie after the war.
2. Walsh, *op. cit.*, 45.
3. *Ibid.*, 16.
4. *Ibid.*, 351.
5. Hildebrandt, *op. cit.*, 32.
6. Walsh, *op. cit.*, ch. I–V.
7. *Ibid.*, 352.
8. Albrecht Haushofer, *op. cit.*, No. 23.
9. Walsh, *op. cit.*, 12.
10. *Ibid.*, 25–6.
11. Hildebrandt, *op. cit.*, 129.
12. Walsh, *op. cit.*, 32–3.
13. Albrecht Haushofer, *op. cit.*, No. 37.
14. Walsh, *op. cit.*, 66.
15. Albrecht Haushofer, *op. cit.*, No. 30.
16. Walsh, *op. cit.*, 33–4.
17. *Ibid.*, 34.
18. G. M. Gilbert, *Nuremberg Diary*, 11; Douglas Kelley, *22 Cells in Nuremberg*, ch. 3.
19. Jack Fishman, *The Seven Men of Spandau*, 26–7.
20. Walsh, *op. cit.*, 23–5.
21. J. R. Rees, *The Case of Rudolf Hess*, 214–24; Kelley, *op. cit.*, ch. 3.
22. Colonel Burton C. Andrus, *The Infamous of Nuremberg*, 73, 121–3.
23. Trial of German Major War Criminals at Nuremberg, *Proceedings*, Part I, 305–6.
24. Gilbert, *op. cit.*, 34, 67; Kelley, *op. cit.*, 32–3.
25. Fishman, *op. cit.*, 27.
26. Gilbert, *op. cit.*, 51.
27. Trial of German Major War Criminals at Nuremberg, *Proceedings*, Part 22, 384–5.
28. *Ibid.*, 487–9.
29. *Ibid.*, 540–1.
30. Ilse Hess, *England–Nuremberg–Spandau, Prisoner of Peace*. See Select Bibliography.
31. Terence Prittie, *Deutschegegen Hitler*, 259.
32. Churchill, *Second World War*, vol. III, 49.
33. *Ibid.*, 48.
34. Albrecht Haushofer, *op. cit.*, No. 41.

Select Bibliography

I. DOCUMENTS AND UNPUBLISHED MATERIAL

1. Hartschimmelhof Papers, in the possession of Heinz Haushofer, containing the letters of Albrecht Haushofer to his parents.
2. The Haushofer Documents, in the German Federal Archives in Koblenz.
3. Hamilton Papers, including letters from Albrecht Haushofer and Reports to the Prime Minister after Hess's flight.
4. The Haushofer Documents, in the National Archives of the U.S.A. and in the Manuscript Division of the Library of Congress, Washington.
5. Hansard 1918–45 and Documents on German Foreign Policy 1918–45.
6. The Trial of the German Major War Criminals before the International Military Tribunal,
   Proceedings vols. I–XXIII, Nuremberg 1947–9
   Documents in Evidence vols. XXIV–XLII, Nuremberg 1947–9.

II. MEMOIRS, DIARIES, SECONDARY WORKS AND ARTICLES WHICH CONTAIN OR MAKE USE OF ORIGINAL MATERIAL

Andrus, Col. Burton C., *The Infamous of Nuremberg* (London, 1969).

Ansel, L., *Hitler Confronts England* (Durham, 1960).

Avon, Earl of, *The Eden Memoirs*, The Reckoning (London, 1965).

Bakker, G., *Duitse Geopolitiek 1919–45* (Assen, 1967).

Baynes, Norman H., *Hitler's Speeches 1922–39* (OUP, 1942).

Benes, Dr Eduard, *Memoirs* (London, 1954).

Bernadotte, Folke, *The Fall of the Curtain* (London, 1945).

Best, Captain S. Payne, *The Venlo Incident* (London, 1950).

Bethge, Eberhard, *Dietrich Bonhoeffer, A Biography* (London, 1970).

Boehm, Eric H., *We Survived* (California, 1966).

Boldt, Gerhard, *In the Shelter with Hitler* (Edinburgh, 1948).

Bowman, I., *Geography vs Geopolitics* (Geogr Rev, 1942).

Bullock, Alan, *Hitler: A Study in Tyranny* (London, 1962).

Churchill, Sir Winston S., *The Second World War*, vol. ii (London, 1942), vol. iii (London, 1950).

——, *War Speeches*, comp. Charles Eade (London, 1952).

Ciano, Count Galeazzo, *Ciano's Diary*, ed. Malcolm Muggeridge (Surrey, 1947).

Crankshaw, Edward, *The Gestapo, Instrument of Tyranny* (London, 1956).

Davidson, Eugene, *The Trial of the Germans, Nuremberg 1945–46* (New York, 1967).

Delmer, Sefton; *Black Boomerang* (London, 1962).

Dietrich, Otto, *The Hitler I Knew* (London, 1957).

Dorpalen, Andreas, *The World of General Haushofer* (New York, 1942).

Dulles, Allen, *Germany's Underground* (New York, 1947).

Fest, Joachim C., *The Face of the Third Reich* (London, 1970).

Fishman, Jack, *The Seven Men of Spandau* (London, 1954).

Fleming, Colonel Peter, *The Flying Visit* (London, 1940).

Freeman, T. W., *A Hundred Years of Geography* (Chicago, 1962).

Gilbert, G. M., *Nuremberg Diary* (London, 1948).

Gisevius, Hans Bernd, *To the Bitter End* (London, 1948).

Goebbels, Joseph, *The Early Goebbels Diaries 1925–26* (London, 1962).

Gyorgy, A., *Geopolitics* (Berkeley, 1944).

Hamilton, I. B. M., *General Sir Ian Hamilton* (London, 1966).

Hanfstaengl, Ernst, *Hitler, The Missing Years* (London, 1957).

Harbeck, Karl Heinz, 'Die Zeitschrift für Geopolitik 1924–44', thesis, (Kiel University, 1963).

Hassell, Ulrich von, *The Von Hassell Diaries 1938–44* (London, 1948).

Haushofer, Albrecht, *Sonnets of Moabit* (Berlin, 1948).

Heiden, Konrad, *Der Fuehrer* (London, 1967).

Herbert, A. P., *Let us be Glum* (London, 1941).

Hess, Ilse, *England–Nürnberg–Spandau* (Druffel-Verlag, Leoni, 1952).

——, *Prisoner of Peace* (London, 1954).

——, *Gefangener des Friedens* (Druffel-Verlag, Leoni, 1955).

——, *Antwort Aus Zelle Sieben* (Druffel-Verlag, Leoni, 1967).

——, Rudolf, *Reden, NSDAP* (Munich, 1938).

Hesse, Fritz, *Das Spiel Um Deutschland* (Munich, 1953).

——, *Hitler and the English* (London, 1954).

Higgins, Trumbull, *Hitler and Russia* (London, 1966).

Hildebrandt, Rainer, *Wir Sind die Letzten* (Berlin, 1950).

Hitler, Adolf, *Mein Kampf* (New York, 1939).

——, *My New Order*, ed. Raoul de Roussy de Sales (New York, 1941).

——, *Hitler's Secret Conversations*, ed. H. R. Trevor-Roper (New York, 1953).

Hoare, Sir Samuel, *See* Viscount Templewood.

Italiaander, Rolf, *Besiegeltes Leben* (Germany, 1949).

Jacobsen, Hans Adolf, *Nationalsozialistische Aussenpolitik 1933–38* (Metzner, 1968).

Jo, Yung-Hwan, 'Japanese Geopolitics and the Greater Asia Co-Prosperity Sphere', *University Microfilms* (Ann Arbor, Michigan, 1964).

Kelley, Douglas M., *Twenty-Two Cells in Nuremberg* (New York, 1947).

Kersten, Dr Felix, *Memoirs* (Essex, 1956).

Kirkpatrick, Sir Ivone, *The Inner Circle* (London, 1959).

Kohn, Hans, *The Mind of Germany* (London, 1965).

Laack, Dr Ursula Michel, *See* Michel, Dr Ursula.

Leasor, James, *Rudolf Hess, The Uninvited Envoy* (London, 1962).

Mattern, J., *Geopolitics* (Baltimore, 1942).

Mau and Krausnick, *German History 1933–45* (London, 1964).

M'Govern, James, *Martin Bormann* (London, 1968).

Michel, Dr Ursula, *Albrecht Haushofer and National Socialism*, thesis (Kiel University, 1964).

Nicolson, Sir Harold, *Diaries and Letters 1939–45* (London, 1967).

Norton, Donald Hawley, 'Karl Haushofer and his Influence on Nazi Ideology and German Foreign Policy', *University Microfilms* (Ann Arbor, Michigan, 1965).

Paret, Peter, 'An Aftermath of the Plot against Hitler, The Lehrterstrasse Prison in Berlin 1944–45', *Bulletin* of the Institute of Historical Research, vol. 32 no 85 (1959).

Percy of Newcastle, Lord, *Some Memories* (London, 1958).

Price, Ward, *I Know These Dictators*, (London, 1937).

Prittie, Terence, *Deutsche Gegen Hitler* (Tübingen, 1965).

Rees, J. R., *The Case of Rudolf Hess* (Surrey, 1947).

Reitlinger, Gerald, *The SS-Alibi of a Nation* (London, 1956).

Riess, Curt, *Joseph Goebbels* (London, 1949).

Ritter, Gerhard, *The German Resistance* (Stuttgart, 1954).

Roberts, Stephen, *The House that Hitler Built* (London, 1937).

Ryan, Cornelius, *The Last Battle* (London, 1966).

Schellenberg, Walter, *Memoirs*, ed. Louis Hagen (London, 1956).

Schmidt, Dr Paul, *Hitler's Interpreter* (New York, 1951).

Semmler, Rudolf, *Goebbels, the Man Next to Hitler* (London, 1947).

Sherwood, Robert E., *Roosevelt and Hopkins* (New York, 1948).

Shirer, William L., *The Rise and Fall of the Third Reich* (London, 1964).

Simon, Viscount, *Retrospect* (London, 1952).

Speer, Albert, *Memoirs* (London, 1970).

Strausz-Hupe, R., *Geopolitics* (New York, 1942).

Stubbe, Walter, 'In Memoriam Albrecht Haushofer', *Vierteljahreshefte für Zeitgeschichte* (July, 1960).

Sykes, Christopher, *Troubled Loyalty* (London, 1969).

Taylor, Griffith, *Geography in the XX Century* (New York, 1951).

Templewood, Viscount, *Ambassador on a Special Mission* (London, 1946).

Thyssen, Fritz, *I paid Hitler* (London, 1941).

Trevor-Roper, H. R., *The Last Days of Hitler* (London, 1947).

Valckenburg, S. van, *Geography in the XX Century* (New York, 1951).

Vansittart, Sir Robert, *Black Record: Germans Past and Present* (London, 1941).

Walsh, Edmund, *Total Power* (New York, 1948).

Warlimont, Walter, *Inside Hitler's HQ, 1939–45* (London, 1964).

Weigert, H. W., *Generals and Geographers* (New York, 1942).

——, and others, *Compass of the World* (New York, 1944).

——, *New Compass of the World* (New York, 1949).

——, *Principles of Political Geography* (New York, 1957).

Weinberg, G. L., *Germany and the Soviet Union 1939–41* (Leiden, E. J. Brill, 1954).

——, 'Secret Hitler–Benes Negotiations in 1936–7', *Journal of Central European Affairs* (January, 1960).

Weizsaecker, Carl von, *In Memoriam Albrecht Haushofer* (Hamburg, 1948).

——, Ernst von, *Memoirs* (London, 1951).

Welles, Sumner, *The Time for Decision* (London, 1944).

Werth, Alexander, *Russia at War 1941–45* (London, 1964).

Wheeler-Bennett, Sir John, *The Nemesis of Power* (London, 1964).

Whittlesey, D., *German Strategy of World Conquest* (New York, 1942).

Wulf, Joseph, *Martin Bormann, Hitler's Shadow* (Gutersloh, 1962).

INDEX